MW01277945

LIVESHOT

Journalistic Heroism in Philadelphia

Tom Kranz

TK Books LLC

BOOKS

Thank you to all the journalists, photographers and technicians who contributed their insights to help me tell this story.

Thank you to Pete Kane for the photos and for his support throughout the process of putting this story together.

Thank you to my wife Marianne for her patience as I tap away on my laptop, oblivious to everything else.

CONTENTS

PREFACE TO THE
THIRD EDITION

More than half of Americans answering a 2020 Pew Research survey said they didn't have confidence that journalists were serving the public interest. Only 9% had "a great deal of confidence." So, what better time to revisit a story of journalistic heroism?

The fact that this story took place decades ago is irrelevant. It happened, it's true and the story of these journalists deserves to be told. It is a tale of journalistic achievement for all those who doubt that local television is capable of telling the most difficult stories.

The story I witnessed and retell in this book is how the men and women at a television station put their heads together to bring the man-made cataclysm that climaxed on May 13, 1985, directly to the people of Philadelphia, sometimes at great risk. It was an effort that earned those men and women an Alfred I. duPont-Columbia University Award, one of the highest achievements of broadcast journalism.

This account draws on actual experiences and conversations, air checks of WCAU-TV (denoted in caps), transcripts of the MOVE Commission hearings, my own recollections and other sources as noted. In 1985, personal cellular phones didn't exist. There was no computerized newsroom, so there was still the clatter of typewriters and wire-service teletype machines. The internet was not a daily part of our lives. Portable video cameras were bigger and bulkier and required outboard recorders. WCAU was owned by CBS and people, places and things in Philadelphia may now be moved, renamed or deceased.

In the ensuing decades, the City of Philadelphia has tried to close this chapter of its history without success. It stands as a monument to the failure of government and, to many, a cautionary tale about police violence against people of color. But it remains a stunning success story of local journalism at its best.

TK
2021

TOM KRANZ

PART ONE

WILD IN THE STREETS

"THEY'RE REALLY GOING AT IT NOW. IT'S, UH, IT'S AUTOMATIC WEAPONS, IT'S, UH--"

POW. A heavy shotgun blast right nearby made me jump.

"Look out," someone in the crowd yelled and everyone ducked, including the police officer right at our spot.

"AT THIS POINT, PEOPLE ARE STARTING TO SCATTER."

Harvey was immovable and unflinching.

"PEOPLE ARE STARTING TO PANIC, THEY ARE STARTING TO RUN."

Several diehard TV groupies now hauled ass up Pine Street. Others remained in kneeling positions behind the TV news vans.

"POLICE HAVE TAKEN AN ARMED POSITION RIGHT BEHIND US NOW AS YOU CAN SEE."

"Move it back, move it back," shouted an officer. "Take it on up there; get the hell away from here!"

"YOU CAN HEAR IT, IT SOUNDS LIKE--"

A roar of shooting cascaded like a tidal wave.

"IT SOUNDS LIKE--"

Charles: "THERE IS MORE OF THAT SMALL ARMS FIRE,"

Harvey: "--ANOTHER--"

Charles: ANOTHER SMALL CALIBER--"

Harvey: "ANOTHER VIETNAM HERE!"

Charles: "IT'S UNBELIVEABLE!"

Harvey: "IT'S UNBELIEVABLE THE NUMBER OF ROUNDS THAT HAVE BEEN FIRED AT THIS POINT!"

The roar of war filled the air and people ran for their lives. Eyes darted everywhere, especially the rooftops. Cops cowered next to us as their own machine gun's firing bellowed just a short distance away. The cement sidewalk was a hard place for knees to land. We weren't reporters and spectators anymore, but targets.

Just as suddenly, the shooting would stop and we would check each other over for, well, anything that wasn't there before. Part of me was frustrated that the actual battle was happening around the corner, just a few dozen yards away, out of sight. The other part said stay there, god damn it, and leave me alone.

Reporters Harvey Clark and Charles Thomas stood their ground for the good of the live shot. That was a joke-- live television vs. your own life, which to choose. Isn't this why we're here? But there are moments, like when the cell phone rings during a pants-shitting moment and it's the news director suggesting a brilliant idea for a story about what might be going on "behind the scenes".

"They're fucking shooting at us, Jay, that's what going on!"

This wasn't how anyone wanted the standoff with the people in the MOVE house to end after all those months. At least, that's what the mayor and his boys said in all those news conferences. But their own words and actions—and inaction-- over the months and years leading up to May 13, 1985, set the stage for that day. And, few tears were shed for the adults in that house who practically begged for bullets and bombs to be dropped at their doorstep. There was no reasoning, no talking and no negotiating with them. In the end, you can look at their words and actions and conclude they got what they wanted.

But the children didn't ask for it. Their choices were made for them and they got killed. For that, all the adults are to blame, the ones in the house on Osage Avenue and the ones at City Hall.

FUEL FOR THE FIRE

My first contact with MOVE occurred in 1975 at Temple University. I produced a weekly public affairs program for Temple's FM radio station, WRTI. One day I was contacted by telephone by a caller suggesting a topic for my show. He said his group, called MOVE, might provide for an interesting discussion. I had heard of MOVE in occasional news reports about a so-called "back to nature" group in West Philadelphia that sported long hair, torn clothing and lots of pets. I agreed to set up a taping.

Three MOVE members showed up for the session, two men and a woman. We sat down in Studio A and had a one hour discussion on tape. I actually only interviewed the two men, who were black and whose hair hung in long, matted braids. The woman, who was white with long, blond hair, sat in the rear of the studio listening.

They were very interested in promoting their makeshift car wash where, for a couple bucks, anyone could drive up to their "headquarters" and get his car washed to support their cause. Their cause was to begin a revolution, to begin a society based on total honesty to one's self and others, to cleanse themselves of the evils of modern society, especially foods that poisoned their bodies. They would respect all forms of life. Most of all, they would shun all belief in gods, laws and authority, except that of John Africa.

"Who is John Africa?" I asked. John Africa, they explained was their leader, their god, and their authority. John Africa led their revolution and gave them their strength. John Africa's teachings were the only laws they respected. All of his followers took his last name as theirs.

"How do these beliefs affect your everyday life?"

The answers: no processed or store-bought foods, except raw fruit and vegetables; no manufactured soaps or detergents to be used on the body or hair; only the simplest clothing such as jeans, sweatshirts and T-shirts. As I mentioned, their hair was long and uncombed. For the blacks, it matted into long dreadlocks, which to my untrained eye looked like small braids. For the whites, it was simply long and stringy. Later, when there were no longer any white members, dreadlocks became associated with MOVE. Their hair became their trademark.

Their professed respect for life extended to vermin. They fed the rats that lived in and around their house in West Philadelphia and allowed the roaches to thrive. They kept many dogs and cats in their house and yard. Conditions on the property raised eyebrows in the neighborhood.

During my interview, their answers were peppered with obscenities. I asked why they used the words motherfucker and god dam so liberally in an interview they knew was to be aired on the radio. The answer: you and your society are hypocrites. You all think of those words and use them in hushed tones. In reality they are simply part of the language, so why not use them openly?

The one-hour program took much longer than usual to edit because of the obscenities. Even so, I thought this was an interesting group of people putting their ideas into practice in a relatively harmless way. It was just a radio program. I had no reason to remember the names of these people, or even to save the tape.

A year after my interview, a new component was introduced to MOVE life. That component was open defiance, demonstrated by the blatant display of weapons. Co-founder Donald Glassy became concerned because the other co-founder, Vincent Leaphart, began advocating violence. So, Glassy left MOVE. Vincent Leaphart, who had assumed the name John Africa, professed violence as a viable road to revolution.

1977 was the year MOVE became more than a neighborhood

nuisance. One day in May, police spent nine hours in a tense standoff with MOVE members armed with rifles over the eviction of a member. It ended without gunfire but signaled the beginning of 24-hour police surveillance at MOVE headquarters. The surveillance went on for 10 months, at a cost to Philadelphia taxpayers of over a million dollars. Following the display of the guns, weapons charges were filed against eleven MOVE members. In June of that year, federal agents raided a house in the West Oak Lane section of the city, miles away from MOVE headquarters. They turned up raw materials for bombs and an arsenal of weapons. Vincent Leaphart was charged in that raid, even though he was nowhere to be found. MOVE's founder was now a fugitive, wanted by the FBI.

Inside MOVE headquarters were Leaphart's revolutionaries, and some of them had guns. They had stopped paying their utilities in a show of defiance against "the system". They erected barricades around their front porch to show their neighbors they didn't need them and, in fact, scorned them. They created a military-style compound in the heart of that quiet, residential neighborhood called Powelton Village. Up until that point, their neighbors had no real problems with MOVE because it was simply an extended family living in peace. Now, MOVE members with rifles were seen patrolling the front porch as neighborhood children played in the streets. MOVE had also erected a loudspeaker to deliver its revolutionary message directly to the neighborhood. The message was always laced with obscenities. The bullhorn became a voice for the whole house. "Long live John Africa!" was the frequent cry heard at all hours of the day and night.

The tension became unbearable for the neighbors. Ten months of legal pyrotechnics ensued ending with a ruling by the Pennsylvania Supreme Court giving Mayor Frank Rizzo the legal right to arrest the eleven people who had been charged with weapons offenses.

Thus, one day in March 1978, hundreds of police were sent to the MOVE house at 33rd and Pearl Streets. They spent that day sealing off the neighborhood, erecting barricades of sandbags and steel plates. They cut off all water and electricity to the house, hoping to force the surrender of the eleven. There was no surrender. Instead, MOVE further resolved to fight the mayor who, in their minds, was out to destroy them.

The police presence, the barricades and the relentless tension went on for another five months. There was great hesitancy to storm the building, mainly because of the children. Police Commissioner Joseph O'Neill thought of MOVE as nothing more than a cult, but he also believed the members would kill any or all of the children if necessary to make their point. MOVE exploited the standoff to the hilt. Members made frequent speeches over the loudspeaker as police watched. Negotiations began quietly to try to bring MOVE members to justice without risking bloodshed. At the same time, Commissioner O'Neill began devising a plan of attack on the house that would avoid a wholesale slaughter of the children. O'Neill was a cop, not a politician. But he knew that if even one child was killed by a police bullet, politics would quickly replace whatever rationality was left inside MOVE's world. The police spent the following months practicing an operation against MOVE headquarters.

By August 1978, temperatures had soared, patience had run out and the curtain rose on the final act. A judge signed an order to arrest 21 MOVE members after they refused to fulfill an agreement with the city to lay down their weapons and leave their headquarters. By this time it was routine for reporters and TV cameras to be up the street in their designated area, watching, waiting and wondering what would happen next. Reporters came to work at 33rd and Pearl Streets each day as steel workers would report to a factory. They got to know the cops, who got to know them. The neighbors were caught in a profound Catch-22-- having increased police protection at the cost of a normal life for themselves and their children.

On August 8, acting on the court order, Mayor Rizzo poured hundreds more police into the block and moved in a bulldozer to knock down the MOVE house, which had been condemned by the city. Despite police warnings and attempts at negotiations, the MOVE members refused to come outside and barricaded themselves in the basement with their children. The eviction operation began as firemen stretched hoses from waiting fire engines and trained steady streams of water into the basement windows of the MOVE house to try to flush them out.

Suddenly, a shot rang out. Police responded, opening fire with everything they had. There ensued a sequence of events, captured on film and video, that showed firemen crawling on their bellies to get to cover; reporters scurrying behind parked cars and into neighboring homes; news photographers running for cover; wounded police officers and firemen being dragged away like in a war movie. Police sirens were screaming as cops jumped out of vehicles that hadn't quite come to a stop.

Then, the gunfire stopped. Smoke and dust flew through the air in the momentary quiet. Voices were heard shouting and suddenly, through one of MOVE's basement windows, children were being pushed through into the light of day, naked and scared to death. Police officers rushed to scoop them up while watching their flanks. Then, shaggy-headed MOVE adults crawled through the same window with their hands high in the air, shirtless and shaky.

In a sequence also caught on video, four cops took one of the men behind a police van and kicked him over and over again in the head, a display of brutality shown repeatedly on television, a scene that dogged the police department for years to come.

The children were wrapped in blankets, helped into police cars and taken away while the adults were handcuffed and loaded into vans to be jailed.

The costs of the raid on the MOVE compound were high. Police officer James Ramp died of his wound that day. One MOVE member was wounded. Another, Delbert Orr Africa, took months to recover from the savage beating the four policemen had inflicted on him as he lay on the ground. All of the MOVE children were physically unharmed, but who could say what emotional and psychological damage was done?

The house on north 33rd Street was bulldozed the same day. Ten MOVE members were tried and convicted of murder and other crimes. They were dragged kicking and screaming through a court system they didn't believe in. They were each sentenced to terms of at least 30 years in prison.

Vincent Leaphart was not inside MOVE headquarters the day it fell. He was still a fugitive. He was caught several years later and stood trial. The trial coverage was not as sensational as one might have thought. The city had been deeply scarred by the MOVE shootout and it took years before it was out of the public's daily consciousness. The trial of John Africa was more of a curiosity than anything else.

In July of 1981, Vincent Leaphart was found innocent of federal weapons offenses and he walked out of the U.S. Courthouse in Philadelphia a free man. He told reporters outside the courthouse, "We're on the MOVE," as he climbed into a waiting taxi.

The imprisoned MOVE members saw themselves as symbols of injustice, martyrs to John Africa. Their release became the primary goal of the organization.

But with ten MOVE members in jail and a complete lack of public sympathy for their cause, MOVE became dormant for several years.

ROW HOME
NEIGHBORHOOD

T hree hundred years before the political and racial upheaval that spawned MOVE, the Lenni Lenape Indians lived in a vast swath of the eastern United States that included what is now eastern Pennsylvania, all of New Jersey, northern Delaware and the southern tip of New York State. They were peaceful, and their domain included the parcel of land William Penn called "Philadelphia".

Through a portion of this land ran a creek which the Lenni Lenape called the Kararikong, or place of the wild geese. By 1683, English settlers renamed it Cobb's Creek, for mill owner William Cobb[1]. And by the 1800s, Cobb's Creek formed the western border of West Philadelphia and became a haven for slaves fleeing to the north via the Underground Railroad. Those turbulent years brought race wars, segregation and political uncertainty but the neighborhood called Cobbs Creek never lost its basic structure as a working class community.

"When this community developed, it developed for working people," recalled the Reverend Leonard Smalls of the Church of Christian Compassion, "but it was also for people who worked in center city who needed housing. Blacks moved in and bought the homes, turning it into primarily a home-owning community, not a renting community. It has become the largest home-owning, black community, per capita, in the city of Philadelphia."

"When my family moved into Cobbs Creek in the 1960's," remembered Bennie Swans, "it was one of the most exclusive areas of the city for black folks. Wilt Chamberlin lived down the street!"[2]

Like many Philadelphia neighborhoods of the 20th century, Cobbs Creek was made up primarily of row homes on perpendicular streets like Osage Avenue, Pine Street, Larchmont Street and the numbered streets from about 58th to 63rd. A typical row home is only about 15 feet wide but stretches back from the front porch through to the back door about 60 feet. The first floor typically has a front porch or patio, living room, dining room and kitchen, all connected and lined up front to back. On the second floor are probably three small bedrooms, a bathroom and very little closet space. In New Orleans, similar one-story versions are called shotgun homes because you could fire a shotgun in through the front door and the shot would go all the way through the back door in a straight line.

I grew up in a row home very similar to those on Osage Avenue, except instead of a front porch we had a small outdoor patio and a small back porch attached to the kitchen. Like the homes on Osage Avenue, ours had a number of steps that took you from the sidewalk up to the front door. Much of everyday life on a row home street takes place on those steps and front porches and patios. Because you share your front steps with your next door neighbor, you tend to meet them there a lot. Kids gather on the steps to play. On warm summer nights we sat on the front steps and watched our neighbors sit on their front steps. Sitting led to talking and talking led to familiarity. For better or worse, people who live on row home streets get to know their neighbors pretty well.

Behind the homes on Osage Avenue there were tiny "yards", fenced-in areas that measured about ten by ten. There was no driveway, but a narrow walkway separating the rear of Osage Avenue and the rear of Pine Street to the north. Imagine two rows of shoe boxes. Each row has about 25 boxes, and each box sits tightly next to the other. The two rows are parallel, one to the north and one to the south, spaced about a foot apart. This could be a model of an aerial view of the 6200 block of Osage Avenue, a small street with a row of houses on each side. Add a third row of shoe boxes spaced about two inches north of the north row of boxes and you'd have the south side of Pine Street. The two inch space is a tiny alleyway. Completing the aerial view would be the perpendicular streets that act as borders, 62nd Street to the east and Cobbs Creek Parkway to the west.

Within this block and a half of row homes lived about 250 men, women and children who embodied the dreams, ambitions and memories of three generations. Each person knew some of his neighbors, but not all. Mostly, the people here, like in most row home neighborhoods, knew their immediate neighbors on either side and across the street and maybe a couple folks up the street. On the 6200 block of Osage Avenue, some people didn't even know that MOVE had made its new home here.

MOVE AWAKENS

It was Christmas morning, 1983. Betty Mapp was celebrating the joy of the day with her husband and three children. It was early in the morning and still dark outside their window at 6241 Osage Avenue.

"We were inside making Santa Claus with the kids, when we heard this loud noise," Betty recalled. "At first I thought it was someone playing Christmas carols. So we went to the door and with this loudspeaker, this cursing came from the MOVE house saying they wanted their sisters and brothers out of jail."

Ten houses down the street, at 6221 Osage Avenue, MOVE had reawakened, complete with a new loudspeaker, choosing Christmas morning to deliver the message that their members, jailed five years earlier, should be freed.

"It went on a pretty long time," Betty recalled. "The neighbors began to call each other and we decided to call the cops. We called the cops and told them that this obscene language was coming out of this loudspeaker at the MOVE house."

So the police came to the block on Christmas morning, drove up the street and parked on the corner.

"They never went up to the house," Betty remembered. The cursing stopped around 7AM.

For Lloyd and Lucretia Wilson, MOVE's rebirth began the night before, Christmas Eve. They lived next door to John Africa's children. Lloyd heard banging coming from next door.

"We couldn't understand what it was," he recalled. "They began to board up the front of the house."[3]

Just hours later, they heard the same vile cursing as the rest of the street, except it was much louder, much stronger. Living next door, the loudspeaker bellowed into their bedroom.

The sound of an amplified voice was a weapon MOVE had found useful in keeping Powelton Village on edge. The speakers were the type that tended to reproduce mostly the high frequency components of the voice. They were designed for volume.

Thus, the end of 1983 signaled the end of peaceful living for the people of Osage Avenue. With the Christmas loudspeaker tirade, MOVE made it clear they were re-establishing themselves in a Philadelphia neighborhood.

The house at 6221 was owned by a woman named Louise James who had lived there since 1958. She was a small woman with an afro and a brow etched with defiance.

"Prior to coming into the MOVE organization," she related, "I was the type of person always looking for something that would help me to find justice. I have never ever liked the injustice, the prejudice, the oppression in this system. However, I have never thought of myself as a leader, but I felt that I could be a good follower. And because I felt that way I was constantly seeking out people to follow.

"Prior to, MOVE for example, I followed and supported the Panther Party. Prior to MOVE I followed Angela Davis. I mean I was just mesmerized by that woman. I thought she was brave and courageous, and a black woman with a purpose. I felt she had been used and abused. I also followed both George and Jonathan Jackson.

"A brother by the name of Larry Cross was killed. This brother was going down Vine Street one day and a police officer had stopped and Larry had passed him. When the cop stopped him, he gave Larry Cross a ticket. Larry tore up the ticket. That was his crime. Somewhere between two and three hours later, that brother was dead. I mean, he was hung. And they said he committed suicide and I was outraged!

"There was a big meeting at White Rock Baptist Church at 53rd and Chestnut. Hardy Williams was there, and Cecil Moore was there and David Richardson[4] and big people were there and little people were there. And everyone was gathered because they wanted something done about this brother's murder. At some point somebody said, 'OK, the meeting is over,' and I remember hearing a voice scream, and I didn't even know that it was my own voice until I came back to myself. And I said, 'No! This meeting is over?' I said, 'I will not allow you to have me go out of this meeting as frustrated as I was when I came in. You're gonna have to tell me something!

"As I continued to be disillusioned and as I continued to see nothing working in this political system for me, I continued to search. When I came upon the teaching of John Africa, my search ended."[5]

Louise James had one more compelling reason to join MOVE. Her brother was John Africa, Vincent Leaphart. Her maiden name had been Louise Leaphart. She had been among those who accompanied Leaphart out of the federal courthouse in 1981 when he was found not guilty of federal weapons charges. She helped him into the taxi to freedom. Louise James was devoted to her older brother. He moved in with her sometime after his acquittal, and by the end of 1983 had begun converting her row house on Osage Avenue into his new fortress. She had taken the name Louise Africa. Her son Frank, whom she had raised in that house, keenly felt the influence of his uncle. A young, strong man in his early 20's, Frank James was one of the new warriors in the MOVE revolution. Once a precocious child with a puppy named Buttons, he was now Frank Africa and he often carried a gun.

Others soon moved into James' house, and brought children with them. Neighbors frequently began seeing long-haired MOVE adults taking the children for walks to nearby Cobbs Creek Park. Occasionally, the MOVE children ran free in the neighborhood, but they mostly kept close to their own house. For the first couple years, there was relatively peaceful coexistence between MOVE and the rest of the residents. But after the Christmas 1983 bullhorn barrage, things degenerated quickly.

Lucretia and Lloyd Wilson got to know their next door neighbors well.

"The things I complained about were the trash and garbage on our property," recalled Mrs. Wilson. "I complained directly to them. At first they were cooperative. They would say OK and move things. But as time went on, conditions just grew continually worse. Then we had to contend with the things inside our house.

"Bugs just totally took over our house, so we had to adjust to the situation. We exterminated all the time until the air was heavy with the smells of extermination in our house. And it did no good. It got so bad my children woke up in the middle of the night from bug bites, crying from things biting them in their beds."

Mrs. Wilson never used her washing machine.

"I didn't go into the basement. I would rather go to the laundromat, which I did, rather than even go down there."

The basic act of cooking a meal became a bizarre ritual.

"Before I could cook I had to turn on the stove and let the bugs evacuate it. This was daily before I could use the stove. But even then sometimes there were bugs in my food after it was cooked. And this went on. I did this for months."

So Lloyd Wilson thought the best way to get rid of the bugs was with what he called a sulfur bomb.

"Being a good neighbor," Lloyd remembered, "I went to the MOVE people [to tell them of his intention to infuse the house with sulfur fumes]. As a matter of fact, I spoke to Conrad Africa about it. He went completely berserk. You know, 'The bugs are our brothers and sisters. If you exterminate the bugs, you exterminate us!'"

This prompted an argument outside between the two men.

"One of the neighbors called the police," said Wilson. "They didn't know what was going to happen. And as the police arrived, I told them we could handle the situation. It was just something between neighbors."

Enter Gerald Ford Africa, MOVE's Minister of Information.

"Mr. Ford got indignant," continued Wilson. "Basically, they told me if I set those sulfur bombs off that when the revolution started, our doors would be the first ones to be kicked in. Our family would be the first to go!"[6]

The verbal conflicts continued. The loudspeaker tirades became more frequent. The neighbors' curiosity soon grew into annoyance and irritation. Then came a disturbing new twist-- sightings of MOVE members with guns.

Cassandra Carter lived at 6233 Osage.

"During the summer," she recalled, "I walked my dog down to the park. One day I happened to turn around and I was standing at an angle where I looked straight up and someone was standing on the roof with what looked like a rifle. Another neighbor came by and I asked him, 'Do you see him? He's just standing there as if he was watching to see what was going on on the block.' And that frightened me, to blatantly stand on top of a roof with a weapon showing. I mean, he could have just as easily turned around and said, 'Well, I'm going to shoot her, or shoot whoever is walking by.'"[7]

There had been several sightings by neighbors and news people of what looked like MOVE people on the rooftops with rifles. One of those sightings resulted in the sudden arrival of several dozen police officers on May 3, 1984. The report was of a hooded man on the roof, carrying a shotgun. About 40 heavily armed police rushed to Osage Avenue, training weapons on the house and blocking off the street. The police did not enter the house and did not see the man with the gun. After an hour and a half, the police left.

For 17 months after Christmas 1983, frequent loudspeaker harangues boomed through the neighborhood. For much of that time, Officer George Draper of the police Civil Affairs Unit was assigned to the surveillance team on Osage Avenue.

"On any given summer day," he recalled, "you had the children playing in the street. You have a mother and baby, sitting on the steps, neighbors talking to each other. All of a sudden on the loudspeaker, all of a sudden you'd hear a voice that would say, 'You mother fuckers! What the fuck are you doing out here now? Do you know what's going on here? You son of a bitches, you're around here fucking everybody up. You're going back and forth to the police telling them all kinds of trouble-tales. What the fuck is going on?'"[8]

The voices over the MOVE loudspeaker had the staccato characteristics of an old recording of a Hitler speech--dynamic and defiant, yet strained and hysterical. The voices were younger and had urban accents. Sometimes it was Ramona Africa. Sometimes it was Frank Africa. Whoever it was, the agenda was the same: release MOVE members jailed after the 1978 shootout or the Mayor, the police and anyone else getting in the way would be killed.

After the gun sighting that brought police in May of 1984, there was a lot of talk on the street that MOVE was preparing something for August 8th of that year, the sixth anniversary of the 1978 shootout. On that day, hundreds of police officers assembled at a city-owned building a few blocks away, apparently preparing to do something. But neither MOVE nor the police blinked. There was some bull-horning by MOVE, but no action. The police spent most of the day, then left. There was no comment from the police commissioner or the Mayor about why the police had assembled.

The media's attention didn't turn to MOVE again in any real way until eight months later. April 29, 1985, was the day that became the turning point in the city's relationship with this reawakened MOVE group. Police were called to Osage Avenue because the loudspeaker had been fired-up again. Civil Affairs officer Raymond Matthews was there and told the District Attorney what he heard.

"Frank James Africa called [the mayor] a 'nigger motherfucker' and said that 'we have a bullet for him...to blow his mother fucking head off'. MOVE members threatened policemen who had responded to the scene: 'Them mother fucking cops with shirts on, with guns under their coats, we are going to kill them if they come to our front door or our back door. We will kill any mother fucking cop that comes to the front, back or our god damned roof.' A neighborhood resident stated that he heard Frank James Africa, Conrad Hampton Africa, Ramona Johnson Africa and Theresa Brooks Africa threaten, over the loudspeaker, to kill the neighborhood children if the neighbors did not go along with MOVE's program. The MOVE members also accused the neighbors of inviting police in and announced that the neighbors would 'die from a bullet' and that 'the reason was to get our people out of jail.'"[9]

Although sightings by neighbors of MOVE members with guns were common by now, on this day someone saw a man with a rifle inside the wooden shack on the roof of the MOVE house. The purpose of that shack was clear to the police now: they were targets. Even worse, they could be sitting ducks. It was that same day when the news media finally woke up to what the neighbors had been seeing for months.

WCAU-TV reporter Harvey Clark went to Osage Avenue after the newsroom got calls that the MOVE bullhorn was active again. I tended to be cynical of these reports from Osage neighbors because it seemed they were always complaining about the MOVE people. I was no less cynical this time. The videotape of the scene that day made me a believer. It showed a small, quiet row home street. It reminded me of my own street in northeast Philadelphia with all the rhythms of inner city, row home life--kids in the street playing ball and mothers on the front steps talking with each other, keeping one eye on the kids and the other on everything else. The sun was shining. Suddenly, the rhythm of the street was broken by the sound of the public address system, the words nigger motherfucker and mother fucking cops tore holes in the air. The kids stop playing, the mothers on the steps stopped talking and life on the street froze. The loudspeaker tirade dominated all.

The mothers began climbing off the steps. Men and women started peeking out their doors, some calling their children to come in off the street. Many of the adults gathered into little groups. Everyone was talking about the noise from the speaker, the voices threatening the Mayor with death.

The video photographer panned over and up to the roof of the MOVE house and the ugly tumor that sat atop it. It was nothing less than a bunker, glaring down at the street below, daring someone to do something about it. The rooftop shack had been fortified with metal plates and lumber with slots cut into the walls, presumably for gun barrels. It sat on top of a house that looked like a fortress, its windows and doors barricaded with wooden slats. The compound foreshadowed a war between its builders and those who would tear it down. It was a war that seemed certain to be fought, but when?

FRIDAY, MAY 10, 1985

At 6:05 on a Friday evening, no one wanted to hang around the newsroom. I guess it was superstition but there was a general belief that if you hung around long enough, some breaking story would come along to keep you there longer than you wanted to be. The superstition was unfounded on this particular Friday. It had been an average news day. WCAU covered the trial of a respected brain surgeon accused of sexually assaulting a 17 year old patient. Ticket sales were brisk for the Chagall exhibit at the Philadelphia Museum of Art. A policeman named Ed Quinn became one of the few indicted Philadelphia cops to be found innocent of corruption charges. Vice President George Bush cast the tie-breaking vote in the Senate to approve President Reagan's budget.

And there was an item that we didn't even report in our 5 o'clock broadcast, but only in the 6. Mayor Goode had promised people in the Cobbs Creek neighborhood that he'd meet with them next week to ease tensions caused by the presence of MOVE.

Karen Fox had been following the MOVE story closely during the past week. Fox's title at Channel 10 was news editor, the point person in the newsroom for getting inside information on big stories. She was a woman who had survived in a man's world of journalism for over 20 years and learned to take care of herself in a newsroom very well. She made it her business to cut through the crap and get to the bottom line of a story. She would think nothing of making a dozen phone calls to confirm one fact. Karen believed it didn't matter where the truth came from, as long as it was the truth.

Recently, she had returned from a vacation in her home

state of Iowa and was catching up on the news in Philadelphia when she read an Inquirer article about Osage Avenue and the demands by residents for the city to do something about MOVE. The article contained a small, simple map of the area showing the block in relation to Cobbs Creek Park. As she read it, she remembered that one of the bloodiest weekends in the history of the Philadelphia police department happened in this very neighborhood. On an August night in 1970, a group with ties to the Black Panthers called the Black Unity Council decided to carry out a plan to assassinate police officers and blow up a police station. They targeted the station in Cobbs Creek Park. At that time, the park was patrolled by a branch of the police department called the Fairmount Park Guard.

On the night of Saturday, August 29, 1970, Sergeant Frank Von Coln was at his desk in the guard station. He never knew what hit him. Someone sneaked up behind him and pumped six bullets into his head. Outside, Officer James Harrington pulled up in his wagon and was met by one of the killers. Before he knew what hit him, he was shot in the mouth and critically wounded.

The following night, two other officers were wounded in another incident during a car stop in the same area.

The murder of Von Coln and the shootings of the other officers prompted Police Commissioner Frank Rizzo to stage simultaneous raids on three houses in the city believed to be Black Panther headquarters. During the raids, three more policemen were wounded by shotgun fire.

Karen Fox had covered the Von Coln shooting for KYW radio. She had previously done stories involving a church near 55th and Pine that had been a meeting place for the Black Unity Council. She had also followed the other police shootings and the Black Panther raids. Now, MOVE had taken up residence in the heart of this neighborhood with a history of violence against police.

Putting it all together as she read her Inquirer, Fox was amazed that no one had caught the historical significance of the current scenario on Osage Avenue. She felt in her gut that this time MOVE would play for keeps, on the same streets where the blood of four police officers had been spilled.

She became determined to make herself a student of the current MOVE situation. She pulled out a reverse phone directory and began calling people whose addresses were near 6221 Osage Avenue. Many were frightened to talk. Some were not. One was Howard Nichols, an outspoken defender of the neighborhood who led the efforts to get City Hall to listen. Nichols lived across the street from MOVE. He was afraid of an explosion because he had recently seen the MOVE men bringing gasoline into the house and hauling it up to the bunker. He also witnessed them loading lumber and bags of dirt into the house, apparently to fortify it from the inside. From Nichols and a few other neighbors, she now had a clear picture of what was happening on Osage Avenue.

On the evening of Thursday May 9th, 1985, Karen and her husband, Inquirer columnist Tom Fox, went to dinner in downtown Philadelphia. They were driving back home to Delaware County when they began talking about MOVE 1978, Osage Avenue, Sgt. Von Coln, et al.

"But you know," she said idly as they drove, "I can't picture where Osage Avenue comes in out there."

Immediately, Tom veered the car into that direction for a look. They had to drive through West Philly anyway to get home to Delaware County. They approached Osage Avenue and turned onto it. It was 10PM.

MOVE members and their children were out that night. So were other people from the block.

"Holy shit," Karen said. She couldn't believe how tiny the street was. They kept driving and went around the block. On the second pass, neither she nor Tom could imagine the police getting any kind of elbow room on this miniature street. They would certainly have to take over a number of private homes just to get close enough to the MOVE house to get a clean shot. It would be totally inaccessible to the press during such an operation and that would make Channel 10's job very difficult.

The challenges piled up before her eyes, and the next day she went to the News Director, Jay Newman.

"You went out there?" Jay snapped excitedly, moving closer to her face with his, violating her personal space as he often did when he was excited about something.

"Yes, and you'd better go out there, too. There is no way you can cover this story when it breaks. The street is tiny. The cops will have everything closed off for a block around. It's gonna be a real pain in the ass."

Now it was Friday and Karen made one more call before leaving for the weekend. She called Joe O'Neill, the former police commissioner who was now head of security for Conrail. She asked him, as a veteran of fighting MOVE in a street battle, how would he plan an operation on this tiny street of row homes? He said the key would be to control the rooftops and find a way to knock off the bunker, perhaps a wrecking ball dangling from a helicopter. He'd need tear gas and water to confuse the enemy and obstruct their vision. And somehow, he would have to avoid slaughtering the children.

On Friday, May 10, there was no public talk of any action against MOVE by the mayor, the police or anyone else. But behind closed doors, it was later learned, the OK had been given. The warrants had been sworn out for the arrests of Ramona, Theresa, Frank and Conrad Africa. Fox did not know at the time, nor did anyone in the media, that Mayor Goode, District Attorney Ed Rendell and Police Commissioner Gregore Sambor had had a short meeting at which they agreed to take action on Monday, May 13th.

Publicly, the Mayor talked of a meeting he would have with the Osage neighbors within the next few days because tension was about as bad as it could get. Plainclothes police officers were now stationed at both ends of the small street 24 hours a day. A yearlong, hands-off policy by the Goode administration had allowed the home at 6221 to become a runaway menace, a stinking hole where rats and roaches thrived. The loudspeakers remained active, bellowing threats and obscenities day and night. The house was an infected sore swelling up and ready to explode. It was the center of unwanted attention for a neighborhood that had lived with threats and anxiety for two years, and a city that had lived with MOVE's legacy of hate and violence since 1978. Now, the infection was beyond a cure and Mayor Wilson Goode was preparing to do radical surgery.

By May 10, the bunker had existed in its finished state for several months, although the press had essentially been oblivious to it. As recently as May 9, reporters and neighbors could see MOVE members climbing onto the roof to measure, hammer, raise cans of gasoline and apply whatever finishing touches were needed to, ostensibly, make the bunker impenetrable. Officials of the city had watched the bunker being built and had records of its construction almost to the day the first supports went up. A city inspector for the department of Licenses and Inspections saw the supports being erected on the roof as early as October 1984. L&I is the agency which enforces building codes. The observation was reported by the inspector to his superior who then reported it to the proper authority under the mayor. Since the mayor's policy towards MOVE was "hands off", the bunker's construction continued, unfettered by the laws of the city of Philadelphia.

And so, in the spring of 1985, the bunker emerged in its full, fearsome entirety, a terrible blotch of defiance challenging an entire neighborhood and an entire city. The bunker would become a focal point for the coverage of the MOVE story from that point on. It became the focus of the police operation and a symbol of the paralysis of the Goode administration.

The neighbors expressed their fear any way and every way they could. They held town meetings to which the media were invited. Some went directly to the Mayor's office. They had meetings with the district attorney. They complained to the plainclothes police officers watching over them. But each time the neighbors took what little action they could, MOVE retaliated by turning on the loudspeaker and unleashing a torrent of obscenities and threats. The threats were made against individuals by name. People heard their neighbors berated, humiliated and threatened over and over again. Anyone walking down the block past the MOVE house risked becoming the target of vile taunts and curses. The loudspeakers had become a more powerful weapon than any gun because through it, the entire neighborhood was terrorized and kept in constant fear.

Although the threats mounted and the loudspeakers seemed to get louder, no official action of any kind was taken. This was the subject of repeated questioning of Mayor Goode by reporters during the final days before the confrontation. In each case the answer was, "We have no legal basis to remove the people from the house. To arrest people we need warrants." In one Interview with Harvey Clark, he said he could imagine what it must be like to live in such an environment but that as Mayor he must uphold the law and the rights of all citizens, even MOVE.

Was it possible that MOVE had a legal right to shout over a loudspeaker at all hours of the day and night? The city's ordinance on noise and criminal statutes on terroristic threats indicated they did not. Was it possible that MOVE had a right to not only board up their windows and doors but build a fortified bunker of metal and wood on the roof of their house? The city's building code indicated it did not.

And, there were the MOVE children. Up to six children were present in the house at any given time. They were raised in the shadow of John Africa, taught to eat raw fruit and vegetables and to fear outside authority. Thirteen-year-old Birdie Africa longed to play with the other children on the street. He often peered out of the windows of MOVE headquarters at those children, wishing he could be like them. If he were still the boy named Michael Ward, he would be out there playing, going to school, eating Big Macs and getting into adolescent mischief. As a child of MOVE, his playmates were all named Africa-- Katricia, who he knew as Tree, little Tomaso, Zanetta, Melissa and Phil. This was Birdie's extended family.

The children looked like their parents-- bare-chested with their hair in dreadlocks. Their ages ranged from nine to the teens. They had no points of reference in life other than those offered by their adult role models. They helped build the bunker on the roof. They played and slept in it. They knew about the meetings the adults had upstairs. They took turns cleaning the "dog yard" in the back of the house. Each child cleaned his own clothing using scrub brushes and water. Sometimes, they would sneak cooked food. When they were caught, the adults had a "meeting". At the meeting, the offending child would be "hollered at", but never spanked.

"They don't believe in spankings," Birdie remembered firmly.[10]

Sometimes they were taken to Cobbs Creek Park to swim in the creek or just to run around for exercise.

At one point the police had been ordered to scoop up the children if they were ever seen alone without their parents, perhaps walking in the park. But police assigned to the surveillance insisted the opportunity never presented itself and that the order was ambiguous. The concept of snatching children off the street was of questionable legality, although some officials thought a case could be made for it if it could be proved the children were in imminent danger of failing health or bodily injury. But child welfare investigators would have to go to the home and see first-hand whether children were being abused or neglected. Again, the standing order from Mayor Goode was that no one was to risk any kind of violent response by knocking on the door at 6221 Osage.

"It was my judgment at the time," recalled Mayor Goode, "that 6221 Osage Avenue was an extremely dangerous, explosive situation that would require very careful, very delicate handling, that it could not be done quickly and overnight, that there was potential for great loss of life if we did not approach it in the proper manner. I did not want the risk of any inspector going to their house, pushing a button that could end up with a loss of lives, of that inspector, of children in their neighborhood, of civilians in that neighborhood."[11]

The hands-off policy even applied to the city-sponsored agency whose sole function it was to help keep the peace in tense situations. The Crisis Intervention Network, directed by former gang member Bennie Swans, had proved itself over and over again in mediating neighborhood disputes including racial problems and neighbor versus neighbor situations. CIN had people all over the neighborhoods getting information and then mediating peaceful solutions. Bennie Swans himself spoke many times with MOVE members, particularly Gerald Ford Africa whom he knew from school. Swans knew MOVE well, yet was ordered to cease ongoing talks.

Now, on May 10, 1985, the people of Osage Avenue said they could not and would not live with MOVE for another summer. They would take care of things themselves if someone didn't do it for them. The faces of Osage Avenue residents Howard Nichols, Milton Williams, Clifford Bond and Earl Watkins became nightly fixtures on Philadelphia television news programs. They and other MOVE neighbors talked often with reporters, because they had no one left to talk to. They knew the end would come soon. They had no idea just how soon.

MOTHER'S DAY

I t was our first Mother's Day in our first house in the Philadelphia suburb of Ardmore. It was a beautiful spring Sunday, May 12, 1985. We were barbecuing ribs, chicken and burgers for my mom and dad. It was still too early in the season for the zoysia grass to turn green. All my other grass turned green weeks ago, except for that big patch in the backyard that remained yellow. The saving grace of the backyard was the blooming roses and the ripening raspberries.

The picnic table was just slightly too small for the four of us and all the food. The grill was cooking burgers, the sun was shining brightly, the breeze was just right and you never saw four people more relaxed.

At 1:30 the phone rang. My wife Marianne went inside to answer it as I flipped a burger on the grill.

"It's Mike Archer on the phone", Marianne said.

With those words, my weekend ended. Everything around me seemed to melt into the background. It was a complete intrusion and I hadn't even picked up the phone yet.

"Hello," I breathed into the phone.

"Archer here. Sorry to bother you at home."

He was trying to be sincere.

"The police are evacuating about two blocks around 62nd and Osage," he said. It had begun, on Mother's Day, for Christ sake.

"What are they telling the people down there?" I asked.

"They're only telling them to be out of their homes by 10 o'clock tonight, to go stay with friends or family for 24 hours. No one is saying anything to the media, officially. Of course anyone who lives in that neighborhood knows what the police are getting ready to do and so do we."

"So, no one's talking officially?" I was a bit incredulous.

"You got it." Mike paused a moment. "I think you should come in this afternoon."

He was telling me to come to work on a Sunday with two hours' notice. We speculated together for a couple of minutes. If history were to repeat itself, the police would actually make their move in the morning. Therefore, the real fun was still at least twelve hours away.

"Wouldn't you rather have me come in tonight and work through the morning," I suggested. I could tell the suggestion registered because there was a moment of silence on his end.

"Let me call you back."

As I hung up, I held the phone tightly and stared at the kitchen wall. Holy shit.

I walked back into the yard where my burger was turning into charcoal and Marianne and my parents wanted to know what the phone call was about. I told them and made an empty attempt to eat my burger. About 20 minutes passed when the phone rang again.

"Why don't you be in around three in the morning," said Archer. "You'll go to the scene and field-produce the live coverage. Harvey and Dennis will be there reporting and you'll have a live van."

"OK, Mike. Talk to you tomorrow."

I played my cards right by suggesting I not come in this afternoon. I could now complete my Sunday with my family, and be right in the middle of the biggest story of the year tomorrow morning when the shit would surely hit the fan.

A phone was always ringing in the Channel Ten newsroom.

"Channel Ten News, may I help you?" Coming from Terri Stewart, the question was usually sincere.

"Is this the news?" asked the voice at the other end.

"This is Channel Ten News," she answered.

"Hey, they all gettin' ready to move us out of here on Osage," said a man with urgency in his voice.

Terri's eyes grew wider. "What do you mean move you out?"

"They tellin' us to leave the house so they can deal with them MOVE people. Damn, on Mother's Day!"

Terri hung up. She sat alone in the newsroom.

In a row house on the 6200 block of Osage Avenue, Earl Watkins wiped the sleep out of his eyes, climbed out of bed and peered out the window. There were police officers everywhere. He and Pearl went to church and asked the minister to pray for the neighbors, pray for MOVE and pray for the police and firemen. When they got home from church, a policeman told them to leave by 10PM.

Around the corner on Pine Street, Mrs. Margaret Lane got a phone call from a police officer.

"We have reason to believe there is going to be gunfire in your neighborhood," he told her.

"By whom?" she asked.

"By MOVE," was the answer.[12]

Back at the assignment desk at Channel Ten, Terri Stewart was taken over by the force that guides most assignment editors--controlled fear. It is the fear of failure, tempered by the control that comes with experience and trust in your instincts. Immediately, her inner alarm sounded and she began making a mental list of station people she should call. Several more calls came in from the neighborhood and she was able to get confirmation from the police radio room that an evacuation was underway. Based on her calls from the neighborhood and the few facts she got from the radio room officers, she found out a few things. Police were actually going door to door, telling people to leave their homes by 10 that night and that they'd be back home in 24 hours. Streets were being closed off to traffic but people were still allowed to walk around the neighborhood. Terri, like the rest of us, knew there was the possibility of action against MOVE at any time, so the evacuation didn't come as a surprise to her. But now that it was reality, it was time to move.

She notified the manager on duty this weekend, Mike Archer. He told her to call in extra people including reporters Charles Thomas and Harvey Clark, both of whom had done most of the recent reporting on MOVE. Arrangements were made by phone with Dave Harvey, manager of technical operations, to get extra technicians to work on a Sunday and to get one of the three vans with live capability rolling to the scene. This was all done with quiet urgency, much like the evacuation of the neighborhood immediately surrounding 6221 Osage Avenue.

News managers made phone calls to staffers at home. Police officers on Osage and Pine Streets walked up steps and knocked on doors. Producers, reporters and technicians were being called at home to report to work. Mothers, fathers and children were being advised to leave their homes. Most of the staff of WCAU-TV was put on notice: come in ready to cover the big one. People living within three blocks of the MOVE house were put on notice: get out and make way for the big one.

From the rear of his house on Pine Street, Philip Burch noticed something that stayed with him in the months that followed.

"During the time the police were setting up their perimeters, I would look out the back door and see the MOVE children. They were playing in their back yard and they were up at the fences." He paused as the full picture was recreated in his mind and heart. "It struck me that they were almost like lookouts."

Photographer Pete Kane got his phone call as he was making Mother's Day dinner for his wife. Like everyone else, he was alerted that something could happen at any time in West Philly, so the call was no surprise. But it was ironic that before this moment, Pete had never shot a story on Osage Avenue. Even during his early days as a free-lance still photographer for the city newspapers, he went out of his way to avoid assignments at the old MOVE house on 33rd Street. Here was a man who grew up in gang territory in North Philadelphia, lived on the border between the Morocco Gang and the Seybert Street Gang and somehow avoided joining either one. Of course, he paid plenty of extortion money to prevent getting beaten up. But he was smart enough to survive that environment.

More recently, he had been smart enough to work his way up the ladder at Channel Ten. He started in the mail room when he was 19, continuing to take still photographs on the side. He had wanted to become a policeman and scored well on the test four times. But each time he was beaten by the legions of applicants who were service veterans and had points added to their scores under civil service law. So for Pete, being a news photographer was the next best thing to being where the action was.

While working in the Channel Ten mail room, he learned videotape photography and editing, setting his sights on the goal of being a street photographer. Now, eleven years later, he had reached that goal. He became one of the coveted one-man-band photographers, assigned a station car with a two-way radio, his own set of camera gear and the freedom of the street.

It turned out Pete had talent for the work. It was a talent that resulted in great pictures, but danger, too. There was the time in 1983 when a tank truck exploded on the Schuylkill Expressway and he was assigned to shoot it. He got so close he suffered smoke inhalation and collapsed. He was carried away by stretcher, and was counted among the injured in that accident.

Today, he would make some nice overtime by working on a Sunday. His wife Adrienne was not pleased but she knew Pete. This was his thing. So, he left her to make her own Mother's Day dinner and headed in his station car to 62nd and Osage. He took his special bag with him that contained his binoculars, candy and cigarettes. He also took with him a piece of optional equipment available to all street photographers who wanted them--a bullet-proof vest.

◆ ◆ ◆

1:00pm. Barricades were up around the neighborhood. They were wooden, yellow sawhorses labeled *Philadelphia Police*. They blocked several streets to traffic, although pedestrians still came and went as they pleased. The officers actually in charge of the evacuation were from the plainclothes Civil Affairs Unit brought to prominence in the 1960's and 70's by the late, legendary Inspector George Fencl. He was known for his skill as a negotiator, his concern for the rights of both sides in a confrontation and above all, his great compassion. He brought to Civil Affairs the image of peacemaker, an image that stuck, even after his death. On this day, George's officers were in short sleeves and wore their revolvers in holsters that clipped to their belts. They were gently but firmly telling the residents to leave their homes and go somewhere else for the night.

Across town, the usually sleepy Sunday newsroom took on the air of a situation room. The entire management team was there. Telephones rang with more frequency. The police scanner had more chatter than was normal for a Sunday.

There was no doubt who was in charge at Channel 10. Jay Newman was a hands-on news director who infused himself into every aspect of any big, breaking story. Sometimes, this quality made him a giant pain-in-the-ass because he'd be climbing all over people, telling them what to do when they already knew what to do and shouting orders across the newsroom when shouting wasn't necessary. He didn't mean to be an irritant, but sometimes he just was.

Jay had not become a news director at a CBS owned station by accident. He was very smart about planning. His competitive nature was second to none. He had experience at a half dozen TV stations before coming to WCAU including a stint as a reporter. At 34, Jay was doing pretty well.

But this story was too big for Jay to handle by himself. It was born years before he worked in Philadelphia and had cooked in a pot tended by many of the people that worked for him today. He called a meeting in his office.

"I want to own this story from start to finish," he said firmly to his executive producers and assignment editors. "I want full coverage, not the usual weekend treatment. I want people to know that Channel Ten has its arms around the MOVE story."

When Jay said "full coverage", that inevitably meant a special report that would interrupt regular Sunday programming. It was done in mid-afternoon, a live report on the fact that evacuations were underway and that something was probably going to happen at the MOVE house within the next 24 hours.

The wheels of the machine were now well in motion. Jay was satisfied everything possible was being done at the station to prepare for the next 24 hours. The right people had been called in. He had live capability at the scene. Yet, there was something bugging him. He sat quietly in his office with the door closed, the TV turned down and his chin resting on his folded hands. It gnawed at him for a few minutes until he was finally able to put his finger on it.

His mind went back to a Saturday many months ago, right there at the station. WCAU had sponsored a media seminar in which invited guests including Philadelphia Police Commissioner Gregore Sambor sat on panels with reporters to discuss hypothetical situations involving the media. One scenario involved a terrorist takeover of a local nuclear power plant. Question: Would you, Commissioner Sambor, enlist the aid of the media in disseminating information to the public concerning such a takeover? Answer: No, I would want to retain complete control of any information released concerning such a situation. The debate among the panelists focused on whether people living near the plant should be warned to evacuate and whether reporters should be given frequent updates by police. It even got as far as the hypothetical instance in which a reporter placed a call to a phone inside the reactor building, got a terrorist on the phone and broadcast that conversation. Thank god it was just a fantasy.

One thing emerged clearly and returned today to trouble Jay Newman. Commissioner Sambor did not view the press as an ally in any way, shape or form. He viewed the press as a hindrance. Thus, he probably would retain total control of all information to be released during a police operation against MOVE.

Jay had tried repeatedly just days ago to call Sambor to suggest a meeting between reporters and police to discuss accommodating the press's needs in West Philly while staying out of the way of the police. He never did get the commissioner but did get a spokesman who implied such a meeting would probably not be high on the commissioner's list of priorities. And that was the end of that.

As these disconcerting memories bubbled to the surface in Jay's mind, he knew what he had to do. Karen Fox had said it herself just two days ago. To reassure himself that he was doing everything possible to insure the best coverage and the safety of his people, he would have to go to Osage Avenue to see for himself. He grabbed a portable two-way radio, jumped into a station car and drove to the scene of the evacuation.

Jay's visit to 62nd and Osage, by all accounts, was as calm as the evacuation. He was not the pushy, impulsive, sometimes overbearing boss who had irritated almost everyone who worked for him at one time or another. He was instead patient, a learner, a person who did not appreciate the immensity of the MOVE situation until he actually witnessed it with his own eyes.

"I regarded MOVE as an isolated, bizarre group and didn't understand until that day what we were dealing with," Jay recalled.

One day in 1951, five-year-old Harvey Clark and his six-year-old sister Michelle were dropped off by their parents at a friend's house in Cicero, Illinois. The reason, said their parents, was that the local white folks were coming to burn them out of their home and that they would have to stay away for a while.

The Clarks had gotten used to sitting inside their front door with guns ever since they moved into the apartment in Cicero, the only black family in town. After the first couple of days of stoning, brick-tossing and random gunfire, word spread through the town that it was finally time to get the niggers out.

The Clarks were indeed burned-out, stoned-out and chased-out of their home by a vicious mob. There was extensive media coverage. A young lawyer from the NAACP named Thurgood Marshall fought their cause before a federal judge, and won.

Thirty-four years later, Harvey Clark stood before an audience at a Jewish community center in northeast Philadelphia. The Oxford Circle Jewish Center had its traditional Men's Day on May 12, 1985. It was the day for the men to make breakfast for the women. And this year, Harvey Clark from Channel 10 was the guest speaker. He stood before several hundred people on a Sunday morning, talking to them about being a TV reporter. They asked about his roots, about being nervous on television and about MOVE.

As if on cue, Harvey's pager-radio began beeping loudly. The beeping stopped after a few seconds and was replaced by the tinny voice of Terri Stewart: Harvey, please call the station right away. Something is happening at MOVE, we don't know what but they're evacuating. Please call.

Harvey made his apologies and left a group of people who, in a small way, shared a bit of the excitement of the MOVE story.

At 40 years of age, Harvey had come a long way since Cicero. It was a road filled with detours and awful tragedy. After Cicero, his family moved to Nashville where he spent his youth before joining the U.S. Navy. He served on the U.S.S. America, spending almost six months on that ship in the waters off Vietnam. The Navy taught him how to be an air traffic controller, a skill that became his career after the service.

His sister Michelle had broken into the broadcasting business as a television reporter. By the time Harvey got out of the Navy, Michelle had become one of the only black reporters for CBS News and was destined for greatness.

By 1972, Harvey was 27 years old, Michelle was 28. She had become a co-host of the CBS Morning News. John Hart anchored from New York, Michelle Clark from Washington, D.C. She had just finished covering the Republican National Convention in Miami when CBS News president Richard Salant elevated her to the position of correspondent, a title that carried with it the full weight of CBS News prestige and a nice salary increase. In subsequent conversations, Salant told her it was his intention to see her become the first female correspondent on 60 Minutes.

By then, Harvey had become a customer service supervisor for United Airlines in Chicago. It would be as close as he would ever come to his dream of being a pilot.

The 1972 Christmas season arrived and it was time for Michelle Clark to fly home to Chicago. She boarded a United flight for Midway Airport, looking forward to a holiday visit with her family. In heavy weather and under severe icing conditions, the plane crashed short of the runway at Midway, killing Michelle and 40 other people. Her brother Harvey, a United employee, was one of the first to find out. Again, the Clark family was thrust into the media spotlight under tragic conditions.

There was a memorial service in a small chapel in Chicago. It was standing room only. Harvey delivered the eulogy before hundreds of people including CBS executives who had chartered a plane from New York. Michelle Clark, who at age 28 had just begun turning heads as a promising network correspondent, was gone in a tragic accident. Her brother Harvey, who had always admired her beyond words, was now forced to find words to express his feelings before a crowd of hundreds of people dressed in black.

Afterwards, there were handshakes and condolences. CBS News President Salant approached Harvey with his hand outstretched.

"I hired your sister and brought her to the network," he told Harvey with pride. It was one more handshake, one more person praising Michelle.

"You know, you have a tremendous speaking voice," said Salant. "If you ever find you have the desire to get into the broadcasting business, give me a call." He gave Harvey his card. Harvey put it in his pocket and forgot about it.

Two years passed and Michelle's influence on her brother became more pronounced. He found himself getting more and more interested in his sister's work, perhaps believing his life experience helped qualify him to relate other people's stories. By the mid 1970's, the demand was higher than ever for capable minorities in broadcasting and Harvey thought this was the time to make his move.

To become enrolled in a special minority training program sponsored by the three (at the time) major networks and several major newspapers, an applicant needed to already be employed somewhere. Harvey was a student at Vassar College, one of the first class of male students at the formerly all-female college. He remembered he had Dick Salant's card. He called and immediately Salant put him on the CBS payroll. Salant was essentially being Harvey's sponsor for the minority training program. Salant helped place Harvey in his first job as a television reporter in 1975 at WCCO, the CBS owned station in Minneapolis. When Harvey began working there, his fellow reporters were Susan Spencer, Jerry Bowen, Barry Peterson, Phil Jones and Bob McNamara, all of whom went on to become CBS News correspondents.

Ten years later, in 1985, Harvey had become a Philadelphia television institution. One former Channel 10 news director referred to him as "our gutsy, metropolitan reporter." His first story for Channel 10 was the 1978 MOVE shootout in Powelton Village. He covered it as a stranger in a strange town. In the years since, Harvey became identified with the stories of the streets-- crime, urban blight, minority struggles and everyday people struggles. He had also grown in his knowledge of MOVE and was now the main reporter assigned to that story.

◆ ◆ ◆

There was plenty of activity at 62nd and Osage on that warm and pleasant May 12, 1985. People were walking by with suitcases and boxes of belongings. Earl Watkins' wife Pearl was walking slowly up Osage Avenue with a small suitcase. Cars pulled away with people and boxes inside. Lots of men in shirtsleeves and ties were walking around, pistols strapped to their belts. At the yellow police barricades stood uniformed officers with dark blotches of sweat staining their starched, blue shirts. They were making sure only the neighborhood residents were coming and going, not strangers who might start trouble. Most of the faces in the neighborhood were black. Those that were white belonged to some of the police officers and reporters.

In the middle of the activity were the mobile news vans of the three (at the time) major Philadelphia television stations. Channel 10's was at the corner of 62nd and Pine. The sliding door was open and Pete Kane was standing at it with one foot resting on the van floor, the other on the ground and his arms folded. This was the new van called Mini 2. It was parked right outside Dee's Market, a classic Philadelphia corner store that sold candy, cold sodas, newspapers and cigarettes. Business was pretty good, between the warm weather and all these strangers around.

The name mini for the vans was a shortened form of mini-cam, which is what hand-held, portable television cameras were called at first. One former news director thought it was demeaning to call the vans minis, and always referred to them as mobile 2, mobile 3, etc. He was the only one who ever did. The label mini stuck.

Each van was capable of transmitting a microwave signal that would carry live or videotaped pictures. A minivan was equipped with a camera, tripod, lights, portable radios, various cables and a gasoline-powered generator. Total price tag at the time: about $175,000.

The reporters would be going live from Mini 2 for tonight's broadcasts. To do so, the technicians had to raise its transmitting antenna to a height that would clear the row homes. The antenna on the van was mounted on a telescoping aluminum mast that extended vertically to a maximum height of about 50 feet. The microwave signal then had a clear, line-of-sight shot to a receiver mounted on a tall, receiving antenna. Receivers were located in various high spots in Philadelphia. From there, the signal was piped back to the station by land line, and then put on TV.

Jay had arrived on the scene in mid-afternoon and began looking around. The mast on Mini 2 had already been raised since a live shot was done for the special report earlier in the afternoon. The tripod was sitting there on the sidewalk, without its camera. Pete Kane had it on the ground next to him as he was preparing to shoot video of the evacuation. Photographer Chuck Satiritz had arrived earlier with reporter Dennis Woltering after being detoured from their other story in Pottstown. Photographer Bob Roncaglione had also been detoured to the scene from a story he had been shooting with reporter Roseanne Cerra. He had dropped Roseanne off at the station and driven Mini 2 to the scene. He got there quickly and grabbed the choice parking spot in front of Dee's.

Jay turned his gaze upward. Looming high above the neighborhood, affording the best view of Cobbs Creek, was a church steeple. St. Carthage's Church at 63rd and Cedar was a neighborhood landmark anchored in bedrock. It wasn't just a house of worship, but a house of friendship. It linked the neighborhood's past with its present, its old members with its young. Father Charles Diamond, the pastor, was a leader in the neighborhood. Born and raised in Philadelphia, Father Diamond had been assigned to St. Carthage's by the Archdiocese a number of years ago. He was soft-spoken but bright and funny. He didn't look anywhere near 50 years old and had striking blue eyes. He had found it a challenge to be the white pastor of a mostly black parish, but he loved it. Recently, he had been visited often by a short, chubby Jewish man with curly hair who did a Santa Claus act at Christmas. That man was Channel 10 photographer Frank Goldstein.

Frank had been Harvey's photographer for most of the recent MOVE stories on Osage. Frank realized almost from the beginning that the only way to get pictures of what was going on at the MOVE house was to get a camera up high. Early on, his eyes had scanned the geography and stopped at the St. Carthage steeple. His relationship with Father Diamond at first made him hesitate to ask him what was on his mind. But before long, he did. At first Father Diamond thought it would be a neat idea to have a TV camera in his church steeple. He couldn't see the harm in it. But a few days later when Frank brought it up again, Father reminded him that lots of pigeons roosted in the steeple and that it was probably pretty filthy up there, not to mention dangerous. Although he hadn't ruled it out, it appeared he was starting to waver. That was how he left it when Frank was assigned to cover the Flyers in an out-of-town playoff game on May 12.

As Jay surveyed the area immediately surrounding Mini 2's location, he saw how impossible it would be to cover anything because of how far away the police kept reporters. The MOVE house itself was actually around the corner from where reporters were allowed to remain. They couldn't even see the house. This was definitely going to require a creative approach. This was one story where almost simply wouldn't be good enough. Jay remembered what made the difference in the video he had seen of the 1978 shoot-out--cameras in high and secret places. So, he too looked upward and spotted St. Carthage's steeple.

By now, Harvey had gotten an eyeful of Jay and thought to himself, "Oh, shit, what's he doing here?" The other members of the crew also regarded Jay skeptically.

"What is this guy possibly gonna do here?" fretted Roncaglione who, like the others, was used to doing his work in the field without interference. "Although I guess if he's here, something big must be getting ready to happen."

Bob was a photographer who believed in shooting first and asking questions later. He kept his elbows up when making his way through a crowd to clear a path while he shot. Once when I was the assignment editor, I sent him to the airport to get a shot of The Who arriving in Philadelphia. I seemed to be the only person in town who knew the exact time the charter was landing, and at which gate. He knew it was important to me to get the video. He arrived at the gate and walked right past a police guard towards a waiting limousine. The plane had already touched down and the four members of the group had deplaned. They had to walk past Bob's rolling camera to get to their limo. They did so and drove away, thinking nothing of this lone TV photographer. But the police guard was not pleased at all. She stormed over the Bob, threatened to arrest him and told him to get the hell out of there. Later, Bob told me, "Sometimes you have to step on their faces, then apologize for not wearing sneakers."

Jay sought out Harvey, whom he considered the authority on MOVE. Almost immediately, the talk turned to finding a spot to put a high camera, and Jay's first idea was St. Carthage's. Chuck Satiritz went to the church and sought out Father Diamond. The final answer to Frank Goldstein's idea was a definite no. The Archdiocese had ruled against placing any camera in the church steeple. It felt it would be better not to get involved. Chuck reported this information back to Jay. Undaunted, Jay decided to scout other nearby locations. Harvey went with him reluctantly, knowing Jay was right to be preoccupied with getting a high spot for a camera. Now was the time to do it, when things were still relatively calm, not at the last minute when there would be no more time to think.

They walked about a block over on Pine Street towards 61st and spotted a three or four story building that was higher than other buildings around it. They walked closer and soon realized it was virtually uninhabitable, burned out by fire and rotted out by neglect. Still, they went inside.

This was bad. It was a shell of a building, littered with garbage and stinking of urine. They stepped carefully over the stuff lying on the floor, mercifully inanimate and, hopefully, dead. Up the steps they climbed through the condemned building, making their way slowly and cautiously to the roof. Finally, in a spasm of logical thinking, Jay said, "This just isn't safe. Let's get the hell out of here."

Back outside on solid ground, Jay and Harvey walked back to the corner and got into one of the station cars. Harvey knew of a building known locally as the geriatric center, an apartment building for the elderly at 63rd and Walnut Streets. Harvey remembered it from 1984 when police used it as a command center for another operation against MOVE that was aborted when MOVE made no threatening gesture.[13] Really, it was probably too far away, but it was the only other tall building in the area.

They parked around the corner from the main entrance on Walnut Street, got out of the car and approached the door. Jay was carrying his portable two-way radio as they walked through the main entrance and approached a woman sitting at a guard station.

"The other officers are all inside," she said to them. "They're setting up down the basement."

"Actually," offered Jay, his eyes fixed fast on Harvey's, "we could really use access to the roof."

"Right this way, officers." The woman showed them the way, no questions asked. Harvey and Jay walked quickly and with no small amount of paranoia. Neither said a word.

There they stood, on the roof of the police command center, looking out towards Osage Avenue and the MOVE bunker. As they suspected, it was too far away to see anything. Even a zoom lens on its tightest setting wouldn't work. Besides, this charade wouldn't go over big once the guard started checking IDs. Harvey and Jay gave the woman a pleasant good-bye as they left, heading back to Mini 2 at 62nd and Pine, some five blocks back.

As they approached the van, Chuck and Bob were already there. Harvey and Jay told of their treacherous walk through the abandoned apartment building down the street and their temporary promotions to police officers at the Geriatric Center. Including the church, they had now ruled out the only three, obvious places where it was physically possible to a put high camera. Jay emptily suggested they rent a cherry-picker, which was immediately ruled out as too obvious and impractical.

"We absolutely must get a camera high," asserted Bob. "The cops are never gonna let us close enough to get ground shots of what's going on down there." The fact that reporters and cameras were not permitted beyond the barricades almost assured that somehow, someone would do it.

"When they tell me I can't take a picture, you know I'm going to try my darndest to get that picture," declared Chuck, whose resourcefulness had come through for the station on many occasions. Chuck was a former film photographer who made an effortless transition to videotape photography when the news department started phasing out film in the late 1970's. In the process, he also became an expert technician who learned how things worked. Now, Chuck was eyeing Mini 2's 50-foot high, aluminum mast.

"Here's an idea, but you probably won't like it," Chuck offered Jay. "We stick a camera on top of that mast, pointing at the bunker."

To Chuck's surprise, Jay did not immediately reject the idea.

"Will the mast support the weight of a camera?" asked Jay.

"Not the cameras we have here, but there's a smaller one back at the station that would probably hold." Chuck was talking about a lightweight camera the station purchased as an experiment a couple of years back to see how the photographers liked it. Its video quality was inferior to the big Sony's that were standard equipment, especially in situations with limited available light.

"It's not the greatest camera in the world," said Chuck, "but it would probably sit nicely on top of that mast. And at only $5,000, it's expendable!"[14]

Jay thought about what could happen to it. It could get shot down. It could fall down. Worst of all, it could be discovered by the other stations.

"I could lower the mast and tape it to the antenna, point it in the right direction, raise it back up to 50-feet, do it all when it gets dark so on one else sees." Chuck was selling, Jay was buying.

"Do it," said Jay.

Al and Edna Parker[15] had moved onto 62nd Street in 1957. It was the last stop in Al's travels as a dock builder, a job that took him many places. Officer George Draper had come to their door once the night before and twice today, pleading with them to take a few things and leave their home. Draper, of the Civil Affairs Unit, was as much a fixture in the neighborhood as the MOVE people. He was on the surveillance team for a long time and he knew everyone on Osage Avenue and 62nd Street. He was hated by the MOVE people and on evacuation day he was looked upon with some suspicion by the residents.

Saturday night he knocked on the Parkers' door and said, "I'm just notifying you that you might have to evacuate your home tomorrow because of MOVE."

Bullshit", said Al Parker. These kinds of warnings had come a couple times before from the police in recent years.

Sunday morning, the Parkers got ready for 11 o'clock mass when Officer Draper came around again, and again they brushed him aside, determined to go on with their lives despite MOVE, despite the reporters and despite the dozens of police officers swarming through their neighborhood. If they didn't sell their house during the worst of the bull-horning, they weren't going to be chased out today.

The Parkers were looking forward to Mother's Day dinner after church with their grown daughter and her two little girls. After coming home from church, they spent a couple of hours relaxing, if that was possible with the police everywhere and their neighbors leaving their homes. At 3 o'clock, Officer Draper came by one more time, pleading with them to leave for the night.

"I'm not leaving and that's that," said Al. Draper left, frustrated again. By now, Al had made it clear to Edna and their daughter that he would not be going to dinner with them, but would stay with the house. It was not exactly the kind of Mother's Day dinner Edna had hoped for, but she was resigned to it. She, her daughter and two granddaughters went to dinner in the afternoon.

When they returned it was early evening, about six. The evacuation was reaching its peak. There were more cops than ever. There was a knock on the Parkers' door. It was Father Diamond, who was in the process of knocking on every single door where families still remained, pleading with them to leave.

"I don't want any funerals at my church," he said good-naturedly but quite seriously.

It was a tribute to the respect Father Diamond commanded in this part of the world. Al Parker wouldn't leave after three warnings by the police, but he agreed to leave after one visit by Father Diamond. Al Parker had a niece in the Germantown section of the city and it was agreed they would all spend the night with her. He was not happy about leaving his home of 28 years.

◆ ◆ ◆

6:30PM, Channel Ten News, Sunday, May 12, 1987. Kris Long, anchors:

"GOOD EVENING, GLAD YOU'RE WITH US. A LONG-FESTERING PROBLEM IN WEST PHILADELPHIA MAY BE RESOLVED SOON. NEIGHBORS OF THE RADICAL GROUP MOVE HAVE BEEN GIVEN UNTIL 10 O'CLOCK TONIGHT TO VACATE THEIR HOMES, AS PHILADELPHIA POLICE PREPARE TO COME TO GRIPS WITH MOVE MEMBERS WHO, NEIGHBORS CLAIM, HAVE MADE LIFE MISERABLE ALL ALONG OSAGE AVENUE. IT HAS BEEN AN ORDERLY EVACUATION SO FAR, NO VIOLENCE

HAS BEEN REPORTED, AND OFFICIALS HOPE THEY CAN REACH A PEACEFUL SOLUTION TO THE PROBLEM."

Harvey Clark reported on the evacuation. Dennis Woltering concentrated on interviewing neighbors as they gathered their belongings and left their homes. Anchorman Long promised that Channel Ten would be following the developments closely on Osage Avenue, and would break in with any further information. The MOVE story ate up the first seven minutes of the broadcast, and then, "IN OTHER NEWS..."

The live shots were done. Harvey and Dennis put down their microphones, removed their little earphones and stepped away from the camera that was set up on the corner of 62nd and Pine Streets. By 7 o'clock, it was still light. It had cooled off nicely and a pleasant, spring evening set in.

As millions of Americans settled down to watch 60 Minutes, a small pocket of the Philadelphia population was preparing for a terrible unknown. The cool night did not cool the anxiety that breathed through the streets of the Cobbs Creek neighborhood. Now that the events of Mother's Day on Osage Avenue had been broadcast for all to see, spectators began gathering at the police perimeters. They walked or drove from neighborhoods near and far. They stood at the yellow barricades, craning their necks for a glimpse of some kind of activity, or to see the many police officers or maybe even a dreadlocked MOVE member. Couples came. Women with their children came. Kids from who-knows-where came. They pointed. They chatted. They laughed and giggled. Their eyes darted from place to place, drinking in with awe the realness of what had just been on live TV.

It never fails that part of any crowd at a big story chooses to hang around the television crews. A glimpse of a famous TV reporter is just as good, if not better, than a glimpse of a body-bag. If the TV crew has its live van, so much the better-- all that fascinating stuff inside, the monitors, the radios chattering, the police scanners-- so many gizmos, so many questions.

Bob Roncaglione thought it was strange. He had covered fires in which children were burned to death, brutal strangulations and shootings, all manner of pain and suffering. Yet, the macabre curiosity of bystanders at these scenes always troubled him. Who were these people and why did death hold such fascination for them? What was there to see--a dead person? A shrieking mother whose child had been killed? Was it enough just to be at the spot where a crime had been committed?

Around him, as police were orchestrating the evacuation of a neighborhood for a probable battle with MOVE, people on the sidelines seemed detached. One woman had just been voted mother of the year at some local bar and she let everyone know it. She hung around Mini 2, bragging non-stop.

Across the street at a competing station's live van, there was joviality. It was just another live shot to them. But that was fine with Bob because he knew he was part of a plan that could competitively kick their asses out of town.

For now, Bob was assigned to reporter Charles Thomas, who knew where to find Louise James, owner of the MOVE house. Charles had interviewed her before and had established a rapport with her. Bob and Charles set off to do what no one else would do this night--get an exclusive interview with John Africa's sister on the eve of his last stand.

Harvey and Dennis both checked in with the station for further instructions. They would both be relieved for the night and were to report back early the next morning. Before he left though, Harvey had an important, secret meeting to go to, just a few feet away.

By now, the "toy" camera, as it was affectionately called, arrived at Mini 2 from the station. It came in a black case, carrying all the cachet of a secret weapon. Chuck began examining it, checking out how best to fasten it to the top of the mast.

Sitting on a barricade just a few feet away from Mini 2 was a man named Gary. He had been hanging around the truck much of the afternoon and was still there as night descended. Pete Kane found himself caught up in idle conversation with this young man. He did not appear to be a threat. As their conversation became more focused on the events around them, Gary revealed he had relatives in the neighborhood. In fact, he knew quite of few of the people who lived here. Some of those people lived right down the street on 62nd where it met Osage Avenue. Imagine that letter "T" again. Osage Avenue is the vertical line, 62nd Street the horizontal line. Where they intersected were several homes on 62nd Street with front-window views right down Osage Avenue.

It was Pete's fantasy to be inside one of those homes with his camera rolling when the police tried to arrest the MOVE people. It was the lesson of the 1978 shootout. There would be no other way to record the arrests on videotape. Even the camera mounted on the mast would only afford a shot of the bunker. A camera needed to be behind the police lines, in someone's home, shooting through a window towards the MOVE house when the police would launch their operation. Of course, there was the chance that all the action would happen in the alley behind the MOVE house, out of range of this secret camera. But the layout of the alley wasn't known to Pete, who had never been here before to shoot a story. The whole thing was a long shot anyway.

"Do you know any of the people who live in those houses that look down Osage Avenue?" he asked Gary.

"Yeah."

"I would love to get into one of those houses with my camera."

"What do you mean?"

"I want to set up my camera inside one of those houses and aim it through the front window so I can get pictures of whatever happens in front of the MOVE house. Looks like about four of the houses have a clear view down Osage. I'd have to go in tonight and stay there until it's all over."

Gary hardly hesitated. "I'll go find out for you."

He left the van and started down 62nd Street. He was not challenged by the police because he looked as though he belonged there. Had Pete tried it, he would have been immediately stopped since the police knew by now he didn't live there. Pete lit a cigarette and thought about what he was attempting to do here. It sounded kind of illegal.

Gary returned a few minutes later. Of the four doors he knocked on, the occupants behind two said no. The other two weren't home. They chatted a while longer and he offered to try the other two again in a little while.

Harvey was just around the corner, out of earshot and eyeshot of everyone, having a meeting with a friend. It was a friend he had come to know during his years as a reporter in Philadelphia. It was a friend whom he saw socially. His friend was a Philadelphia policeman assigned to the Civil Affairs Unit, on duty in West Philadelphia. He told Harvey the entire plan for the assault on MOVE headquarters: that it would be tomorrow morning at 6AM; that the warrants for the four members accused of crimes would be read; that a chance would be offered for those four MOVE people to surrender; that upon refusal of surrender, a smokescreen would be sent out in front of the MOVE house so two teams of police officers could get into the homes on either side; that those officers would try to blow holes in the adjacent walls with explosives and pump tear gas into the MOVE house to force the occupants out. No one saw Harvey and his friend together. After their chat, they went their separate ways, both to return at 3am Monday.

Gary had since gone back down 62nd Street to knock on those two doors where he got no answer before. Pete figured he'd give this one shot, then forget about it and just move on. Harvey soon appeared from the shadows and Pete started telling him what he wanted to do. Harvey had become familiar to the people in this neighborhood after doing so many stories there. A couple of random spectators would say "Hi, Harv." Harvey was used to that. It was part of being a local celebrity. One person, a pretty young woman, approached Harvey and struck up a conversation with him. She had seen him around because her parents lived down the street on 62nd. Did he have any inkling what the police might do here, she wondered.

It was time for Pete to call the station and tell someone what he was planning to do. After all, he was placing himself, and the station, at some risk of criminal prosecution, not to mention the risk of physical harm to himself. Pete dialed the station on the cellular phone in the van. He got Terri Stewart on the Assignment Desk and told her what he was up to.

"Hold on, let me get Jay," she said and put him on hold. Jay had returned to the station in time for the early news. A couple of minutes passed but being on hold always seems longer than it really is. A click on the other end and Terri's voice said, "Jay says OK, but only if you are 100% comfortable with the arrangements."

"Tell him I want to offer the owner of the house $100," said Pete.

"Hold on." Another click, another wait, another click.

"Jay says OK."

The Parkers spent a while sitting on their front steps, watching the evacuation proceed. It was that time of year when twilight set in around seven or so. On the stoops up and down Osage Avenue, 62nd Street and Pine Street, thoughts turned to leaving home. It had finally come to this, being chased out. But who was doing the chasing, MOVE or the police?

As the Parkers sat on the stoop, waiting for something to begin or end, the young man Gary approached them.

"How you doing," Gary asked them cautiously.

"Well, we're not sure right now," answered Mrs. Parker.

"Yeah, I see what you mean. Um. . ." The question trailed off into uncertainty. This was not something he could just come up to people and ask them as they were about to be kicked out of their home. But he did anyway.

"There's a guy I know down the street from Channel Ten. He's looking for a place to shoot some pictures with a good view of Osage Avenue."

The Parkers looked at him quizzically.

"I'm asking if he can use your house as a base to take pictures of whatever happens at MOVE."

"No way," exclaimed Edna. She shot up from the stoop, turned around and went inside to begin gathering the few things they'd need for the overnight stay at the niece's house.

Up the street the Parker's daughter had gotten involved in a conversation with Harvey Clark. Soon, Harvey drew Pete into the discussion and soon the discussion centered on Pete's career as a TV photographer. Yes, it went, Pete is at a stage in his career where he really has to show the boss he can do it. Here he is, a young black man from the ghetto, trying to make good at the big TV station, trying to show he's as good as everybody else. This MOVE thing is his chance to show them. And besides, there would probably be some money in it for her parents.

The young woman was touched and impressed. This was Harvey Clark, one of the most trustworthy newsmen in Philadelphia, the pride of the black community, right here on 62nd Street. Before she knew it, the idea of having this photographer in her parents' house taking pictures out the window sounded plausible, even desirable, for it might be good to have a young, strong man to watch the house while god-knows-what was going on.

As Edna Parker was getting things ready to leave, her daughter came in and talked to her about Pete. Pete and Harvey kept their distance. Al Parker heard, and was furious.

"If I can't stay, no one can stay, do you hear me?" It was tough enough for him to agree to leave his home. To allow a total stranger to stay in it alone was outrageous.

"But he's offering money. And he won't tell anyone except his boss where he is. Our names will be kept out of it." Al's daughter was giving him the hard sell on the idea. "He's a nice, young man. He can watch the house for us."

Al was not sold but Edna was starting to weaken. Her daughter had spoken to this man. He was out there with Harvey Clark from Channel Ten.

"He just wants a clear view of Osage Avenue and this is the only place he can get it," was the final plea from the daughter.

It was so absurd that Edna Parker thought something good just had to come of it.

"He better call us every hour to tell us everything's alright," she said crossly. Al Parker couldn't believe what he was hearing but by now this thing had become bigger than all of them. A young man he didn't even know would be along in a little while to set up shop in their home to take pictures for TV. It was hard to believe.

At that moment, Officer Draper knocked on the door. This time it was an order, not a request. It was time to go.

Pete figured Adrienne wouldn't like this at all, especially since he had already left her on Mother's Day. But he would have to call her later.

After hanging up the phone with Terri in the newsroom, he started moseying over to an alleyway a few feet from the van. It was the alley behind 62nd Street. He would have to go down that alley to get into the house through the Parkers' back door so the police wouldn't see him. There seemed to be no surveillance on the alley, probably because the police had no reason to believe anyone would try to get into a house tonight. He gazed down the alley, trying to pick out which back door would be his target when Bob Kravitz, a photographer from Channel Six, wandered over. Kravitz was friendly with many of our technicians, even though they were his competition. He was also a very smart person and knew that if you stay on good terms with the competition, some day it might come back to you in kind. Today, however, was not the day.

"What's happening, Pete," he asked amiably. He was such a sweet guy; it was a shame to have to lie to him outright.

"Nothing's happening, man. The cops just told me if we don't stay out of that alley they'll kick us all out of here. I'm telling you man, stay away from that alley!"

Pete was an equally sweet guy, which made his lie so much more believable. But did Kravitz believe him? They chatted for a few minutes when he finally left, looking over his shoulder as he walked away. Did he know something was up? Pete wondered.

Pete went back to the truck and gathered the things he would need for an extended stay in the stranger's house-- camera, recorder, three tapes, four batteries, Snickers, Almond Joy and cigarettes. He stared at his bullet-proof vest. With his camera loaded with a fresh battery and his recorder loaded with a fresh tape, he waited until full darkness.

A block away and around a corner, Chuck Satiritz was busy in the van, sizing up the small camera for its journey 50 feet up. He decided he would tape it to the antenna on top of the mast using the wide, gray duct tape each truck had stashed inside. Chuck did every job without griping. He had a neatly trimmed moustache with neatly coiffed, slightly longish black hair. He spoke tersely and with purpose, a total professional, sometimes unforgiving in his perfection. His brother Nick was also an excellent photographer and editor at the station.

As Chuck began ripping lengths of tape, his mind wandered back to a moment the day before when he had been in this same neighborhood shooting a Saturday MOVE story with reporter Lorrie Yapczenski. A little boy from the neighborhood came up to them, proudly showing off a turtle. He told them he was going to take care of the turtle and bring it to school on Monday. Now, that boy had probably left his home and his turtle behind. He would surely be sad if he couldn't show it off in school tomorrow.

◆ ◆ ◆

Charles Thomas didn't know when or where it would happen, but he knew sooner or later he would interview Louise James. From the first time he did a MOVE story several weeks ago, he thought it was important to talk to the owner of 6221 Osage Avenue. He even got one of the neighborhood old-timers to get Louise's phone number for him. He tucked it away.

Charles had always felt certain sympathy for black revolutionaries, even as far back as high school when he published his free paper, "The Dark Side" in 1969. He wrote about the ways in which blacks should go about gaining the rights they should've gotten 200 years ago.

"There were two basic schools of thought at that time," he told me later, "burn it all down, or build it up from the inside. My position was somewhere in the middle."

One July 4th during his youth, he and his friends declared a holiday they called Independence Day for Blacks. They put up posters of Malcolm X, Stokely Carmichael, and H. Rap Brown around St. Louis. They were arrested and later released.

After college came several jobs in broadcasting including stints as a reporter at TV stations in Kansas City, Missouri and San Francisco. He viewed the 1978 MOVE shootout as many people did outside Philadelphia--a battle begun by crazy Frank Rizzo and his militaristic police force. Since coming to Philadelphia and experiencing the MOVE story as an insider, his opinion changed considerably.

"By 1985, MOVE was intransigent," he recalled. "They were a cult of confrontation. They confronted society on every level and left no room for compromise."

On May 12, 1985, Charles Thomas found himself on the phone with Louise James. He had dug out her phone number and called her, figuring maybe today she'd feel like talking.

"Charles Thomas called me and asked if I was aware that they were evacuating the neighborhood," she recalled, "and I told him that I had heard it on the radio. He asked if there was anything that he could do. I told him that if he could contact the Mayor for me I would appreciate it because I wanted to talk with him and see if I could prevent it in some way. He said he would attempt to do this."[16]

As he sat in the Channel Ten newsroom with the phone to his ear, Thomas heard an angry, bitter woman speaking of the violence and death she was sure would come. She agreed to be interviewed but would not allow him to go to her directly. She told him he would have to call her sister Laverne, go to her house and have Laverne take Charles to where Louise was. Jay Newman didn't like the idea at all.

"No way," he told Charles. "I need you to stay at the scene and report on the evacuation."

"But this is a shot at an exclusive," Charles pleaded. "I think she trusts me." Back and forth they went for a couple of hours until Jay finally agreed around four o'clock.

Charles made one more call to Louise to firm up the meeting with Laverne. He was about to embark on an exclusive interview with John Africa's sister on the eve of his last stand.

Photographer Bob Roncaglione came back to the station, picked up Charles and off they went to an apartment at 39th and Reno in West Philadelphia, the home of Laverne Simms. Laverne was a taller, broader woman than Louise with sadder eyes and a quieter way. She met Charles at the door to her apartment and followed him into the station car. Bob was at the wheel. She directed them to another apartment building, the Chestnut Arms at 40th and Chestnut. They parked close by and got out of the car. Laverne led them into the building through a series of doorways into a tiny, hot apartment loaded with junk. There, in a corner, sat Louise James, a tiny woman combing a big afro. Charles approached cautiously, and she received him cautiously. There was some pre-interview chatter, mostly about whether Charles had gotten through to the mayor yet.

"She immediately struck me as crazy," he remembered, "and here I was stuck in this hot, tiny room with her."

Charles explained to her that he had put in a call to the Mayor before he left the station and hadn't heard back yet. He sensed he had better hurry up and do the interview before she changed her mind. He positioned himself in a chair directly in front of her. Bob sat behind and to the left of Charles, his camera aimed at Louise. He focused, framed the shot of Louise's face and said to Charles, "Go."

Charles had heard that Louise was no longer a MOVE member because of some kind of falling out. That was why she didn't live on Osage Avenue any more. But he never would have known it to hear her today. A defiant Louise James was spitting threats and rhetoric into the rolling camera. She knew of the evacuation, knew the people of Osage Avenue and environs were leaving their homes and knew that her house was the center of an evil that was yet to take place.

"If this thing kicks off, I am very much afraid you are going to have blood-soaked streets," she coldly declared. "You are going to have bodies thrown every which way. You're going to have children killed. You're going to have adults killed for no other reason than complaints from the neighbors!"[17]

The interview lasted about seven minutes. Charles looked at Bob and said, "OK, that's it." He put down the microphone and Bob took a few setup shots and reverses of Charles for editing purposes. Again, Charles offered to try to approach the Mayor on her behalf, without making a firm promise. All the talk of Charles going to the Mayor made Bob's ears perk up. He thought if Charles was willing to even think of doing that, this must be real. At that moment Bob wanted more than anything to be back at 62nd and Osage and stay there until the end.

"I called the station and was told my message had been received by the Mayor's office but that the Mayor was out of town," Charles remembered later. "But I did promise her that if I got a response, I'd get back to her right away."

Charles admittedly showed her sympathy for two reasons. First, he identified with blacks trying to make their way in society and learned that unconventional methods were sometimes necessary. Second, he wanted Louise to continue trusting him so that he could eventually get into 6221 Osage Avenue and interview John Africa himself.

"MOVE didn't care if you were black or white," he told me. "They were real interested in people wanting to learn more about them. Ramona liked that the few times I interviewed her on the street at Osage. Once I asked her if John Africa would talk to me. She thought for a moment, and went inside the house. About 45 minutes later, she came back with a handwritten document a few pages long stating the goals and purposes of MOVE. Ramona implied that John Africa had written it. At that moment, I was convinced that John Africa was alive and living in that house."

An Interview with John Africa's sister was nothing to sneer at either, as far as Charles was concerned. He was excited about getting an exclusive with Louise. He and Bob left her apartment and drove to the scene where Charles prepared to do his story for the 11 o'clock news.

It was night in Philadelphia. The forecast called for rain. Some of the uniformed police officers now wore yellow slickers.

The pace of the evacuation was quickening as the 10PM deadline approached. Though they were fearful of what might happen after they left their homes, most of the Osage neighbors were also relieved that one way or the other, the siege was about to end. And they were impatient that the police get on with it.

"I don't want to see anyone hurt or killed. But better them than me," Milton Williams was telling a reporter in an interview. "They came into OUR neighborhood. Now we want them out."[18]

As the evacuation reached a crescendo, the MOVE bullhorn remained strangely silent. There had been scattered sightings of the MOVE children in their backyard and maybe one or two adults on the roof, but no bullhorn.

There were no more live shots scheduled until the 11 o'clock news, so now was the time to put "mast-cam" into service. Chuck lowered the antenna mast. It worked on an air pressure system that prevented it from collapsing too quickly into itself. The 50-foot, telescoping mast atop Mini 2 was now slowly being lowered. When it was fully collapsed the antenna atop the mast stuck out of the roof of the van just a foot or two, easily accessible to anyone who could climb the ladder on the rear of the van.

In the darkness it was impossible to tell why Chuck was on the roof of the van. It looked like he was tinkering with the microwave antenna. He held the small camera and the roll of duct tape. Bob had since returned from the interview with Louise James and was on the van roof helping Chuck. It was simple enough to do, tape the camera to the metal fitting that held the antenna onto the top of the mast. They taped the hell out of it to make sure it wouldn't come loose. Then they pointed it in the direction of 6221 Osage Avenue and slowly raised the mast again.

Chuck loved that they were doing this, but there were two drawbacks. First, the camera worked on a battery which would eventually need replacing. Second, the video cable that connected the camera to the switcher inside the van might be visible. An experienced technician from another station might notice the video cable dangling from the top of the mast and put two and two together. All he could do was pull the cable as close to the mast as possible.

Chuck opened the camera's lens to let in as much light as possible. It was now turned on and he looked at the picture on the TV monitor in the truck. It needed adjusting. He had to lower and raise it two more times before it was finally aimed correctly. The third and final time he raised it, he left it up for the night. The big test would come in the early morning anyway, when presumably the action would start.

The other hidden camera in this master plan was now on its way to its secret perch inside the house on 62nd Street. Pete strapped his recorder to his shoulder, threw his accessory bag over his other shoulder, picked up his camera like a briefcase and quickly but quietly slipped into the alley behind 62nd. He glanced over each shoulder as he walked down the narrow alley to the back door of a house he had never been in, occupied by people he had never met and who were hopefully expecting him.

He had decided he would take Gary with him for company. He also decided at the last moment to leave behind the bullet-proof vest.

❖ ❖ ❖

Jay Newman was doing some heavy thinking back at WCAU. He had just given one of his photographers permission to violate a police perimeter, secrete himself in a private home and possibly expose himself to gunfire, all to get pictures for a news story. How could he justify it to himself and others? It was unquestionably the right thing to do from a competitive standpoint. The station stood to gain exclusive video. He had given Pete full discretion and full veto power. It was, after all, Pete's idea. But his overwhelming concern was for Pete's safety. He could be shot.

Yes, it was a risk. But every time any journalist goes to the scene of a news story, he or she places him or herself at risk. Reporters and photographers do get hurt while covering the news. They die in helicopter crashes. They die in wars. They get shot, or shot at. Is it ever worth getting the story or the picture? ABC'S Bill Stewart thought it was worth it, or he wouldn't have gone to Central America. Channel Ten's Sid Brenner thought it was worth it or he wouldn't have been in that helicopter the day it went down near Harrisburg. Pete Kane thought it was worth the risk, or he wouldn't have volunteered to hide in a house in MOVE country.

Jay concluded Pete was as safe as he could be. He would be the only person to speak directly with Pete. His sole job would be to shoot pictures of whatever happened at MOVE headquarters, then get the tape back to the station for playback after the fact.

The phone rang in Jay's office. It was Harvey calling from home. He had tried to go to bed early, but couldn't sleep. Jay started babbling excitedly into the phone, asking a hundred questions at once almost incoherently when Harvey barked, "Jay will you just shut up for a minute and listen to what I have to tell you!"

Harvey related the whole police plan to Jay and told him he would be on the scene by 3:30 in the morning. Jay figured he'd better be in pretty early himself.

"Are you sure your friend knows what he's talking about?"

"Jay," Harvey answered a bit impatiently, "I've known the man for nine years. We are friends. He knows exactly what's going to go down, count on it."

"OK, if you're confident, so am I. Talk to you in the morning."

8:30pm. In deepening darkness, Pete Kane quietly stole down the back alley behind 62nd Street, his new best friend Gary in tow. He had thought over and over again about whether Gary should come. He was a stranger to him. He didn't even know his last name. Yet, he thought it might be important to have a companion, or a witness. He did trust him and without him, he wouldn't be taking this walk right now. They carefully counted the houses so they wouldn't barge into the wrong one. They were met at the back door by the Parkers' daughter who had made this whole thing possible. Soon, they were inside the house, arriving as the rest of the neighborhood was leaving.

Pete introduced himself. Mrs. Parker greeted him cordially. Mr. Parker looked upon him suspiciously, but gave him a half-hearted greeting as well.

"May I see the windows?" Pete asked. The Parkers granddaughters were fascinated by Pete and his equipment. He made friends with the children quickly and their acceptance of him helped the situation. He was now walking a fine line. He had to show these folks that he, a total stranger, was OK. But he had a job to do, also.

Peeking out the living room window, he had a good view of Osage Avenue. He could see just about the entire length of the street. In the foreground was the small, front lawn of the house he was now in and the steps leading up from the sidewalk. The window was very close to the sidewalk. He feared he might be seen.

"Do you mind if I check out the upstairs?"

"No, go ahead," said Mrs. Parker, who by now had accepted the situation.

Upstairs, the same view of Osage Avenue was afforded from the master bedroom. It was modest, but nice--flowered bedspreads, a clock on the wall, a TV in the corner, sheer curtains on the front window. He moved the curtains aside and was pleased. The view was a bit elevated and out of direct line of sight of anyone on the street. He had an unobstructed view of MOVE's front porch and its boarded-up windows. He could also see the large bunker on the roof. It hung over the eaves, glaring down at the sidewalk below. If it was going to happen in the front of the house, Pete thought, he would definitely get it on video.

"This is perfect," he said, satisfied as he could be with the efforts to get him into this home. "I'd like to set up right here, looking out this window."

"Fine," responded Mrs. Parker. "Just clean up your own mess and you better call us and tell us what's going on."

"Absolutely," said Pete.

"There's pork chops in the icebox if you get hungry, and stuff to drink."

"Thank you, I'll be fine. Listen, I got my boss to pay you $100 for this. We're very grateful for your help."

"You just keep our name and address off the TV. We don't want any more publicity than MOVE has already brought us."

"I promise. No one will know I'm here except my boss. I'll call you all the time. Thank you so much."

Pete's gratitude was apparent to the Parkers. This obviously meant a lot to him. Maybe it really was a good thing. For Pete's part, he was in awe of his good fortune. He was in a spot so prime, he almost couldn't believe it. He was already fantasizing about the exclusive pictures he would shoot. No one else would have the shots of the street battle, the arrests, he thought. Then again, maybe he'd be seen and be shot for a burglar or a MOVE member. Stay back from that window, he thought. Make them wonder afterwards where you got that video.

A few doors down, Pete was aware that Channel Three had been trying to negotiate a similar deal with another family. He didn't know the outcome of that situation and didn't really care. He had the chance of a lifetime to be right on top of a heavy, history-making story.

9:00pm. The Parkers had gathered their things and said good-bye to Pete and Gary. Pete again assured them he would take good care of the place and call them often. They were about to leave through the back door.

"Wait," Pete said. "If you leave by the front door, the cops will know you've gone. They won't come by again to check up."

The Parkers were obliging. They walked out of their home through the front door. A couple policemen saw them. One of them checked them off a list. The Parkers walked away from their home, leaving it in the hands of two men they had only known for about two hours.

Now it was night, and Pete felt uneasy in a strange house, in a strange neighborhood. Not even his wife knew what he was up to. He'd have to call her soon, he thought. Gary had gone downstairs, keeping a healthy distance from the windows, looking for something to eat.

Pete set his camera on its tripod and spent a few minutes aiming it for the best picture of the MOVE house. He loaded a fresh, 20-minute tape, put his recorder on standby and sat back to think about things for a while. He finally called his wife to tell her he wouldn't be home tonight. Then he called Jay Newman, and told him he owed the Parkers $100 dollars.

◆ ◆ ◆

The city plan to eliminate MOVE from Osage Avenue had been worked out the previous week. Mayor Goode had ordered his police commissioner and managing director to come up with a plan, based on arrest warrants, to take into custody those MOVE members wanted for crimes. Of course, everyone knew that to arrest four MOVE members they would probably encounter resistance. Police intelligence told them there could be a dozen or more MOVE people in the house, including the children. Past experience with MOVE showed they banded together and would resist any attempt to arrest brothers and sisters. It was very likely the arrests would have to be made by force. To deal with this probability, the plan called for a forcible entry into the MOVE house by experts of the police Stakeout Unit, known in other cities as the SWAT team. The plan was the product of brainstorming by several members of the Stakeout Unit, led by Lieutenant Frank Powell, who had been entrusted by the police commissioner to devise a safe but effective plan for entering the home and arresting anyone inside.

But when it came time to present the plan to top city officials, Mayor Goode evidently was uninterested in the details. District Attorney Ed Rendell was in the final planning meeting on May 9, as Commissioner Sambor began to relate the plan.

"He started to explain a little bit," recalled Rendell, "and the Mayor said something like, 'Look, I will leave that up to you all. It's your plan, so execute it.' In other words, he cut off discussion."[19]

Now there was urgency in the Sunday evacuation as nightfall reminded the police to make sure every resident was out. By 9pm there were only a few stragglers left, people who couldn't or wouldn't leave earlier. Police tow trucks moved in to tow away any cars that remained on Osage Avenue. Crews from the Philadelphia Electric Company and the Philadelphia Gas Works were being briefed by police on the best time to shut off the utilities to the neighborhood, a precaution against explosions and fires. The final preparations were being made to clear the neighborhood of anything that might get in the way of the violence that was sure to come in a matter of hours.

There was one, final try by citizens from the community to talk to MOVE. A small team of volunteer negotiators walked down the dark, deserted street, under the watchful and slightly nervous eyes of the police, to MOVE's front door. Novella Williams, an outspoken woman who had dealt with MOVE in 1975 and 1976, was among them. So was Bennie Swans, head of the Crisis Intervention Network which until recently acted as middleman in dialogues between MOVE and the city. Bennie went to school with Gerald Ford Africa, one of MOVE's spokespeople. Bennie, Novella and a couple of others ventured down Osage Avenue and approached the MOVE house. Novella rang the bell and Theresa Brooks Africa came to the door and spoke with them for a few moments.

"I'll never forget her face," recalled Novella. "She began to talk about what brought them to this point, which was that their brothers and sisters were in jail and that no one would listen to them. I knew Frank James because my daughter attended Mitchell Prep School in Haverford with him. He used to sit on my steps. The MOVE people are intelligent people. They are basically good people. They're not the animals they've been portrayed as."[20]

Pete Kane sat in the darkened bedroom on 62nd Street, looking through his viewfinder at the shadows walking towards him. He had just gotten off the phone with Adrienne, doing his best to set her mind at ease. He told her he was safe and that he'd be here for a while, but he didn't tell her where "here" was.

Now he was shooting video. He had placed a microphone outside the window to pick up whatever sound it was capable of picking up. Through his viewfinder he saw four or five people walking away from the MOVE house towards 62nd Street. They were Novella Williams, Bennie Swans and the other negotiators, apparently unsuccessful in talking an end to the madness. His recorder whirred as the dark figures ambled their way to the safety of the police checkpoint at the corner. The last cars had been towed from Osage Avenue. The view through Pete's camera was an eerie one, indeed--a deserted, city street with dark houses, no cars and no signs of life.

Suddenly, the bullhorn sprang to life.

"We all know what you mother fuckers are trying to do," shouted a female voice through the speaker. "You been killing MOVE babies for 17 years. You been locking us up when you know we ain't guilty. You been prosecuting this group for 17 god dam years. Let our people go! Y'all let our people go! We ain't leaving our mother fucking house!"

The desperate, shrieking voice was shouting at an empty street. The police who heard it were almost amused. It went on for a good ten minutes, and then stopped.

Pete stopped shooting to go to the bathroom. Gary was somewhere else in the house, perhaps grabbing a snack. Pete himself was thinking about tearing into his candy bars. As he reached over to flush the toilet his hand stopped dead in the air and a look of recognition snapped his eyes wide open. He remembered at that moment that on his old block in North Philadelphia, he would sometimes stand on the front step outside his friends' row homes and hear someone inside flush a toilet. Now, here he stood, having flushed a couple times already during the evening, about to do so again as several police officers stood just feet away from his front door. From that moment on, Pete stopped flushing.

He settled in behind his camera, opened a candy bar, and turned on the TV set in the bedroom to Channel Ten.

11:00pm News, WCAU-TV, Larry Kane, anchor.

"GOOD EVENING, EVERYONE. IT BEGAN THIS MORNING WHEN PHILADELPHIA POLICE MOVED THROUGH THE NEIGHBORHOOD AND ASKED RESIDENTS TO LEAVE BY TEN O'CLOCK TONIGHT AND, IN A SENSE, EVACUATE A SEVERAL-SQUARE-BLOCK AREA SURROUNDING THE MOVE COMPOUND AT 62ND AND OSAGE IN WEST PHILADELPHIA. RIGHT NOW WE BEGIN OUR LIVE TEAM COVERAGE WITH CHARLES THOMAS. CHARLES?"

The picture switched live to Charles at the scene, his dark, mustached face artificially lit, and the words Live/West Philadelphia superimposed under his chin.

"LARRY, OUR BEST INFORMATION IS THAT POLICE HAVE BEEN SWEEPING THE AREA THAT WAS SUPPOSED TO HAVE BEEN EVACUATED. THEY'RE TRYING TO FIND OUT WHETHER ALL OF THE NEIGHBORS ARE GONE, THAT THEY ARE OUT OF THE WAY SHOULD ANYTHING HAPPEN HERE..."

Charles' report was shown, about a minute and 30 seconds long, recapping the evacuation earlier in the day, punctuated by Louise James' angry prediction of death and violence on Osage Avenue. Back live, Charles pitched to reporter Kasey Kaufman, standing next to him and she wrapped her report.

"THAT 10 O'CLOCK DEADLINE TO EVACUATE HAS COME AND GONE. THERE ARE JUST A FEW PEOPLE INSIDE THESE POLICE BARRICADES."

Kasey had spent the evening at the scene and was assigned to one of the primary locations for the early morning coverage.

It was very unusual for Larry Kane to be anchoring a broadcast on a Sunday. He was the station's main anchor. He had established an almost legendary presence in the market since his arrival in the early 70's at Channel Six. He had never worked a Sunday before, so his appearance this night signaled an extraordinary event.

Bennie Swans came to the station to be interviewed live by Larry. He had just come from the final negotiating try with MOVE.

"They've indicated that they want the release of all their

members from jail. And if the members are not released, they are prepared to meet whatever consequences come."

Pete watched TV inside the Parkers' bedroom. There hadn't been any movement on Osage since the negotiating team left over an hour ago. Absolutely nothing was happening now. He still had one candy bar left, which he decided to save for tomorrow. For now, he closed his eyes and waited for some noise to wake him up.

◆ ◆ ◆

3:00am. Osage Avenue was quiet. None of the residents was there anymore. A couple of hundred Philadelphia police officers were getting out of bed to prepare for armed combat.

Chuck Satiritz and Bob Roncaglione were in Mini 2, fine-tuning their aim of the mast camera.

Jay Newman was dead asleep in his condo just a couple blocks from the station when his phone rang.

"Hello?"

"Charles Thomas is in the house with Pete," is all Jay picked out of the torrent of words coming through the phone at him. "Charles is in the house with Pete," the voice said again.

In the recesses of Jay's mind, a vague recollection of Pete Kane started to surface-- a house near MOVE; Pete getting video; no one to know.

"What are you talking about?" he pleaded with the voice on the other end.

"Charles Thomas right now is with Pete Kane in the house on 62nd Street." He recognized the voice as one of his employees, but he simply couldn't place it.

"OK, bye." Jay hung up. He crawled over to where he had the scrap of paper on which Pete's phone number was written. He turned on a light and grimaced. He ambled back to the bed and sat on it as he dialed the number. The phone rang and Jay breathed deeply and yawned.

"Hello," answered the voice on the other end. It was Pete.

"Hello Pete, this is Jay Newman. Is Charles Thomas there?"

There was a silence on Pete's end that spoke volumes. Then, "Yeah, hold on."

After another brief silence, Jay heard what sounded like a hand being cupped over the receiver and a rustling on the phone then, "Hello?"

"Is this you, Charles?" Jay was wide awake.

"Yes, it is."

"I thought I made it clear that everyone was to stay away from Pete Kane."

"Well yes, I know you said that Jay, but I feel this is a situation where a reporter should be present. If anything should break, who would--"

"GET THE FUCK OUT OF THERE RIGHT NOW OR I'LL BLOW YOUR ASS RIGHT THE FUCK OUT OF THIS TOWN!"

Charles left.

One of the last night shots Pete captured was electric company crews climbing up the wooden utility poles to disconnect the power and helmeted gas works men going to each vent in the sidewalk, shutting off the gas. These were the last steps necessary to make the neighborhood safe for the police and MOVE to blow it apart.

PART TWO

THE SHOOTOUT

The alarm sounded nasty and the blue numbers read 2:30 AM. I was half awake anyway. My mind had been spinning all night as I tried to fall asleep. Every time I began to doze, something else invaded my thoughts. I did this to myself every time I was about to embark on a field assignment--drove myself crazy all night, thinking about worst-cast scenarios, imagining the most bizarre, terrible things that could make me fail, thus leading to my termination and subsequent death.

I had no excuse to continue trying to sleep. I got up, showered and dressed quickly. I dressed only by the light leaking into the bedroom from the hallway so as not to awaken Marianne. I dressed the way I usually do for Channel Ten-- blue jeans with a comfortable, buttoned shirt, sweat socks and running shoes. I checked out my beard in the bathroom mirror. Most of it belonged there, but down towards the throat it was overgrown. Hell with it.

I stole into the guest room where my police scanner was. I turned it on in the dark. The red lights blinked sequentially, scanning for any chatter. It was pretty quiet except for an occasional few words from the dispatchers. In this same room, I had a second scanner, a portable, charging overnight. I unplugged it, put it on battery power and programmed it for the Philadelphia police frequencies that might be helpful. I strapped the portable to my belt. I sneaked back into the bedroom, kissed my sleeping wife goodbye and padded down the steps to the living room, then the kitchen. The date on the orange juice container was May 10. I looked at my watch and it said Tue May 13. I chucked it.

I climbed into my orange, 1980 Mustang and drove to the station in the dead of night.

About ten miles away in center city Philadelphia, Harvey Clark tossed and turned, a video loop racing through his brain. The video was of the MOVE operation as he imagined it would go down. Each time it went around, some detail had changed. He studied all the different versions in his dark bedroom. Every ten minutes he looked at his clock-- 2:00, 2:10, 2:20. He was afraid the alarm might fail and he'd miss it all.

"Shit," he said to himself in the dark, whipping the covers away and climbing out of bed. He showered and got his clothes together. He hadn't slept at all. He mechanically groomed, tossed his tie and jacket over his shoulder, walked out the door of his apartment and drove his Corvette to MOVE Land.

I was vaguely aware that it had rained overnight. The streetlights reflected coldly on the pavement. Once I was a few minutes on the road, I turned on the radio. KYW was reporting that the evacuation was apparently complete and all was quiet. There was no talk of what would happen next, or when. I was leaving the serenity of the suburbs and would soon be heading into a zone of urban warfare.

I went first to the station to meet up with a technician who would accompany me to the scene. Inside the newsroom, Hank Stahl was at the assignment desk. Hank was the overnight assignment editor. If anything moved in Philadelphia between midnight and 7AM, he had to know about it. Technician Tony Gore was there, too, sipping coffee and eating a donut. Tony and I were both Temple alums. He was a graduate assistant assigned to WRTI when I first started there as a newscaster eleven years earlier. He was mild mannered, easy going and a competent photographer and editor. He was one of several summer relief people who managed to hang on through the year. He and I were to drive to Osage Avenue together, he to man Mini 2 and me to be field producer. It was now 3:15am.

"Good morning, boys," I said. Tony raised his hand and mumbled through his donut. Hank said, "Morning, TK."

The newsroom's pulse was steady, but weak at this time of day. There was the constant drone of KYW in the background; occasional chatter on the scanners; the flickering of the TV monitors tuned to Channels 3, 6 and 10; the harsh, blue light of the overhead fluorescents; the muffled pecking of the old UPI wire machines and the distant wheeze of a vacuum cleaner. A dozen typewriters sat idle. A dozen desks sat with papers and wire copy piled in varying amounts on top. The newsroom sat at the corner of the ground floor of the building in what was once the huge, glass-enclosed lobby. On the two corner walls that separated the newsroom from City Avenue were huge glass panels that stretched from floor to the 30-foot ceiling. Outside was the intersection of City Avenue and Monument Road, usually busy with traffic heading onto or off the Schuylkill Expressway and US 1. At this time of day, it was an empty, asphalt expanse.

Tony had grabbed the keys to one of the unmarked station cars. The station had a fleet of Ford LTDs, chosen because they had huge trunks to hold a typical one-man-band's camera gear and huge, V8 engines that could tolerate the hard driving they would undergo in their three or four year lifespan. Some of the cars were plain white; others were painted with "10 News, Live At Five."

On the way out, I stopped in the station cafeteria. The word *cafeteria* was used more as an affectionate term. It was really an eating room with machines containing toy food. I put a quarter in a machine and got a cup of "fresh brewed" coffee. I put in 50 cents and got a Tastykake. Tony put in 50 cents and got a red light. He banged the sucker until he got a Tastykake, too.

Tony drove with one hand and fiddled with his Tastykake with the other. I played with my portable scanner, which wasn't picking up anything. The empty streets were lit by orange, overhead street lights. The only signs of life were at the convenience stores which were frequent along the way. I began feeling more anxious as we approached the scene and I sensed Tony getting the same way.

We passed the 7-Eleven, Cavanaugh's bar and other City Avenue landmarks until we made the left turn onto 63rd Street, the road to West Philadelphia. From the station it was only a ten minute drive to 62nd and Osage at this time of day.

It was apparent parking would be a problem. It seemed as though more streets than necessary were blocked off to traffic. We parked several blocks away. The Cobbs Creek neighborhood was basically asleep until we got to within a block of the evacuations where there was an undercurrent of anticipation and uneasiness. People were wandering around. It was unclear whether they lived there or were tourists.

We walked to the corner where Mini 2 had been parked since yesterday afternoon. Standing on the corner under a streetlight was Harvey, his necktie draped casually around his neck, his top button open and his jacket nowhere to be seen. He had arrived a few minutes earlier. He also had to park several blocks away. He had only a fleeting concern about leaving his well-preserved Corvette parked on the street. He was chatting with CBS correspondent Chris Kelly. Chris knew Harvey's sister at the network and had covered a couple of trials in Minneapolis for the network while Harvey covered them for WCCO. Chris had taken care of Harvey, helping him with information and insight. Now, it was Harvey's turn to reciprocate.

"So what do you think," Kelly asked him. "The police will bust in and take them quickly, huh?"

"I wouldn't count on it," returned Harvey.

Wandering around about a half block away was Dennis Woltering. He was talking off-camera to a couple of people on the sidelines.

Inside the van was Bob Roncaglione, who was staring at a very dark image on the monitor. He was also playing with the joystick that controlled the antenna mast.

Chuck Satiritz was outside the truck, finding a good spot for the tripod. At that point I had no idea those two had been there for over 12 hours already.

"What are you staring at?" I asked Bob. The screen was

virtually black, except for a couple uneven shadows.

"We have a camera at a special vantage point," he said quizzically with a half-smile as he continued fiddling with controls. Chuck came over to me because he heard my question.

"Don't make it real obvious, but look up on top of the mast," said Chuck, also with an inscrutable half-smile. All I could see was a thin, black cord hanging from the top and running into one of the input plugs in the side of the van. I squinted a bit more and saw a familiar shape at the very top.

"You put a camera up there," I said in loud voice.

"Will you keep your voice down?" implored Chuck. I could see in his eyes this was his baby. "It's the toy camera. It's been up there since last night. And it works."

I got the quick version of the story and understood now that Bob was trying to get a picture from that camera. It was still too dark to get an image.

I walked over to Harvey and Chris Kelly, now joined by Dennis. Harvey related the police plan of attack as he learned it from his friend in Civil Affairs. It looked like 6am was zero hour. Dennis had just worked the onlookers at the barricades. There were plenty of them, even at four in the morning. They were all neighborhood people, some of whom had been evacuated, some of whom lived on Pine Street to the east. They were very worried. A few feet in front of us was the police line. The yellow barricades closed off Pine Street looking west directly in front of us. To our left, they closed off 62nd Street. We had line of sight vision only as far as the corner of 62nd and Osage. We could not see down Osage Avenue where the MOVE house was. Referring back to the letter T again, our position was on the left tip of the horizontal line (62nd Street). The MOVE house would be about a third of the way down the vertical line (Osage Avenue). Uniformed police officers now guarded the barricades as the plainclothes officers wandered within the perimeter, many of them wearing arm bands with the word "POLICE" in red letters on a white background. For the time being, there wasn't much to do besides stay alert. In less than two hours, the police commissioner would come knocking on MOVE's door.

At the other end of Osage Avenue, where it was bounded by Cobbs Creek Parkway, more and more flashing red and blue lights were coming into focus. The Parkway had been closed off between Pine and Larchmont Streets. It became the assembly area for the police, hundreds of them. Many were now arriving from home in their own cars, half in uniform and half in street clothes. At Osage and Cobbs Creek Parkway, one officer was slipping his white, bullet-proof vest over his undershirt, then his blue shirt over the vest. Coming down Cobbs Creek Parkway was a dark brown van with no windows and its side door open. As it passed you could see four officers, their faces blackened, wearing the navy blue jump suit and dark blue, baseball-style cap of the stakeout officer. One held a shotgun pointing upwards. Two had UZI's dangling from their necks. Behind this van were several marked police cars with lights flashing and uniformed officers inside. Off to the side, in the park, were several dozen stakeout officers putting on their blue helmets, body armor and sporting all sorts of weapons-- M-16 semi-automatic rifles, UZI's, shotguns with short barrels, rifles with silencers and an assortment of side arms strapped into holsters. More blue and white police cars with flashing lights arrived, some carrying just one officer, some carrying several. The reflections of red and blue lights on the rain-soaked street darted and bounced everywhere.

Down the street at the corner of Cobbs Creek and Walnut, police officers wearing suits and ties walked quietly into a small, side entrance of the geriatric center. This was the command post and it was now fully operational. A light shone through a tiny window at ground level.

All the activity at this end of Osage Avenue was being recorded by the whirring camera of Tom Watson, a veteran Channel Ten photographer. Watson was an assignment editor's dream. You never had to give Watson directions to get anywhere. He knew the area blindfolded. I never had to tell him what to shoot or how to shoot it. He shot the routine, ribbon cuttings and the major breaking stories. He shot many out-of-town jobs which required quick turnaround but he could also do the longer, artier pieces. Watson seemed to favor breaking news, crime stories, fires, disasters, accidents, anything that was impossible to get to quickly. Somehow, he would get to them quickly.

Tom was shooting pictures of the Philadelphia police force at its most awesome. At four in the morning, he was allowed to roam among them and shoot at will. The police were oblivious to him, preoccupied with the task before them. Some of the officers might even have felt pride in showing off their fire power.

"Get the hell down from there," came a shout from about 30 feet away. Watson turned towards it. A uniformed policeman was shouting at someone trying to climb up the front of one of the row homes on Cobbs Creek Parkway.

"Get down from there right now!" the officer shouted.

Watson squinted to see who he was shouting at. There, with a foot up on a window sill and another on a front step was Kasey Kaufman, trying to climb up onto the roof. The officer walked briskly over to her gesturing urgently.

"If you don't get off there right now, I'm gonna lock you up!"

"Well, if you didn't seal off the whole neighborhood I wouldn't have to do this," she shot back.

Watson looked interested. That was the kind of thing he would do to get a good camera location. He didn't think Kasey had it in her.

Kasey indeed had it in her since her first TV job in Burlington, Vermont, and was now pushing the envelope to get a good view of the police blockade.

"If you guys weren't so obsessed with managing the news, reporters wouldn't have to go around looking for rooftops to sneak onto," she said. She straightened her skirt, ran her hand through her hair and said to Watson, "Let's go."

Kasey had spent the night at Mini 2 with little to do after her 11 o'clock live shot except schmooze with some of the neighborhood types and check out the lay of the land. By 3:30 when Watson showed up, she was itching to do something. The east end of Osage and Pine were well covered. She and Tom decided to go to the west end onto Cobbs Creek Parkway to see what they could see.

Back at the van, I realized I had not gone to the bathroom, a critical error in planning. I was standing on a street corner at 4am with no public toilet in sight. Would I knock on doors until I found a kindhearted soul who would let me use their bathroom? Would the owner of Dee's Market let me use his toilet? Would I have to hang it out behind Mini 2?

Pete Kane had stopped flushing the toilet inside the Parkers' house hours ago lest someone outside heard. He sat at his camera, looking out over Osage Avenue, waiting for something to happen. It was still early.

At a few minutes before 4am, John Mussoni climbed out of his car in front of the 7-Eleven up the street from the station. He bought coffee for himself and Hank, then drove across the street to the donut shop and bought a dozen. As he drove up city Avenue, he was reminded of the last time he got up in the middle of the night to deal with a big story. He was the assignment editor at a station in Hartford just a couple of years ago. His phone rang one morning at 1:00 AM. The Connecticut Turnpike Bridge had just collapsed into the river below. There were deaths and traffic promised to be log jammed in a large part of southern New England because of it. He had made dozens of phone calls from his home to get the station mobilized to cover the disaster.

But this morning, there was no scramble. There was order. The station's plan was worked out yesterday. As he arrived, he knew reporters and crews would already be on the scene. He hadn't been awakened by a phone call from Hank, so he knew things were quiet.

At the WCAU assignment desk, Hank listened to the police scanners for any clue of activity on Osage Avenue. Yes, it was quiet.

John walked in a few minutes after four, toting coffee and donuts. He had arrived two hours earlier than usual. Hank's briefing was simple. Nothing had happened all night. Harvey had called to say more police were moving in. Dennis had checked in, as I had. No scanner activity.

John took off his jacket, sat down at the desk and had a donut. He kicked a pile of wires, power cables and old videotapes that were under the assignment desk. He turned KYW up to a dull roar, adjusted the scanners' volume and checked the note from the night assignment editor to make sure there would be no surprises. He peered out the window at the early morning darkness.

Ever since yelling at Charles Thomas, Jay had trouble sleeping. Despite what he knew about the plan, he still had doubts. There had been false alarms before with MOVE, most notably the August 1984 incident in which hundreds of police poured into 62nd and Osage expecting a confrontation that never took place.

During his very short drive to the station, Jay was glad he had spent as much time as he did yesterday making assignments and planning for today. The benefit of Harvey's police intelligence and Karen's personal inspection of the neighborhood had gotten him off his ass. Now that the day had come, he felt he was ready.

Harvey also felt ready. Walking slowly within a 20 yard radius of the van, he was absolutely comfortable being here. In recent weeks, Harvey had knocked on MOVE's door, asking for interviews. He talked to dozens of Osage Avenue residents, sat on their porches, shoved microphones in their faces and borrowed their telephones. He had covered the 1978 shootout. Now he would cover whatever would happen in 1985. I belong here, he thought to himself.

As I stood at 62nd and Osage, shifting my weight from one foot to the other with my hands in my pockets, the mobile phone in Mini 2 rang.

"Hello, Mini 2." Funny way to answer a phone.

"Tom?" asked a voice I knew quite well.

"Yeesssss," I answered in a stupid, cheery voice. It was John Mussoni. "Gee, you're in early, John."

"Yeah, some big story, I hear. Anything going on down there?"

"Yes, I have to take a moderately wicked piss right now," I offered. "Otherwise, we're all kind of waiting for the other shoe to drop."

"Well, I'm calling to tell you to get Harvey ready to do a special report at 5:30."

It was now 5am, pitch-black and very quiet.

"OK", I said, "and how much time are we getting for this special report?"

"I'm not sure but I don't think time will be much of a problem. You can probably take as much time as you want."

"Alright, I'll tell Harvey to get pretty."

I hung up and made my way over to Harvey. I told him to get ready to do this thing. We quickly reviewed what he would talk about, what he knew about the plan, the mood of the neighborhood and any perspective he deemed relevant. Fifteen minutes later. the phone rang again. It was Jay Newman.

"Mini 2," I answered.

"Hi, Tom, this Is Jay Newman. You know about the 5:30 special report, I assume?"

"Yeah, John just called about it."

"I want Dennis to do it," said Jay emphatically.

"But I assumed Harvey would do it," I answered.

"I want Dennis to do the special report. He can bring Harvey into it if you think that's best, but I want Dennis to be the primary talent on the special report."

The frigging story hadn't even broken and I already had a problem. After telling Harvey he would do the special report, I now had to tell him that Dennis would do it and that he'd be the added attraction.

It was no secret that Jay favored Dennis. And in all fairness, Dennis was an excellent ad-libber on live reports. But I overestimated Harvey's ego. I told him and he didn't seem to care. Dennis looked at me with a face that asked, "Are you sure?" I assured both that these were the orders. Dennis agreed to do the special report and Harvey agreed to be second man.

Under the early morning darkness, two teams of police officers were gathering for the part of the operation that was central to arresting those inside the MOVE house. One team, led by Sergeant Ed Connor of the bomb squad, would run into the house two doors to the east of MOVE. The MOVE house was at 6221 Osage. Connor and his team would go into 6217 through the front door, under cover of a smoke screen. The other team, under Lieutenant Frank Powell, would enter the house just west of MOVE at 6223. They would do so through the back door. Once inside, the two teams would blast holes through the walls adjacent to the MOVE house and pump tear gas in. The two entry teams would be backed up by heavily armed police at four posts outside--two in homes across Osage Avenue, two in homes across the rear alley. One of the posts across Osage Avenue was equipped with an M-60 machine gun, a heavy, tripod-mounted weapon used in combat. The plan assumed MOVE would not come peacefully.

Mike Archer let out a big yawn as he drove to the station. He had gotten plenty of early morning phone calls in his time, but actually being up and dressed and driving to work at 5AM was rude. Mike was a compact man who drove a compact car. Born in Brooklyn in 1951, he was a native New Yorker, still retaining a tinge of his Brooklyn accent. He had worked at WABC-TV as a producer before coming to Channel Ten in the late 1970's. Now, he was executive producer for the early evening news.

Mike was anal about getting facts right. He tended to favor big, national stories with political flavor. His experience covering local news in New York gave him the requisite cynicism. Mike could be in awe of the stories he covered, a quality that humanized him to me. But he kept his stress bottled up, rarely exploding with anger. I figured he ate such small portions of food at lunch because his stomach was always killing him. Maybe for that reason, he had plenty of gray hair at his temples for a relatively young guy.

He parked in the station parking lot and walked across the

quiet expanse of asphalt to the rear door. Inside sat the guard and the TV tuned to Channel Ten, 24 hours a day. The guard buzzed him in after Mike banged on the door a few times to wake him.

The fluorescent lighting inside the building was like a cold slap in the face. The carpeted floor made the walk down the long hallway too quiet, a bit surreal. Up the 12 steps into the newsroom he climbed.

Assignment editor Mussoni was at the desk with a phone attached to his right ear and Jay Newman attached to his left. Mussoni, like any good assignment editor, spent at least 75 percent of the time on the telephone. Hank was also on the phone, hunched over his desk. Jay was questioning John about logistics. Did he have all the crews he needed? Did everyone show up on time? What are the cops saying? Jay's mind was working a mile a minute. Jay had come dressed in a casual shirt, no tie and no jacket.

Mike hung up his sport jacket and approached the desk where Jay and John were huddled.

"Jay, let's go over this again," urged Mike. "Harvey, Dennis and Charles are at the live location with TK as field producer. Kasey is with Tom Watson on Cobbs Creek Parkway, right?"

"Right," Jay answered. He had gone through this all with Mike and John yesterday, but it was good to review again. His thoughts returned again and again to Pete Kane.

"Who else knows about Pete Kane?" he asked John.

"No one."

"Charles Thomas knows. I had to call there and tell him to get the fuck out." Jay took a deep breath and shook his head. "Pete Kane speaks only to me, you got it?"

"Got it," confirmed John.

The next priority was getting on the air with a special report as soon as possible. It would be done live from the scene with the central control technician simply routing the remote signal directly onto the air. The question now was, which reporter would do it.

"I told Kranz to get Harvey ready to do the special report around 5:30," John told Jay, who grimaced.

"Well, I don't think-- I think I want Dennis to do the special report."

John's eyes opened a little wider. Mike's expression was stoic. Jay's eyes darted between them.

"I already told Kranz to tell Harvey to do it. I figured Harvey would be the primary reporter," offered John.

"Dennis is better live," retorted Jay. "I'll call Kranz myself and tell him to make the adjustment".

It wasn't as though viewers would care whether it was Harvey or Dennis doing a special report at 5:30 in the morning, for Christ sake.[21]

On the streets of West Philadelphia, daylight started to break through. The sky turned from black to deep blue as the sun rose somewhere in the distance. The voice of Dennis Woltering broke the silence on the street.

"WE INTERRUPT REGULAR PROGRAMMING FOR THIS SPECIAL REPORT."

Dennis was holding a microphone with the 10 mike flag as he cut into the CBS overnight news program, Nightwatch. He was dressed casually, with a denim jacket and a white, pullover shirt opened at the neck. Standing to his right was Harvey, also holding a microphone, his tie draped around his collar and the top button of his white, dress shirt open.

"I'M DENNIS WOLTERING WITH HARVEY CLARK AT THE CORNER OF 62ND AND PINE WHERE AUTHORITIES CONTINUE PREPARATIONS FOR AN APPARENT CONFRONTATION WITH THE RADICAL GROUP MOVE, A CONFRONTATION AIMED AT PUSHING THAT GROUP OUT OF THIS AREA."

Dennis ad-libbed as Harvey stood quietly next to him, waiting for a hand off.

"LET ME TELL YOU WHAT'S HAPPENED SO FAR. ABOUT

TOM KRANZ

TWO HOURS AGO, 3:30AM, UTILITY CREWS MOVED INTO THE AREA, SHUT OFF GAS AND ELECTRICITY, PURGING THE LINES IN THE AREA OF ALL GAS SERVICE. YOU CAN SEE A FIRE TRUCK BEHIND ME WITH A DELUGE GUN POINTED BACK THAT WAY."

The fire engines had moved in overnight. They were equipped with a snorkel mounted on a thing like a cherry picker, designed to direct streams of water at tall buildings. We incorrectly called them deluge guns. The actual deluge guns used by the fire department were heavy-duty water cannons mounted at ground level, designed to deliver thousands of gallons of water per minute on a fire. These cherry-picker things were actually known as squirts or snorkels. They delivered about as much water as a regular fire hose.

"THE DELUGE GUN IS AIMED, APPARENTLY, AT THE MOVE HOUSE. WE KNOW OF AT LEAST TWO FIRE TRUCKS POINTED LIKE THAT."

Dennis paused for a moment to breathe and review what was left to tell.

"SWAT TEAMS HAVE BEEN CONVERGING ON THE AREA. IT LOOKS LIKE THE SCENE IS SET. WE'RE TOLD THAT SOMETHING MAY BE HAPPENING AT DAWN."

Dennis continued with more description as I looked on from behind Roncaglione, who operated the live camera. Tony was inside the van, riding the audio level and watching the bunker shot on the monitor. I looked at my watch. 5:35.

Back at the station, Jay Newman watched from his office and thought to himself that this was great. We were the first station on with any live shots from the scene. He began to relax a little, knowing all his best people were out on the street, and his inside management team had things pretty much under control.

In the control room there was only Mike Archer. A director, camera operator, floor director, technical director and audio person were due in soon. Archer sat at the elevated console where the producer normally sat. That seat gave the producer a panoramic view of every video source, two different clocks and the backs of the heads of the control room crew. On the console directly in front of the producer's seat was a bank of switches and a small microphone on a gooseneck. The switches determined whose ear the producer could speak into--the anchor, the live reporter or the photographer. There was also a phone with a bank of pushbutton selectors for the anchor desk, the newsroom, the microwave receiving room, the tape playback room, the editing rooms and a regular outside line for executives to call directly into the control room to harass producers during news broadcasts. The news director had his own, dedicated line directly from his office to the producer's console.

It was a little lonely for Archer to be sitting in an empty control room, the shot being handled by the technician downstairs in central control. To his left was the plate glass window that looked down on the newsroom one floor below. It seemed twice as empty from this aerial view. He turned his attention back to the monitor and noticed Dennis had handed off to Harvey.

"WHAT WE WERE TOLD YESTERDAY IS THAT THE POLICE WILL MAKE THEIR MOVE INTO THE BUILDINGS NEXT TO THE MOVE HOUSE ON EITHER SIDE. THERE'S GONNA BE ONE ATTEMPT TO GET THEM OUT THIS MORNING. THEN IF THEY REFUSE TO COME OUT, THEY'RE GONNA FILL THE BUILDING WITH TEAR GAS. I THINK THOSE DELUGE GUNS ARE IN PLACE IN CASE THEY GO TO THE ROOFTOP ONCE THE BUILDING FILLS WITH GAS."

Harvey's deep voice became strained and louder when he did live shots. His brow became tied in a knot. His eyes fixed on the camera lens with intensity. Behind Harvey and Dennis, the camera picked up random movements of out-of-focus figures, probably police or bystanders. Another two or three minutes went by when Dennis finally wrapped the special report.

"WE WILL CONTINUE TO REPORT LIVE THROUGH THE DAY AS EVENTS WARRANT. I'M DENNIS WOLTERING WITH HARVEY CLARK. WE NOW RETURN YOU TO REGULAR PROGRAMMING."

In the van Tony checked the air monitor and saw that

Nightwatch was back on.

"We're clear," he called out.

Harvey and Dennis placed their mikes on the ground at the base of Bob Roncaglione's camera tripod. Harvey straightened up and began eyeballing the plainclothes officers behind the barricades. He was searching for his friend among the raincoats with POLICE armbands. He was also searching the faces of those around him for any signs of the unusual. Harvey had learned about reading faces from his sister. When they were both children, he remembered going to the doctor with Michele to get shots. Michele, being the elder sibling, was set up as the role model for little Harvey. She had to be strong when the needle came and not show any fear or pain. As the doctor approached her arm with the needle, Harvey's eyes locked on her face, looking for any sign of panic. It was at those doctor's office visits that Harvey learned a person's face could tell more about what was going on than words. Harvey studied faces at 62nd and Pine and saw wariness.

Dennis and I peeked into Mini 2 where Bob had perched himself in front of the monitor again, resuming his fiddling with the joystick that aimed the antenna mast. He was fine-tuning the mast camera shot, which began getting brighter as the sun began to rise. We could now begin making out the silhouette of rooftops. It was still too dark to see the MOVE bunker. Bob began wondering if he had aimed the camera in the right direction.

At the same intersection but caddy-corner from us was the Channel Three live van. Their veteran police reporter Walt Hunter was on the scene, along with anchor/reporter Jack Jones. Walt and I had worked together for several years at WCAU radio. Jack was a former Channel Ten anchorman who left in the 70's for another market, then came back to work for Channel 3 in the early 80's. They were perfect for the assignment. Walt had unparalleled knowledge of the Philadelphia Police Department and experience covering MOVE in 1978. Jack had an ultra-smooth delivery, impeccable ad-libbing ability and his own knowledge of his hometown. I looked around for Channel Six's van but didn't see it. I figured they were someplace else. The cellular phone rang.

"Mini 2," I answered.

"Tom, it's Jay. From now on, have Dennis shoot tape and do interviews with people on the sidelines. He'll do a people story for later. Harvey should do all the live shots with assistance from Charles."

I wondered what made him change his mind about Harvey.

"Charles?" I asked. "Is he supposed to be here?"

"Yeah, I think he spent the night out there. Haven't you seen him?"

"Not yet, but I'm sure he'll turn up." I had learned from assignment desk experiences that Charles enjoyed his independence on the street more than most and protected it jealously. He often went off by himself to talk to people without a photographer in tow. He once told me he liked to see what a scene felt like without being encumbered by the hardware.

"One more thing," remembered Jay. "Do you know about Pete Kane?"

"No," I replied.

"He's in a house looking right down the street at MOVE." I could hear in Jay's voice that he was smiling.

"No shit. That's great. How'd he do that?"

"It took a lot of negotiating yesterday. I'll tell you about it some other time."

I was impressed.

"Just in case," he went on, "here's his address in case you have to tell the cops to get him out or, I don't know, something happens."

"Do you have a phone number?" I asked.

"Nobody gets that phone number but me." He was firm and kind of smug about it.

"OK, so it's a quarter to six, when do you want to go again?" I asked.

"Let's go around five of in case they really do start shooting at six." The way he said it made me realize for the first time that there was potential for danger to us. Did Jay really think we'd all stand around and do live shots if the shooting started?

"Talk to you later," I said and hung up the cellular.

I noticed that Bob and Chuck were on the roof of the van with the mast all the way down. They were trying to be inconspicuous about refocusing the toy camera and changing the battery. I looked at my watch and saw 5:45 and hoped they would get the thing back up quickly.

As the first trickles of daybreak sneaked onto Osage Avenue, the loudspeaker on the MOVE house came alive again. Pete Kane rolled his camera and tried to make out what the crazed voice was saying. Through the closed window he heard only hysteria. The voice was probably female but he couldn't be sure. It could've been Ramona, he thought, since she often spoke for MOVE. The shouts and curses were muffled. The picture he saw through the lens was of an empty Osage Avenue with no cars and no people. In the foreground, directly across the street, were a couple of stakeout officers in their blue helmets with rifles on their shoulders. They were right up against the end house, peeking up Osage Avenue. To the left he saw two other stakeout officers in similar regalia, up against the end house across the street, also peeking around the corner at the MOVE house. He kept the camera locked on the front porch of MOVE, but he allowed his eye to look away from the viewfinder for a moment. He saw several policemen on the Osage Avenue rooftops across the street from MOVE, lying on their stomachs with rifles trained at 6221. He got closer to the window so he could look farther down 62nd street and saw many more stakeout officers carrying rifles. He looked the other way and saw a fire engine with its cherry-picker hose high in the air, pointed at MOVE. He peered straight ahead up Osage Avenue to the other end of the street and saw more stakeout officers, their blue helmets catching an occasional orange ray of morning sun. They were looking up the street towards MOVE. Pete was more afraid of what he couldn't see. Were there stakeout officers on the roof above him? Were they out back? What was going on in the alley behind the MOVE house?

The antenna mast on Mini 2 had been raised back up and inside the van, Bob, Chuck and I marveled at what we saw on the monitor. Enough sunlight was now present to clearly make out the MOVE bunker. It was clear enough to see the gun ports and the wooden slats. The three of us stared at it like children, hoping for a glimpse of John Africa. There was no movement.

"I'm gonna take it down one more time and zoom in more on the bunker," announced Bob after a couple of minutes.

"No way, man," I pleaded, grabbing his arm as he reached for the control that would lower the mast. "Don't fuck with it now. Harvey says 6 o'clock is when they're gonna do it. If we miss it, you'll kill yourself. Then, I'll kill you again."

Bob looked at the picture. He really wanted the shot to be tighter on the bunker.

"That picture right there is more than you could ever have dreamed of under the circumstances," I said. "They will shit when they see it on the air. It's un-fucking believable!"

"Maybe you're right," Bob said and finally backed down. Even during those few moments, the horizon became a little brighter and the bunker became a little more defined.

Back at the station, Rob Feldman had arrived to man the microwave room. Normally a producer, this morning his job was to monitor the remote pictures and stay in radio communication with the van. Rob wandered into the microwave room where all remotes were received by expensive and complex equipment that sucked signals out of the air and put them on television. He was seeing what we were seeing in the van.

"Where the hell is that camera," he asked the technician. He could make out the bunker and the other rooftops. "Did they get onto a roof out there?" The technician didn't know. What he did know was that there was only one van at the scene, so both this camera and the one on the ground used for the live shot must have been switched back and forth from inside the van. Now they at least had two shots to choose from for the next cut-in.

As Rob stared at the picture, it had switched back to the ground camera where Harvey and Dennis stood. Then it switched back to the high camera, then back to ground. Someone in the truck was switching back and forth.

Jay had entered the room and was looking at the shot, too. Rob asked where the elevated camera was. Jay did not respond, suddenly preoccupied. His mind had shifted gears to the next special report.

"I can switch back and forth between the two cameras," said Tony from inside Mini 2 after rehearsing it a few times. "There's a slight roll in the picture at the moment of the switch, but it's not terrible."

"That's great, Tony," I said. "I'll let the director know he's got two shots to choose from and you switch between them when he calls for it, OK?"

"Sure."

On the second floor of 6221 Osage, six children lay sleeping in a hallway. Birdie, Zanetta, Tree, Tomaso, Phil, and Melissa Africa were sleeping in what was, for now, the safest part of the house. They were out of the immediate reach of anyone who would break down the front or back doors or windows. At a moment's notice, they could scramble up the ladder into the bunker.

Downstairs a racket was starting. Ramona and Rhonda took turns at the microphone, yelling curses and threats over the loudspeaker. Frank, Raymond and Conrad made final checks of the fortifications they had spent months building inside the house--pieces of heavy lumber and logs lining the walls of the basement and a makeshift bunker inside the front of the first floor.

Birdie began to stir. He was half awake. To him it was still halfway nighttime.

◆ ◆ ◆

Steve Levy was looking at himself in the dressing room mirror as he quickly applied his makeup. He saw a 38-year-old man about to go on live television with no script.

Steve was born and raised in a South Philadelphia row home and worked his whole career in this city except for a brief stint as a reporter in Syracuse. He became familiar to Philadelphia viewers on Channel Six during the 70's where he did sports, weather and a morning talk/game show called Dialing For Dollars. He left Channel 6 under unpleasant circumstances following a contract dispute. Channel Ten had done some audience research that showed, among other things, that Levy's credibility among viewers was high. That research helped him land a job at Channel Ten as an anchorman and reporter.

The night before, Steve read some of the past week's newspaper stories on MOVE. When he arrived on the morning of May 13th, he pulled out the scripts from the previous night's 11 o'clock news and read them. He also familiarized himself with the videotape that was in house. He was preparing himself to anchor a live special report without a script because he felt he could more effectively say what had to be said by simply talking to the viewer, one on one. He would he talking to his friend Harvey on live television. They had become close in their three years together at Channel Ten. They shared many of the same ideas of what television news should be, were about the same age and were both single. They shared many a beer, and many a private moment.

In the main studio, he was the only one sitting at an anchor desk designed for up to four people. Flush with the top surface of the desk was a monitor at each position so the anchors could just glance down to see what was on the air. There were two other, larger monitors in the studio so the anchors could look just beyond the cameras and see air. There were three large cameras in the studio, each equipped with a teleprompter that projected the script on a plate of glass in front of the camera lens. For this cut in, the prompter was disabled because there was no script.

Steve adjusted his earpiece. This morning, Mike Archer would be the voice in Steve Levy's ear. Mike now perched himself at the producer's console in the control room, which was one floor above. He pulled the gooseneck microphone close to his mouth and studied the position of the buttons before him, memorizing the one that put him in Steve's ear. Another button put him into Harvey's ear. It had been a while since Mike had actually honchoed a live broadcast from the producer's chair.

The door to the control room swished open and in dashed Vee Beamon, the director.

"What are we doing? When are we going on," he asked, slightly out of breath.

"In a few minutes," Mike said calmly.

"I just got here and Jay literally shoved me up the steps to do this," Vee complained.

Mike pointed to the monitor and explained that he had a ground shot and a high shot of the MOVE bunker but that he had to call on the technician in Mini 2 to switch between them. Vee rehearsed that a couple of times with Tony in the van. As he did so, a technician quietly took his place behind the audio board and the technical director sat down behind the video switcher.

Mike now saw before him the backs of the heads of his control room crew.

Mike ran it through his mind one more time: Harvey on the ground camera, the MOVE bunker on the high camera, Steve anchoring. The only missing element was someone in the newsroom to work the phones and that problem would go away as soon as Karen Fox came in, which would be in about an hour.

Mike took a deep breath.

The picture on the monitor inside Mini 2 was now bright and clear. The horizon cut about halfway across the picture with the MOVE bunker in the center of the screen. Tony and I now gazed at the picture as Bob readied his shot of Harvey. Chuck Satiritz had been summoned back to the station and would be relieved by another, fresh one-man-band. It didn't seem fair that he should have to leave just as his mast-mounted camera began showing its stuff. I was sorry to see him go, but he was being tapped by Mussoni for another job somewhere that probably required his particular ingenuity. Replacing Chuck would be Artis Hall, who had already arrived. Artis lived just a few minutes away and came right from home. He was another veteran one-man-band who would now he paired with Dennis Woltering to shoot taped interviews of the people watching on the sidelines.

Harvey had tied his tie and straightened himself out to be on television. This was a moment Harvey had readied himself for since the day his sister died. This, Harvey thought, was his story, and he was going to tell it as only he could. There could be no written script for him here. He had only to reach into his mind and retrieve that which he knew so well.

"Something's happening," shouted Tony from inside the truck where he was watching the monitor. I went over to see. One of the cherry-picker fire hoses had been turned on and the stream of water was being haphazardly aimed at the MOVE bunker. I whipped the cellular phone off its cradle and dialed the station madly.

"Channel Ten news," answered Mussoni.

"It's started," I barked into the phone. "John, it's TK. It's started. Tell them to come to us now."

"OK, bye," chirped John.

At almost the same moment, Archer spoke calmly into Harvey's ear.

"Harvey this is Archer. Do you hear me OK?"

"Yes," Harvey answered into the microphone, nodding his head into Bob's camera. Archer was watching from the control room. He saw the water go on and began talking to Harvey the same second I phoned the station.

"Stand by. We'll go to you in about one minute."

"Let's go, it's happening," Harvey warned, his voice rising a little.

Watching from the van, I saw the stream from the snorkel now shooting directly onto the bunker, hitting its rear wall full-force and causing water to deflect many yards in all directions. "Stand by," the director now said in both Harvey's and Bob's ears.

"Here we go," announced Harvey to those of us who had nothing in our ears. I looked around quickly to record the moment. Harvey stood poised with the mike in his hand, his eyes shifting from the camera in front of him to my face and back to the camera. Bob was gazing into his viewfinder at Harvey. Tony sat in the van, gazing at the bunker shot, his finger on the button ready to switch to it at the director's command. Some newspaper reporter was peeking into the van's open door. Behind Harvey stood a couple of uniformed officers in yellow rain slickers, guarding the wooden barricade that was the police line. Down along the other barricades stood a few dozen onlookers. I was now uncomfortable from holding it in for three hours.

"Thirty seconds," shouted Roncaglione. The live shot machine was just about up to speed. A small TV tuned to Channel Ten at Harvey's feet was tilted up so he could just glance down at it when necessary. Through his earpiece, he heard air, punctuated by the verbal cues of the director and Archer.

"Ten seconds," he heard. He closed his eyes and breathed deeply. "Five."

A recorded voice broke the silence and Channel Ten's air crackled to life.

"WE INTERRUPT OUR REGULAR PROGRAMMING TO BRING YOU A CHANNEL TEN NEWS SPECIAL REPORT."

Birdie Africa heard a bullhorn. But as he started waking up, he realized it sounded different and was coming from somewhere else. He was hearing Police Commissioner Gregore Sambor on a megaphone, giving MOVE its ultimatum.

Sambor had a broad face, eyes that squinted most of the time and a mouth that rarely smiled. He was a big man, probably a hell of an athlete in his younger days. Yet, his big frame and imposing appearance in uniform belied his scratchy, monotone voice. He sort of whined when he spoke. He was in his 50's and a Philadelphia police veteran. He was appointed by Mayor Goode because of his reputation as a tough, honest cop.

Grim-faced and resolute, he personally walked down the alley to MOVE'S back door, wearing body armor and flanked by other officers. They stopped and Sambor read from a piece of paper.

"Attention, this is the police commissioner," he began through a megaphone. "We have warrants for the arrest of Frank James Africa, Ramona Johnson Africa, Theresa Brooks Africa and Conrad Hampton Africa for various violations of the criminal statutes of Pennsylvania."

Sambor's terrible monotone cut through the deadly silence in the Osage neighborhood.

"We do not wish to harm anyone. All occupants have 15 minutes to peaceably evacuate the premises and surrender."

He paused, awaiting a response, then said, "Wake up, MOVE. This is America!"

Inside, Birdie heard the megaphone chatter, but couldn't hear Sambor's side of it clearly. Suddenly, he heard Ramona answer him on the MOVE bullhorn.

"If one house gets it, all these houses gonna get it", she shrieked. "We are ready to respond to your mother fucking police force!"

A moment passed.

"This is your only notice," Sambor continued as though he had heard nothing. "Your 15 minutes starts now."

He turned off his megaphone and stepped back a considerable distance. All bullhorns remained silent.

Birdie listened from the upstairs hallway where he and the

other children were huddled. The silence was not a good sign.

Suddenly, several of the adults came up to the hallway, woke up the rest of the children and began ushering them into the basement.

"GOOD MORNING, I'M STEVE LEVY. POLICE HAVE SURROUNDED A HOUSE IN WEST PHILADELPHIA THAT IS THE HEADQUARTERS FOR THE GROUP CALLED MOVE, A GROUP THAT HAS MADE THREATS AGAINST NEIGHBORS AND CITY OFFICIALS FOR MONTHS, WHILE DEMANDING THAT OTHER MOVE MEMBERS BE RELEASED FROM JAIL FOLLOWING THEIR CONVICTION IN THE 1978 SHOOTING IN POWELTON VILLAGE THAT LEFT A POLICEMAN DEAD. POLICE SPENT ALL YESTERDAY EVACUATING THE NEIGHBORHOOD, AND NOW WE ARE TOLD AN ATTEMPT WILL BE MADE TO ARREST MOVE MEMBERS. LET'S GO LIVE TO 62ND AND OSAGE WHERE HARVEY CLARK HAS BEEN SINCE VERY EARLY THIS MORNING. HARVEY?"

Thousands of gallons of water were pounding the MOVE bunker from the snorkels. Pete Kane's camera recorded ground-level video of the water rushing over the bunker, throwing an occasional plank into the street. I was leaning into Mini 2, watching the mast-camera shot. Harvey was on live doing a brief synopsis of the recent events which had brought us to this point. The director alternately called upon Tony to switch between the mast camera and the ground camera. Archer marveled at the fact that he had this extraordinary camera angle to go to.

5:58AM. Harvey Clark: "THE POLICE WENT IN ABOUT 5 MINUTES AGO, ABOUT 5 MINUTES TO SIX." Harvey had gotten a high sign from his policeman friend when the operation actually started. Pete shut down for a minute to scratch his nose and sip the coffee he had made for himself. Birdie Africa and his brothers and sisters were hoarded into the basement of the MOVE house, surrounded by railroad ties and planks.

Suddenly, Pete heard a pop and a hiss. He looked out his window and saw smoke begin billowing in front of the MOVE house. His eye locked onto the viewfinder. The police had fired a smoke screen into the street to mask the entrance of Sgt. Connor's team into 6217 Osage. The smoke spread quickly and within seconds the entire street was filled with it. All Pete could see was billows of white.

In the MOVE house, Birdie figured the police had begun tear gassing. He and the other children were told to lie down on the basement floor. The adults covered them with wet blankets to filter out the gas.

I stuck my head out from inside Mini 2 and looked past Harvey. As he stood there talking on live TV, police officers behind him ran down 62nd Street toward Osage while others ran down what looked like a small alley connecting Pine Street with the alley behind MOVE. They had their rifles drawn.

The first shot sounded like someone's screen door slamming.

"IT APPEARS THAT THERE MAY HAVE JUST BEEN A GUNSHOT. THAT SOUNDED LIKE A GUNSHOT." Harvey turned his head slightly, distracted for a moment by the sound. He was pausing to listen, his earpiece barely hanging in his ear, his brow knitted into a terrible lump as the first gunshot turned into more.

"THE GUNSHOTS ARE STARTING RIGHT NOW."

The sound was like the first pops of popcorn in a microwave oven-- first one, then a few more, followed by silence for a few seconds, then a lot more. Live gunfire, which I had never heard before, sounded like so many other, everyday sounds. I was watching Harvey's report on the monitor at his feet while hearing it happen around me for real.

Pete was pushed so hard against the viewfinder the bone around his eye began to ache. He saw the smoke begin to clear and he heard a lot of shooting. There were several machine guns pumping-off many rounds at once. There was the blunted sound of a shotgun and the high-pitched rattle of UZI's. There were many single shots. The most disturbing thing was that he couldn't see anyone firing. There was no pitched battle on Osage Avenue. Not even the cops right in front of him, perched at the end of the block, were firing. In fact they looked rather relaxed. It was obvious the shooting was coming from up the street, probably from inside other houses or rooftops. But it sounded so close.

At the live location, the sound of battle was very loud now. Again, we all found it disturbing that we couldn't actually see anyone shooting. I peeked quickly into the van. The stream of water had not eased on the bunker. The machine gun fire was now intense. The shotgun blasts really delivered blows to the gut. They began to come one after the other, rapid fire, as though many shotgun rounds were pounding against a target that wouldn't fall. Here and there, higher pitched shots were heard, some sounding like they were almost over our heads.

A block away on Cobbs Creek Parkway, Kasey Kaufman was crouched behind a parked car, her photographer Tom Watson next to her, rolling tape. Tom's camera had just recorded them running for cover as the shooting began. Bullets sounded like they were whirring overheard. Uniformed police officers assigned to the perimeter were on their bellies behind parked cars, their police Specials drawn. No one could see a gun pointed at them, yet the sound of bullets was so close, they believed they were in danger.

"It's right up on the roof there," a newspaper photographer said over his shoulder to Watson who kept rolling. "Right up on the roof there."

The print guy's motor driven camera snapped three quick frames and he scurried off to where a policeman was on the ground, guarding a couple of bystanders who were also on their stomachs. The shots sounded so close, yet no gunman could be seen. Bullets ricocheted and police uniforms whizzed by Kasey as she remained crouched behind the car.

Harvey live: "THEY'RE REALLY GOING AT IT NOW. IT'S, UH, IT'S AUTOMATIC WEAPONS, IT'S UH--"

POW! A heavy shotgun blast sounded close by.

"Look out," someone in the crowd yelled and everyone ducked, including the uniformed officer right at our spot.

"UH--AT THIS POINT, UH, PEOPLE ARE STARTING TO SCATTER."

Harvey was immovable and unflinching. His eyes searched my face and evidently saw no panic. He was a statue in front of the camera. Roncaglione had been hunched over the tripod with his eye on the viewfinder for about ten minutes now. He peeked up for a moment, as if to make sure a bullet wasn't coming straight for his nose.

"I DON'T THINK THAT WE'RE IN ANY REAL DANGER, BUT, UH, THERE'S NO REAL WAY OF TELLING AT THIS POINT."

Harvey's voice did not rise, there was no emotion.

"PEOPLE ARE STARTING TO PANIC, THEY ARE STARTING TO RUN."

Several diehard TV groupies now hauled ass up Pine Street away from the gunfire. Others remained in kneeling positions behind the TV news vans.

"POLICE HAVE TAKEN AN ARMED POSITION RIGHT BEHIND US NOW AS YOU CAN SEE." Additional uniforms suddenly appeared behind Harvey.

There were more single shots, an occasional burst of heavy machine gun fire and more shotgun blasts. Plainclothes officers now chased onlookers away from the barricades where we stood, yelling at them to move farther up Pine Street.

"Move it back, move it back," shouted one civil affairs officer. "Take it on up there. Get the hell away from here!"

Two other officers moved the barricades farther back. This set off an alarm in the back of my brain. It occurred to me I might get shot, or Harvey might get it in the back of the head. I began looking around on the rooftops, wondering whether I would see John Africa aiming his rifle at me. Single shots kept ringing out through the chaos. Single shotgun blasts ripped the air.

The cellular phone rang. I climbed into the van, looking behind me as I did so. I snatched it off its cradle.

"Yeah?"

"TK, it's Jay," in a hushed and rushed tone. "Bring Dennis into the shot."

"Huh?"

"Bring Dennis into the shot," he insisted. "Have him report what's going on in the neighborhood."

"They're fucking shooting at us Jay, that's what's going on in the neighborhood!"

"Yeah, it's really wild, isn't it?"

I was speechless.

"I'll look for Dennis." I paused and swallowed. "Look, we may have to move, Jay." I tried to look out the window. "This is really dangerous."

"Look, do what you gotta do to stay safe. But find Dennis. And where the hell is Charles?"

Charles had wandered over to the van by now. I leaned out the door with the phone to my ear when some asshole in the crowd tossed firecrackers into the street just a few feet from us.

"Holy Shit," I yelled into the phone. Jay gave a start on his end, too.

"I'll let you go. Bye." He hung up.

It was 6:14 and suddenly, there was silence. Harvey had been forced to move a few more feet up Pine Street. He caught his breath for a moment and Steve jumped in from the studio. He and Harvey went back and forth with some Q and A for a few minutes.

Phone again. I answered.

"What."

"I got some information from Pete Kane," said Jay. "Tell Charles to report that a Channel Ten reporter with closer vantage point sees debris on Osage Avenue in front of the MOVE house, and teargas."

"OK," I answered.

"Don't identify who it is or where he is."

"Bye."

As Harvey and Steve continued their banter, I pulled Charles to the side and told him what to say. As I did so, the shooting began again.

Harvey: "CHARLES THOMAS JOINS ME NOW. HE'S BEEN IN THE AREA SINCE LAST NIGHT. CHARLES, WHAT CAN YOU TELL US?"

Charles: "HARVEY, WE HAVE SOME NEW INFORMATION FROM ANOTHER CHANNEL TEN REPORTER WITH A CLOSER POSITION THAN US. THAT REPORTER TELLS US THERE ARE SIGNS OF BATTLE ON OSAGE AVENUE. AH, DEBRIS IN THE STREET IN FRONT OF THE MOVE HOUSE AND SOME TEAR GAS IN THE AIR." Charles' eyes darted every which way.

"IT SOUNDS TO ME LIKE SHOTS ARE BEING FIRED FROM THE ROOFTOPS. IT APPEARS AS THOUGH, UH, GUNFIRE IS BEING RETURNED."

The sound of shooting penetrated Charles' narration and began dominating his report. More intense gunfire now, shotgun blasts pounding away again and single shots that sounded ever so close to us.

Charles: "WE HEAR THE DISTINCT, STACCATTO--"

"Move it back!" A police officer shouted at Charles and Harvey live on the air. "Let's go, beat it. Move it back now!"

Charles: "THE POLICE ARE MOVING US NOW, HARVEY, BUT WHAT I WAS SAYING--THE STACCATO OF AUTOMATIC WEAPONS, THEN WHAT APPEARED TO BE--"

"C'mon, Harv, move it out of here," insisted the cop, pushing Harvey and Charles out of the way as they tried to continue their live shot.

"--WHAT APPEARED TO BE SINGLE SHOTS--"

Charles twisted his head back to the policeman who was pushing them out of the way.

Harvey tried to maintain his composure and jumped in.

"OK, CHARLES. AH, STEVE AT THIS POINT--"

Harvey was being shoved off-camera by the officer.

"--AT THIS POINT, UH, WE ARE BEING FORCED TO LEAVE OUR POSITION--" Charles tugged at Harvey insistently.

"C'mon, Harvey let's go," implored Charles.

"WE'RE BEING FORCED TO MOVE NOW. AH, WE'LL GET

BACK WITH YOU WHEN WE CAN."

Charles now had a death grip on Harvey's mike hand and was pulling him along as Harvey was trying to do the live shot. Gunshots rang out everywhere.

"C'mon, Harvey!" pleaded Charles. "Let's go. LET'S GO!"

Charles pulled so hard on Harvey's mike that it came out of its connector, leaving Harvey standing there with just the cord in his hand as Charles ran up the street carrying the mike.

Single shots rang out and Roncaglione captured another flurry of police movement down the street before he was also forced to move.

In the control room, Archer was mesmerized by what he was seeing. He thought for a moment that Harvey or Charles might actually be shot live on the air. What the hell would I do then, he thought.

In the newsroom, there were now more people-- producers, desk assistants, a writer, and Karen Fox. All eyes were riveted on individual TV sets scattered throughout the newsroom.

In his office, Jay had fallen silent, awestruck. As he watched Harvey and Charles get chased away on live television, he realized for the first time this was more than a spot news event. It was life and death on a 25-inch screen.

Archer watched as Harvey and Charles were chased away and quickly flicked the switch that put him into Steve's ear.

"Take it from them now. Do a recap and kick rocks for as long as you can until we get them back up."

Mike watched Steve's face on the monitor. He nodded and began talking.

"YOU CAN SEE WHAT IS TAKING PLACE THERE NEAR MOVE HEADQUARTERS. THE PHILADELPHIA POLICE ARE NOW MOVING HARVEY CLARK AND CHARLES THOMAS FROM WHAT HAD BEEN CONSIDERED A SAFE POSITION, WHICH IS ACTUALLY AROUND THE CORNER FROM MOVE."

Steve glanced down at his monitor. The shot of the bunker being sprayed with water appeared. He described what he saw.

"YOU'RE LOOKING NOW AT THE DELUGE GUNS WHICH

ARE PUTTING VAST AMOUNTS OF WATER, CERTAINLY MORE AMOUNTS OF WATER THAN ANY HUMAN BEING COULD STAND UP TO, AND THEY ARE PUTTING THOSE AMOUNTS OF WATER ON THE BUNKER, AS IT'S BEEN CALLED, ON TOP OF THE HOUSE DOWN THERE AT MOVE HEADQUARTERS."

Archer had no idea how he still had the bunker shot but he asked no questions. All he had to go to for the moment was Steve on the set and that one picture coming from god-knows-where. The little word "Live" was superimposed on the top left corner of the screen.

"This is some serious shit," he said aloud to no one in particular.

"But you can't see where the shooting is coming from," said the director. "Did you see how calm the cops were behind Harvey?"

Mike didn't answer because he was now in the midst of his second worst fear: having no live reporter to go to. His worst fear was having no reporter to go to because the reporter had been shot. Levy would just have to take the ball and keep it in the air because now there was no choice-- Mike and Jay both agreed separately and tacitly--we have to stay on.

The news director's hotline rang on Archer's console.

"Yeah," snapped Mike.

"Stay on that bunker shot," ordered Newman. "Tell the director not to touch it!"

Steve kept talking. He recapped, reviewed, relived and retold the 1978 story. He paused once or twice to swallow, to gaze at the shot of that aerial hose pummeling the bunker with tons of water. During one of those pauses, Archer popped into his ear.

"Stay alert. Keep your eyes on that bunker for movement or anything." Mike saw him nod on camera three.

Now, the microwave room was calling.

"We're getting Harvey back up now," said a voice on the phone.

"Great. Thanks," answered Mike as he saw the ground camera turn on again and Harvey coming back into focus.

"Can you hear me, Harvey?"

"Yeah. We're OK, just moved another few yards away."

"Stand by, coming to you."

Mike jumped into Steve's ear and said urgently, "Go back to Harvey now."

Steve thought thank goodness, Harvey's OK.

Steve live: "LET'S GO BACK NOW TO HARVEY CLARK WHO IS, I ASSUME, AT A MORE SAFE LOCATION. HARVEY?"

The shot was switched to Harvey's camera.

Harvey: "THE SHOOTING HAS APPARENTLY STOPPED NOW, AND THE CIVIL AFFAIRS POLICE OFFICERS BEHIND ME SAY THEY HAVE NO IDEA AT THIS POINT WHO MAY HAVE BEEN INJURED. IT WAS A ROOFTOP BATTLE. CHARLES THOMAS IS, UH, WITH ME." A nervous chuckle escapes. "OF COURSE YOU SAW BOTH OF US--". Several more shots were heard in the distance.

"A FEW MORE SPORADIC SHOTS, BUT MOST OF THE SHOOTING HAS ENDED."

There was a natural pause here and Charles jumped in.

"HARVEY, WHAT REALLY CONCERNED POLICE HERE-- THERE'S ANOTHER SHOT--WAS WHAT SOUNDED LIKE SMALL ARMS FIRE, 22-CALIBER FIRE, INTO THIS AREA WHERE WE WERE STANDING AND, UH, THE OTHER REPORTERS. THAT REALLY SCATTERED THE CROWD, THAT'S WHAT HAPPENED TO US RIGHT BEFORE WE LEFT THE AIR."

Suddenly, like a tidal wave, a roar of gunfire shook them.

"SHOTS HAVE PICKED UP AGAIN. IT'S NOT OVER, HARVEY."

Charles' delivery became more urgent, more nervous sounding. He yielded again to Harvey.

"STEVE, YOU CAN HEAR IT, IT SOUNDS LIKE--"

The roar of shooting filled the pauses.

Harvey: "IT SOUNDS LIKE--"

Charles: "THERE IS MORE OF THAT SMALL ARMS FIRE,"

Harvey: "--ANOTHER--"

Charles: ANOTHER SMALL CALIBER--"

Harvey: "--ANOTHER VIETNAM HERE."

Charles: "IT'S UNBELIVEABLE!"

Harvey: "IT'S UNBELIEVABLE THE NUMBER OF ROUNDS THAT HAVE BEEN FIRED AT THIS POINT."

Archer had now decided what to do if any of his people got shot. There was only one thing he could do.

Into Steve's ear he calmly said, "Follow closely. If anything happens, just describe it. Do you understand? Just describe anything that might happen." Steve realized he was being told to stay on if any of our people got shot on live TV.

Inside 6217 Osage Avenue, Sergeant Ed Connor had just taken a bullet to the back. It lodged in his bullet proof vest. It felt like a bruise and it ached, but he was OK. Not so OK was one of his men who was pinned down in 6219, the house between Connor's team and MOVE. Connor and his men had spent the past hour returning what they believed to be machine gun fire from MOVE. They had used several small, explosive charges to blow holes in the walls as planned. Now, they had nowhere to go because of intense gunfire they believed was coming at them. They were pinned down and unable to inject tear gas from their position.

On the other side of MOVE, inside 6223, Lt. Frank Powell's group made its way up from the basement and was now on the front porch next to MOVE's. The only thing separating them from MOVE was the thin, common wall between the two porches. This wall was pocked with bullet holes. Powell and his men were on their backs and stomachs, ducking gunfire. Powell would frequently call by radio, asking for cover from the backup post across the street. When he did so, the officers at that post opened up with the M-60 machine gun, firing a short burst, then stopping to let the air cool it and then firing another short burst. The officers manning that post believed their cover fire was keeping Lt. Powell and his men alive.

Both Powell and Connor never actually saw any MOVE

member during the gun battle. They did report seeing muzzle flashes from handguns or rifles and both heard automatic weapons firing. They were strongly convinced that MOVE was armed to the hilt and was shooting at them. They were returning fire, but couldn't see who was firing at them.

In the MOVE basement, Birdie and the children were huddled in a corner. They heard the shooting amid the occasional, small explosions coming from upstairs. They did not move.

◆ ◆ ◆

Pete Kane was feeling fear and frustration. The intense gunfire started getting to him a little. And, he was annoyed by the fact that there was no battle happening in front of his camera. His phone rang.

"Hello?"

"Pete, It's Jay. What's going on out there?"

"There's a lot of shooting but it's all happening either inside or on the roofs or in the back alleys. I hear it, but I can't see it."

"You alright?"

"Oh, yeah."

"OK. Call you later." Jay hung up and dialed the cellular in the van.

"Hello?" I answered in a hurry.

"Hi, it's Jay. Pete says the shooting is pretty intense, but he can't see anything. They must be up on the roofs or fighting within the houses, maybe in the alley."

"OK."

"Remember, just attribute that to another Channel Ten reporter with a closer vantage point."

"OK, Jay." We hung up.

Jay saw Harvey and Charles huddled together with gunfire breaking out around them and thought about what he would do if they got shot. He didn't know. His phone rang.

"Hello?" It was me.

"Jay, it's TK." I paused. "These shots are close. Um, I'm

starting to get concerned about--"

Jay interrupted. "Listen to me. You guys have final say. When you think it's getting too dangerous, get the hell out."

6:50am, almost an hour since the first shot rang out. Harvey is on live.

"THERE IS NOT AS MUCH SHOOTING NOW AS BEFORE. UH, NO WAY OF TELLING FROM OUR VANTAGE POINT EXACTLY WHAT'S GOING ON. AS YOU CAN SEE BEHIND ME, POLICE ARE GOING IN AND OUT OF THAT SMALL ALLEY LEADING BEHIND THE MOVE HOUSE. THEY APPEAR TO BE RELAXED, AS THEY MANEUVER AS CLOSE AS 20 OR 30 FEET FROM THE BACK DOOR OF MOVE."

It was quiet. I peeked into the van at the mast camera shot and noticed the water continued pouring onto the bunker.

"STEVE, UH, THERE APPEARS TO BE A CLEANUP NOW. AH, THERE'S PEOPLE CRYING HERE."

A number of bystanders were locked in embraces as they stood by the police barricade. There was slow, but steady movement of police officers behind Harvey as he narrated the scene around him. There was a feeling that it was over. The guns had been silent for almost ten minutes. Behind Harvey, police officers could be seen leaning into the open trunks of their patrol cars, loading equipment back into them and slamming them shut. A couple policemen took off their helmets and wiped their brows.

Karen Fox had listened to KYW in the car on the way to the station and heard their live report. It was virtually a recreation of the radio report she heard seven years ago describing live gunfire in Powelton Village.

She arrived at the station and went right to her desk, hardly saying hello to anyone.

"Who's down there?" she asked Mussoni. He told her what she needed to know.

"As far as I'm concerned," John told her, "your one job today is to work this story."

"Fine," she answered. That was the way she liked it, she as the point-person for information on a breaking story. She was already armed with the information she had gathered last week from MOVE neighbor Howard Nichols, from former police commissioner O'Neill, from her visit to Osage Avenue Thursday night and from her experience in 1971 covering the Von Coln murder. Now she had to establish a beachhead on the breaking story. From her early days in the newspaper business to radio reporter in the 1970's to news editor at Channel 10, Karen lived by one rule when gathering information: find someone who is right in the center of the action, a primary source, not necessarily a top official or bureaucrat but maybe a lower level individual who is right at the epicenter.

Her first few calls to the police radio room, detective headquarters and police public affairs yielded no information except the phone number at the command center. She called it, and after being put on hold several times was routed to Inspector John Kramer[22], her old friend from homicide. Score! She had found her primary source. Kramer was in the very room where City Managing Director Leo Brooks communicated with the police commissioner and the mayor. Kramer was hearing radio and telephone conversations. He couldn't tell Fox what was going to happen but he could tell her things after the fact. He did so in whispers. From my own experience with Kramer, he was never one to hide from the press. He was never afraid of the truth coming out as long as it didn't jeopardize an investigation or the lives of police officers.

Fox had struck gold. She got what little information Kramer had to give, typed it up as he related it, thanked him and hung up.

The phone in the live van rang again.

"Mini 2", I answered.

"Tommy? Hi, it's Karen."

"Boy, am I glad to hear your voice."

"Is it really crazy down there?" she asked.

"I've never been at anything like this," I answered. "Are you guys getting any information back there, because we're getting shit."

"I'm getting a little from my cop buddy in the command center," she said.

"The command center is talking?"

"Oh, not officially. This is from Kramer. He happens to be assigned there and is whispering shit to me over his desk phone." Good old Karen, coming through again.

"Whaddya got?" I asked eagerly.

"He says they can't get to the people in that house. No one's surrendered, no one's under arrest. They're all still inside there, including the kids."

"Anything on what they'll do next?" I asked.

"Nah, he doesn't know that stuff, only what's already happened. Shit, my other phone's ringing. I gotta go."

"Call any time," I said.

"OK. Bye."

As Harvey continued his description of what was going on around us, his attention turned to a hysterical Louise James Africa who was being escorted away by two police officers. She was screaming and crying, "That's my son in that house! That's my son!"

Harvey: "LOUISE AFRICA, THE WOMAN THAT CHARLES THOMAS INTERVIEWED LAST NIGHT, WAS JUST CARRIED AWAY IN TEARS. PHILADELPHIA POLICE JUST TOOK HER AWAY. LOUISE JAMES FEARED THAT HER RELATIVES, HER, HER FRIENDS, HER SON I BELIEVE, UH, MAY HAVE--".

BLAM!! A thick explosion rocked the neighborhood. I felt it in my stomach, and Harvey was startled.

"OH, MY GOODNESS!"

For the first time all morning, Harvey was speechless. He craned his neck to see if he could see anything. He raised the mike to his mouth but no words came out.

Steve jumped in. "WHAT WAS THAT SOUND, HARVEY? CAN

YOU TELL US?"

Harvey tried to pull the pieces together.

"I, I CAN'T TELL YOU, STEVE. IT WASN'T--UH--I CAN'T--IT, IT'S HEAVY. I DON'T EVEN KNOW IF IT WAS A GUNSHOT, IT SOUNDED MORE LIKE AN EXPLOSION OF SOME KIND."

Steve: "COULD IT HAVE BEEN THE LOBBING OF A TEAR GAS CANNISTER?"

Harvey: "UH, I DON'T THINK SO. TEAR GAS DOESN'T MAKE THAT KIND OF SOUND. THAT SHOOK THE WHOLE BLOCK!"

The explosion echoed through the streets but we saw nothing. There was no flash, no smoke plume.

The teams led by Lt. Powell and Sgt. Connor had now been working more than an hour to try to get enough tear gas into the MOVE house to force them out. They were afraid of getting shot. They couldn't get in position to get copious amounts of tear gas into the house and dodge bullets at the same time. On top of that, some of the officers were now wondering if they weren't being caught in their own crossfire.

The teams were using explosives to take down the walls between MOVE and the houses on either side. We learned later it was the first blast that startled Harvey at about 6:50. Despite the multiple explosions, the two teams were unable to get enough tear gas into the MOVE house to force the occupants out.

"Utter disbelief," said Billie Jo Thurmond, a neighborhood woman being interviewed by Dennis Woltering. "Utter disbelief that this is happening to us." Her face was filled with wonder, her big, brown eyes growing bigger as she tried to understand it. "It's war!" she almost shouted to Dennis. "This is war. I've never seen it, but I've lived through it today. I have lived through it today."

Earl Watkins stood on a porch behind us on Pine Street. It must have been a friend or relative's house since Earl and Pearl were among those evacuated yesterday. He was sipping coffee and standing on this porch, trying to get a better look at what was going on. Across the street from us, sitting on someone's front steps was Inquirer columnist Clark DeLeon. His one leg was extended with his notepad resting on it, his pen poised in his hand. He was writing. In a small laundromat across the street from Dee's Market, one man was doing laundry like it was just another Monday. He loaded a dryer, pumped in a couple of quarters, then sat down with a paper and read it.

All around us were faces frozen in time, eyes and ears recording memories of this scene. Most of the spectators were from the neighborhood and all they could do was watch as someone else took control of their lives.

Inside the house on 62nd Street, Pete Kane stared out the bedroom window. Several things had happened in the past hour since the shooting started. Early on, Pete watched in horror as several stakeout officers turned towards the Parkers' house and appeared to be pointing right at him. He froze, thinking he had finally been spotted through the curtains and was about to get his ass kicked. Instead, the officers rushed the house next door, pounded on the door and found photographers from Channel Three and USA Today. On one hand, Pete felt sorry for them. On the other, he was happy he had the action to himself now. What Pete couldn't see was yet another photographer, from the Inquirer, being escorted from the house directly across the street from MOVE. He was discovered before the shooting even began.

At one point Pete noticed the TV in the bedroom went off by itself. He was too busy shooting at the time to worry about it. Now he checked and discovered that all the power in the house was off. He figured it had been turned off hours ago when the utilities to the block were shut down. The clock radio was dead, too. He picked up the telephone receiver and heard a dial tone. Still had phone service. He also had his portable, two-way radio and could hear communications between the station and Mini 2.

He could switch to another frequency and hear Channel Ten air cue. He was not totally cut off from the outside world.

Pete had been hearing explosions throughout the morning. Now he noticed a pile of debris in front of the MOVE house. It looked like window panes, part of a door frame and some of the slats that once covered the windows.

Water continued to pummel the bunker at about 1,000 gallons a minute, soaking the debris in the street. Now that the photographer hidden next door had been discovered, Pete was extra careful not to get too close to the window.

In a house on Cricket Avenue in Ardmore, Pennsylvania, Marianne Kranz awoke early and turned the black and white television in the bedroom on. It was still tuned to Channel Three from watching Letterman. The sound came on first. She heard Jack Jones and Walt Hunter urgently describing something happening live. Must be MOVE, she thought. Slowly, the black and white picture appeared, revealing the two of them crouched behind their van, wide-eyed. She stood frozen in her nightgown. Walt and Jack were live and there was some shooting going on around them. The camera quickly panned around but showed no one pointing any guns. She switched to Channel Ten. There were Dennis Woltering and Harvey Clark together with this shooting in the background. Dennis was doing the talking.

"ABOUT TEN MINUTES AGO WE WERE WATCHING SMOKE WAFTING AWAY FROM THE MOVE HOUSE. LOOKED LIKE IT MIGHT BE TEAR GAS OR SOMETHING."

A shot is heard close by.

"AGAIN, YOU'RE HEARING SMALL ARMS FIRE."

Marianne quickly ran downstairs to the living room and switched on the color set. She poured herself a Coke, grabbed a pack of cigarettes and settled in, switching back and forth between Channel Ten and Channel Three. Channel Six had on "Good Morning America".

◆ ◆ ◆

I was now getting really anxious about the whole idea of doing live shots in a gun battle. Not only could we not see who was doing the shooting but there was no one in authority willing to give us any information. And now, some moron in the crowd was throwing firecrackers, making everyone even more jumpy. I began hearing a sound like hoof beats.

There appeared behind Harvey and Dennis a mounted police officer wearing a white helmet and white shirt. He looked different from the other mounted police officers. I looked closely and saw he was a sergeant. He was somewhat older than the other officers, perhaps around 50 or so. He had a mean face with a long nose, squinty eyes and a mouth tied up in a sneer. He rode the biggest damn horse I had ever seen.

He came right at us and shouted, "Get the hell out of here right now!"

Dennis got out of the way. Harvey continued to talk on camera. I got into the van with Tony.

"Get the fuck out of here, god damn it! Who do you think I'm talking to?!" He was pissed to shit. He moved his horse closer to Harvey's back. The horse didn't seem fazed by the gunfire or the prodding its rider was giving. Harvey now acknowledged the problem on the air.

"STEVE, IT APPEARS AGAIN THAT WE MAY BE MOVED. WE'RE GONNA TRY TO STAY WITH THIS AS BEST WE CAN." Another, uniformed policeman now came over and shouted at us to move away.

The shooting was coming hard and fast again. Shotgun blasts, single rifle shots and the rattle of machine gun fire cut the air around us. The police were now evacuating our entire area. After being moved twice, a few yards each time, it seemed like they really wanted us out of here now. The sergeant on the horse was screaming at us at the top of his lungs. The sound of automatic weapons fire seemed right over our heads again.

"STEVE, IF YOU'LL BEAR WITH US JUST A LITTLE BIT--"

Rat-a-tat right near us. Was it a machine gun, or was it firecrackers?

The sergeant's horse was now wheeling around our live position, forcing me to cower inside Mini 2 as Tony began gathering up some necessities. Harvey was being shoved out of the frame and the picture began shaking as Bob picked up the tripod to move the camera away. In one corner of my mind, I was wondering how this must be looking on television. The rest of my mind was concentrating on this massive horse, which now seemed to be climbing into Mini 2 with Tony and me.

"Hey, man! Watch the equipment," Bob barked at the mounted cop, who had parked his horse in perfect position to make it impossible for us to continue with the live shot. Bob and Tony madly coiled the cables, unplugged the mikes and the monitor, folded the tripod and started shoving the stuff into the van. Harvey glared at the cop and wondered why they had chosen now to move us away. Was the live television coverage striking a little too close to home for someone? He knew the shooting was really on the other side of a row of houses, that the crowd was more dangerous than the distant gunfire and that the police had remained calm around him. Could they be trying to hide something? Before he could answer himself, he was jumping out of the way of the horse's big ass and feet.

"I'm not gonna tell you one more time, god damn it. Now get the hell outta here!!"

Bob and Tony threw the last bit of cable into the van. Just as Bob was about to slam the sliding door shut, Tony jumped in, punched-up the mast camera so the station could at least have the picture, then jumped out again. Bob slid the door shut and locked it as Harvey trudged away, thoroughly disgusted. He had no microphone, no camera and no telephone. I had gotten out of that horse's way long ago. Operation MOVE was going on around us and we were helpless to report on it. Bob, Tony and I all evacuated the corner of 62nd and Pine, leaving Mini 2 behind, transmitting the mast camera shot on autopilot.

The police were now going up our block of Pine Street telling people to stay in their homes. We were stranded in the middle of the 6100 block of Pine Street with no camera. Artis and Dennis had disappeared when the horse cop got belligerent. We hadn't seen Charles in quite a while.

Around us, people were on their porches, leaning over railings to see where the shooting was coming from. Police officers in yellow rain slickers yelled up from the sidewalk for the residents to stay inside. The faint sound of Steve Levy's voice was coming from a TV somewhere in the distance.

◆ ◆ ◆

The second wave of heavy gunfire made Kasey groan. It seemed like she and Tom had been hiding behind parked cars all morning. Once she saw police officers crawling on their bellies with their guns drawn, she knew she was in trouble. She was reminded that she left politics and got into television journalism to report the news, not to make it.

She picked her head up for a moment to look down Cobbs Creek Parkway when she saw something curious. Three men in sport jackets were walking up the middle of the street without a care in the world. They walked slowly and deliberately and made no effort to find cover. As they came closer, Kasey recognized the man in the middle as Captain Gene Dooley, chief of homicide. She had interviewed him recently for a story on an unsolved murder case. She didn't know what he was doing here but she was relieved to see a familiar face among the police.

"Captain Dooley," she shouted as he walked towards her position. "Am I glad to see you. Kasey Kaufman, remember?"

"Sure, I remember. The Donna Friedman case, right?" Dooley had a thin build, close cropped, receding hair, a square jaw and eyes that could bore a hole in your brain.

"When is all the shooting going to stop?" Kasey pleaded.

He looked her in the eye, took a hold of her wrist and said, "Don't worry. You're OK."

"But the shooting sounds so close," she persisted.

"You're OK," he repeated, grabbing her arm firmly, but gently. "What you're hearing is the bullets going over your head faster than the speed of sound. Each one is making a miniature sonic boom as it passes over you. Believe me, I've come across this same phenomenon in the service."

Dooley was one of the police department's most respected criminal investigators. "Look," Kasey said as she pulled a bullet out from her pocket and showed him. "This sucker landed just a few inches from where I was crouched over there."

He examined it and recognized it as an M-60 round. He wasn't surprised. The M-60 was being fired by police from the second floor of a house across the street from MOVE, towards the MOVE bunker. Dooley knew the M-60 fired bullets at supersonic speed.

"Your fear was quite natural, but don't worry about it," he assured Kasey, as he and his two detectives walked away.

Kasey and Watson set off to find a telephone.

Back on Pine Street, Harvey, Tony and I met on the sidewalk.

"I want to get to a god damn telephone," snarled Harvey, still pissed at the horse cop for chasing us from our live location. Harvey had knocked on many doors in this neighborhood when MOVE was simply a pest. He had no hesitation in knocking on doors now that MOVE was a terror. He looked quickly around, his eyes focusing on the homes immediately behind us. These were row homes much like the others. They all had front porches and a few steps leading up to them. His gaze settled on one and walked up its steps with Tony and me in tow. He knocked on the front screen door and a woman with big cheeks opened the door.

"Excuse me, ma'am. I'm Harvey Clark from Channel Ten. May we borrow your phone?"

"Why, certainly," she said with a grin and held the door open for us.

Inside was a group of people, maybe neighbors or relatives, sitting around the television, watching Channel Ten. The looks on their faces were priceless as Harvey Clark walked off the screen and into their living room. On a small table was a pot of coffee, cups, milk and sugar.

"Please, have some coffee," she offered.

"Thank you," I said. "Actually, would you mind very much if I used your bathroom?"

"Not at all." She seemed so pleased to help. "It's right at the top of the stairs."

"Thank you so much," I said and dashed up the stairs.

"There's the phone, right over there," she pointed for Harvey. Tony found a spot in the room to stand where he wouldn't block anyone's view of the TV. Harvey punched a number on the phone. He sat down in a comfortable chair and waited for someone to answer.

Raylena Fields had been madly logging what she saw on television. Her eyes constantly darted back and forth between the monitor on her desk and the clock on the wall. She noted the time to the second of all gunfire volleys or anything during Harvey's narrative that might warrant replay. Her job today would be to handle all the videotape of the shootout and the first part of that job was to log what was going on the air. Later, she would go to the time-coded air tapes and find the video she needed.

She continued logging as Harvey left the air and Steve stayed on solo. It might soon be time for her to pull chunks of Harvey's live coverage off the air check to replay for filler.

In the control room, Mike Archer was once again left with no live reporter. Yet, the aerial shot of the bunker being pounded with water remained.

"Where is that camera?" he asked out loud. He picked up the phone to the newsroom, which automatically triggered a ring on a half dozen newsroom telephones.

"Newsroom," answered Raylena, the first to grab one.

"Archer here. Start getting some tape ready for Levy to recap.

We've lost our live shot."

"OK." She hung up and began scanning her notes for the "best" of the shooting.

At the assignment desk, John Mussoni picked up a ringing phone and got Harvey Clark on the other end.

"You guys OK?" John asked with sincerity.

"We got shut down at 62nd and Pine. They're closing off another whole block and chasing people off the street here. I think someone somewhere didn't like what they were seeing on TV."

"Where are you now," asked John.

"I'm in a house on Pine Street, watching our air in this living room. Where's Archer, I want to get on." Harvey was driven now. Being kicked off the air by the police was a challenge to him. He would find a way to continue reporting.

The people in the living room with us didn't know whether to watch television or watch Harvey. I glanced around. It was a modest house as most row homes are. There were family photographs and furniture that was OK. The smell of the coffee made it feel warm, along with the friendliness of our host and her guests. Damn nice bathroom, too.

Harvey hung up and immediately dialed another number.

"What's up?" I asked. "Calling the live line?"

"You bet your ass," was his reply. He was calling the number that would put him on a line that could be broadcast live on the air.

"Hello, Archer here."

"Hi, it's Harvey. I'm ready to go live again." He explained quickly what had happened and where we were. There were a few moments of silence as Harvey listened to Archer talk. Then Harvey said "OK" and fell silent for about a minute.

"Would you please turn down the TV?" Harvey asked a man sitting close to it. This was to prevent his own voice from feeding back from the television speaker into the phone.

The scene before me now was surreal. Harvey was sitting back in a comfortable armchair in a strange living room with a phone to his face, watching a television set tuned to Channel Ten. His phone conversation with anchorman Levy was being broadcast live as he described the mast camera picture on the screen, over which was superimposed the words "Speaking: Harvey Clark Live".

Mussoni watched on his desk monitor and knew what he had to do. With the primary live van now effectively useless, he had to get another van to a new spot and hook us up with it. Mini 1 was ready to go, but he needed bodies to put with it. There had been a one-man-band staking out Miseracordia Hospital. With nothing going on there, John sent that camera to the shootout scene to connect with Mini 1. The van would be driven there by Jim Barger, a technician who was experienced with the vans and could shoot and edit. The question was, where would the van go? How close could it get and when would Harvey be able to get to it?

In a modest home some blocks away, Mayor Goode sat in his kitchen with a group of men who would later become known as his Kitchen Cabinet. They included Goode's biggest supporter on city council, Lucien Blackwell, the council president and the state representatives from the part of West Philadelphia occupied by MOVE. They heard the gunfire out the window, just a mile or so away. As far as the Mayor was concerned, this was an operation best left to his police commissioner.

Eventually, the shooting stopped.

CEASE FIRE

Steve Cohen stood at a phone booth in a hallway outside a New York City courtroom. He was about to be a witness in a libel case dating back to 1979 when he was news director at WCBS-TV. It could be a long day for him. No telling when he'd be able to break away from the trial. The timing couldn't have been worse. As General Manager of WCAU-TV he should have been back at the station, glued to his TV set, calling the shots with Jay Newman. Yet, this libel case was important, too. It was a case in which the subject of an interview done on WCBS felt he was depicted as a villain.[23] Steve Cohen had made the decision to run the story and now had to explain why to a jury.

Cohen was born in northeast Philadelphia. On the way to becoming General Manager of WCAU-TV (a position that carried with it the title of CBS Vice President), he had acquired master's degrees in diplomatic history and journalism and became a reporter in a small town in Arkansas. His dream of becoming a foreign correspondent slowly disintegrated when he decided he wasn't good enough to compete with other reporters. He chose the management route, becoming news director or executive producer at several larger stations, including the CBS owned television stations in New York and Los Angeles and the ABC affiliate in Detroit.

Cohen cut an impressive figure. He was trim with broad shoulders. He walked with his head up and his chest out, always dressed immaculately. He had thick, grayish eyebrows that matched his grayish hair. He always looked you in the eye when he spoke to you. Cohen had spent the last 15 years of his career making news decisions. He was frustrated that he couldn't be in

Philadelphia on this day for the MOVE story.

He dialed Newman's office, collect, on the pay phone.

"Hello," Jay answered.

"Will you accept a collect call from Steve Cohen?" asked the operator.

"Yes, of course," Jay answered.

"Hi, Jay. What's going on?"

"Well, they spent the morning shooting up the place, but it looks like it may have finally stopped now. We've been on live since about 6 o'clock." Jay looked at his watch. It was 8:14.

"Good, good. Do you think we should just stay with it?"

"Absolutely."

"How are Pete and Harvey and our other people on the scene?"

"Everyone's OK. Harvey got bounced around a little bit by the police and even had to leave the air for a while, but he's alright. Pete is fine, too."

I've got to go into court soon. I'll try to call you when I can. There's this phone booth right outside the courtroom."

"OK, Steve. I think we're OK for now." Jay wanted to keep his boss as informed as possible, but he also wanted to get the hell off the phone.

"Everyone's safety is my main concern, OK Jay?"

"Absolutely, mine, too."

"Talk to you later, Jay."

"OK. So long."

John Mussoni was at the assignment desk, listening to Karen Fox talk about not inciting a riot in West Philadelphia. Karen thought it was important to present a calm demeanor on the air and that the events should guide our reporting, not the other way around. John's phone rang. It was the direct line from Jay's office.

"Hello," John said into the phone.

"I want to have a brief meeting at 8:30 in my office," Jay said curtly.

In the newsroom, the 5 o'clock producer sat at his desk with his little monitor on, an Inquirer opened to the Metro section and a donut to the side. Across the room was the noon show producer watching her little TV and switching back and forth between our air and the network to see what the CBS Morning News was doing. Rob Feldman, the 6 o'clock show producer, was still in microwave monitoring the live shots. Karen Fox was on the telephone. Terri Stewart was back at her regular weekday job of day planner.

The assignment desk is the central clearing point for all local news stories in a typical television newsroom. While MOVE was the overriding story of the day, there were a few other things going on that deserved some attention and John was listing them on his sheet. A desk assistant suddenly raised her right hand in a wild, waving motion, as her left hand slammed down the telephone.

"You won't believe it," she shouted. "You won't believe it! They've raided another MOVE house in Chester!"

John gazed at her incredulously.

"In Chester?" he asked, not quite believing her.

"I swear to god. That was Mayor Battle on the phone."

Upstairs in the control room, Mike Archer had sweated out a long period of time without a live reporter to go to. When Harvey finally called on the phone, he stayed on doing live Q & A with Steve for what seemed like an eternity. By now, Raylena had cut some video of the earlier shooting and Archer told Steve in his ear to go to the tape replay every now and then. Reporter Terry Ruggles was also brought onto the set to wrap a MOVE history piece he had put together using in-house file video, mostly of the 1978 shootout. At one point, Mike's console phone rang. It was Jay.

"Yeah?" answered Mike.

"It's time we heard from our other reporter behind the police lines," said Jay.

"You mean Pete Kane? What's his number?"

Jay gave him the number to the Parkers' house and said emphatically, "Don't give that number to anyone. You should be the only person to make direct contact with Pete."

"No problem," said Mike. He hung up with Jay and then punched the outside line so he could dial up Pete.

Harvey had done a great deal of talking without having any new information to report. He and Steve did live recap after live recap of what had happened during the shooting. He also talked to the live picture of the bunker being pummeled with water. Eventually, Steve turned his attention to Terry Ruggles and to the videotaped replays and Harvey was finally given a break.

Harvey hung up, and immediately dialed the newsroom. He spoke with Mussoni and was told a second van was being sent to the corner of 61st and Pine which appeared to be the closest it would be able to get to the action. That was almost two blocks away from MOVE.

The time had come to thank our hosts.

"You've been very kind, ma'am. We thank you very much," Harvey said, offering a handshake.

"May I have your name and address," I asked, pulling out a pen and a scrap of paper. Our host obliged without question and I too thanked her for her hospitality. My only regret was that we didn't have a camera with us to shoot pictures of these nice folks and interview them on what was happening around them.

Harvey, Tony and I then left the house, walking down the steps to the sidewalk. It seemed to be quiet. There was no gunfire. We stood on the sidewalk and looked around quickly. To the right at the end of the block was Mini 2 right where we left it. But now, it was on the other side of a newly placed police barricade. To our left was the intersection of 61st and Pine. There stood new barricades, closing off the street we were standing on. A uniformed police officer was walking down the middle of the street, his head panning back and forth to the houses on either side making sure no one was outside. He approached us in an easy manner.

"Fellas, you're going to have to either go inside or get off the block," he said.

"Can't we stay here just for a few minutes?" I asked. I wanted to find Artis Hall and his camera and do some quick interviews.

"Sorry, orders. You're Channel Ten, right?" he asked, looking at Harvey. "I think your van just pulled up on 61st Street. That's about as close as you're gonna get." He continued walking up the street, until he disappeared into the war zone beyond 62nd Street.

Harvey, Tony and I started heading east towards 61st Street. As we turned to leave, Artis emerged from a house about three doors away from the house we were in. He had been practically next door to us the whole time.

Steve Levy: "JOINING US NOW IS A GENTLEMAN WHO ALSO WORKS FOR CHANNEL TEN. HE IS ONE OF OUR CAMERAMEN WHO TAKES SOME OF THE PICTURES YOU SEE. PETE KANE HAS BEEN ON THE SCENE FOR MANY HOURS. PETE, I UNDERSTAND YOU WERE IN A PRETTY STRATEGIC LOCATION WHEN A LOT OF THIS HAPPENED. FIRST OF ALL, ARE YOU ALL RIGHT?"

Mike had jumped into Steve's ear during one of the taped segments, telling him to go to Pete on the telephone.

"YES, I'M ALRIGHT. A LITTLE NERVOUS, STEVE, BUT OTHER THAN THAT I'M ALRIGHT."

"I CAN APPRECIATE YOUR BEING NERVOUS AS I'M SURE ALL OF OUR VIEWERS CAN. NOW, WHERE WERE YOU WHEN ALL THIS HAPPENED, PETE?"

Pete talked on the phone from the Parkers' bedroom while gazing out the window at the scene below: "I WAS IN LINE-OF-SIGHT AND I COULD SEE MOST OF WHAT'S GOING ON OUT HERE. RIGHT NOW THE STAKEOUT COPS HAVE THEIR GAS MASKS ON AND THEY'RE JUST STANDING BY. THERE'S A LOT OF DEBRIS IN THE MIDDLE OF OSAGE THAT'S COMING FROM EITHER THE MOVE HOUSE OR THE NEIGHBOR'S HOUSE. AND

THERE'S BEEN A LOT OF GUNFIRE, HUNDREDS OF ROUNDS OF AMMUNITION FIRED."

There had been a final volley of tear gas and smoke pumped into the street and presumably into the MOVE house. Yet, Pete saw no one emerge. There had been no surrender, at least not through the front door. Stakeout officers stood with gas masks and rifles. Others lay prone on the rooftops across the street from MOVE. In many ways, the scene had not changed since 6AM. The water continued to beat against the rooftop bunker. There was no police activity in the street in front of the MOVE house. Again, he was frustrated at not being able to see more action.

One thing had changed, though. The amount of debris in front of the MOVE house was starting to pile up. Much of it was wooden planks knocked off the roof by the stream of water. Pete also noticed a few pieces of the front porch lying there, along with slats that had covered the front windows and door. He figured the stuff got blown off the house by all the machine gun fire.

Pete continued his description of the shooting and the scene on Osage Avenue while Harvey, Tony and I found our way to Mini 1, now parked at 61st and Pine Streets. Technician Jim Barger already had the side door open and was setting up a tripod. Dave Harrington, the one-man-band who had been staking out the hospital, had arrived and was uncoiling cable and setting his camera on the tripod Barger had set up. Bob Roncaglione was there, too, emerging from the confusion of our earlier evacuation to help set up our new live location here.

"How soon can we get on?" I asked.

"Just as soon as I get air cue working for Harvey," said Barger, who was fiddling with a two-way radio, tuning it to the right frequency. Tony had reached inside the van and found a small, color monitor to place at Harvey's feet. Microphones were tested. Harrington color balanced the camera. The shot through the viewfinder had 62nd and Pine a block away in the background behind Harvey. The camera was set up in front of a police barricade. Harvey was on the other side of the barricade, with a small group of onlookers surrounding him. Harrington worked to frame the shot as best he could, as Barger readied an earpiece for Harvey and Tony tried to shield the monitor from direct sunlight so the picture wouldn't be washed out.

Weather-wise, it was turning into a nice day. Police officers began peeling off their yellow slickers and were now walking around in their blue uniforms. There were a couple of officers assigned to the barricade where we now set up our live location. They were relaxed. There was no presence of the more heavily armed stakeout officers here, no plainclothes officers that we could see. It was much removed from where we had spent the first few hours of our morning and that made me more concerned than ever about getting meaningful information for Harvey. The two or three uniformed cops at our barricade probably didn't know shit and certainly wouldn't be authorized to tell us if they did. We were now a good five blocks from the police command center. It would be more important than ever now for Karen to dig for information, then call me so I could whisper it in Harvey's ear. It was like setting up a bucket brigade to get the information from Karen's source to the people watching at home.

The meeting in Jay's office lasted only about ten minutes.

"First, tell me what's going on besides MOVE," he said to John.

"The Lyness trial is wrapping up. Could go to the jury any time," offered John. "The Delaware River Basin Commission is meeting today to decide whether to declare a water emergency."

"What's going on in New Jersey?"

"I'm not sure what Jersey stories are out there. The bureau hasn't called in, yet. You know, we may need that van on our side of the river for MOVE coverage."

"No, I don't want to do that. We can't fill a show tonight just with what happened this morning at MOVE. We need other news. Anything else?" Jay glanced briefly around the room at the others in the meeting. None volunteered anything further.

"OK, review quickly who's at MOVE," Jay said to John.

"I've gotten a second van to 61st and Pine. That'll be our new primary live location. Harvey should be there any minute with Kranz and that's where Dennis, Kasey and Charles should go, too. That van will also feed all videotape back to the station." John paused for a moment.

"Where the hell's the Mayor?" Jay asked Karen.

"I don't know, but I'll sure find out," she said.

"I want someone at City Hall constantly. Send a van there, wire up that room where Goode always holds his news conferences, have a reporter camp out at his door. Whatever it takes, I want the Mayor to be asked some tough questions. Also, I'm calling Larry in to co-anchor the coverage with Levy. He's the face most associated with our station and it'll give Steve a bit of a break. I want to make something clear now," Jay said, addressing the room. "I am committing this television station to remaining on the air live, non-stop, as long as there is something going on down there. There is nothing anyone wants to know more about today than MOVE, and we're going to stay on until it's over. On the other hand, if it is over, I want to be prepared to go on with a full newscast that includes the other news of the day. Let's have Baldini do Lyness, Ruggles do the water thing and Devlin do a Jersey story."

"Christ, I almost forgot," burst out John. "Cops in Chester have raided another MOVE house. Apparently, they did it to coincide with the Philadelphia operation."

"Who's left to cover that? Let's see. Roseanne. Send Roseanne Cerra to Chester," ordered Jay.

"We also have a MOVE related set-up for John Blunt," offered Mussoni, "a woman who's an expert on MOVE. She's writing a book."

"Good. Let him do it and we'll decide later if we'll use it. Great. I think we've got a good start," Jay told the room.

The room nodded in agreement.

"So far, our MOVE coverage has been remarkable," Jay beamed. "Let's keep it up."

◆ ◆ ◆

Chris Kelly finally got on the air for CBS. All morning, his producer kept reminding me that the network had arranged the use of our van, as long as it didn't interfere with our own coverage. Since Harvey was on almost non-stop from 6am to almost 7:30, there had been no opportunity for Kelly to do a hit for the network. Now, at our new location, she was chomping at the bit for Chris to get on.

Finally, we struck a deal. Sometime between 8 and 9, the network would throw to Philadelphia and our live shot. Chris Kelly would do a scene-setter, then bring Harvey into the shot. That way, both the CBS Morning News and the Channel 10 News could carry the same report.

It worked. Everyone was happy. Shortly after that 8:30 shot, Chris Kelly and his producer left us.

In the back of Bob Roncaglione's mind was the fact that he was supposed to go to Quebec early tomorrow morning to cover a Flyers' playoff game. He had already been up more than 24 hours straight but hadn't really thought about leaving. He and Dave Harrington got to talking about the playoffs, when Dave insisted Bob go home.

"I'll take over for you," Dave insisted. "Go home and get some rest. Otherwise, you'll be worthless tomorrow."

Bob was torn between what he wanted to do and what he knew he should do. This was the place to be, he thought. This is the story, not the damn Flyers. But he knew nobody else would be available to make the trip in his place tomorrow, and by then the Flyers could be just as important.

I was disappointed to see Bob leave. He had kept a clear head all through the night and early morning. He had labored over the mast camera and remained steady behind the viewfinder during the worst of the shooting. Now, he walked away to find a station car he could drive back.

On television, Steve Levy had just hung up with Pete Kane

and turned to the monitor behind him on the set.

"HARVEY CLARK IS ONCE AGAIN WITH US. WE SEE WE HAVE A NEW CAMERA LOCATION. I WANT TO ASK YOU HARVEY, VERY BRIEFLY, UH, WHAT ARE YOUR EMOTIONS AT THIS MOMENT?"

Harvey was a bit surprised by Steve's question. He looked the way I felt, tired. He looked into the camera for a moment, pausing to search for the answer.

"WELL STEVE, I'M GONNA HAVE TO TELL YOU THAT I WAS ONE OF THE SKEPTICS." He looked off into the distance for a second. "I NEVER BELIEVED THAT THIS WOULD END LIKE THIS."

In two hours, it seemed like an entire day had elapsed. Surely this was the end of it. Either MOVE had surrendered, and we just weren't aware of it, or negotiations were underway for a peaceful end.

Pete Kane listened to Channel Ten air on his two-way radio. He shook his head and caught Gary's eye. Pete stepped back from his camera and the two of them left their bedroom post for a while, in search of something to eat. They quietly walked down the steps to the first floor. In the kitchen they found cold cereal and milk that was slowly getting warm in a refrigerator that had no power. It would be their first meal of the day. As they chomped their flakes, they began talking about everything they had seen and heard. It was a good thing to do, replay the mental pictures to reassure themselves what they had seen was real.

A woman carrying an overnight bag walked down the carpeted hallway on the main floor of WCAU, looking for the TV newsroom. She gazed down the end of the long hallway and saw a pair of black, double doors. This was the way the guard had told her to go. She passed a smaller newsroom on her left, probably radio she thought. She passed an office with an opened door and football posters hung on the walls. Sports office, she figured.

There was a water fountain on the left, two unmarked doors on the right, a fire extinguisher and hose on the right and the two double doors at the end of the hallway. She walked through them.

Inside, the carpeting continued. So did the quiet. She walked about 15 feet through the entrance, looked to her left and saw the expansive work area that had to be the newsroom. She walked towards it and stopped for a moment. There were men in ties and buttoned-down shirts sitting at desks, reading newspapers. There were women in business attire doing the same. A dozen television sets were tuned to the same picture. Somewhere in the background was the tapping of wire machines and in the foreground the occasional chatter of police scanners. All she knew about MOVE was what she had heard on the radio during the taxi ride from the train station. It sounded like chaos in the little neighborhood called Cobbs Creek. Yet here, in the newsroom of the television station covering that chaos, there was calm.

She walked into the main work area and looked around for a place to park herself. There was an empty desk, close to the front of the room, next to a woman who had a phone to each ear. That's where I want to be, she thought. She took off her coat and dropped her overnight bag at the vacant desk and waited for the woman to put down the two phones. This person, she thought, looks like she's in the center of things.

"Excuse me," she said guardedly, as Karen Fox hung up both her phones. "I'm Jude Dratt from the CBS Morning News. You look like you know what's going on here."

"Karen Fox," said Karen, extending her hand. "Yes, you could say that."

There was a lull in the action, and Karen shared with the woman all she knew about the morning operation on Osage Avenue. Then she produced a thick file containing the history of MOVE in Philadelphia. Dratt accepted it gratefully. Her main concern was to put together coverage for tomorrow's Morning News. But first, she needed an education in MOVE history, and even some Philadelphia history. She remained with Karen through the day, asking questions and getting the right answers. She realized she had picked the right person to ask for help.

At the new location at 61st and Pine, Harvey and I were now joined by Kasey, Dennis and Charles. Kasey was the last to arrive.

"Could you find anything out back where you were?" Harvey asked her.

"I found Captain Dooley back near the command center but he didn't know anything," Kasey responded. She did find out two officers had suffered what were termed minor injuries, but she didn't know what that meant.

Harvey paused again to listen in his earpiece to what was on the air. Pete Kane was on again. Harvey caught sight of some activity behind him. A police van had come onto the block, along with a number of higher ranking officers--lieutenants and sergeants. And from behind the van came a sight Harvey wasn't happy about. Our buddy the horse cop was back and slowly trotting his way towards us.

The crowd situation at our location was not good. The police barricade that cut-off 61st Street merely cut off traffic. No effort was made to keep pedestrians on the other side. Consequently, a crowd of about 20 to 30 people surrounded Harvey. Each time Harvey went on, you could see these people crowding close to him and looking down at the monitor to see if they were on TV. It was obviously uncomfortable for Harvey to have these people literally breathing down his neck. I walked behind the crowd and asked people to move, trying to assert myself like some kind of bouncer. It worked for about five minutes and then they were back.

There was a break for us now, as someone else was on the air, probably Pete. Harvey wiped his face with his hand, more to wipe out fatigue than sweat. Someone from the crowd handed him a Pepsi, which he accepted gratefully. There was teargas in the air. The wind was blowing it into our area, two blocks from where it was deployed. Teargas in your eyes is the same as someone blowing smoke in your eyes, only ten times worse. It was hard to keep my eyes open and it hurt. As luck would have it, the station came back to Harvey at that moment.

"I THINK THESE GUYS BEHIND US, LIKE ME, ARE GETTING READY TO GET RUN OUTTA HERE WITH THIS TEARGAS. IF YOU CAN SEE RIGHT BEHIND US, A LOT OF THESE POLICE OFFICERS--NOW, APPARENTLY WE'VE HAD A WIND CHANGE THAT'S STARTING TO PUSH THAT TEARGAS DOWN OUR WAY." It bothered Harvey, but he pressed on. "KASEY KAUFMAN WAS ON THE OTHER END OF THIS, AND WE WERE LOOKING FOR SOME KIND OF COMMAND POST HERE. WHAT IS ABSENT OUT HERE IS ANY INFORMATION ABOUT WHAT HAS TRANSPIRED, HOW MANY INJURIES THERE MIGHT BE."

"I THINK THAT WAS INTENTIONAL," Kasey jumped in quickly. "I THINK THE LACK OF INFORMATION WAS QUITE INTENTIONAL ON THE PART OF THE POLICE. A COUPLE OF HOURS AGO I WAS STANDING ON THE OTHER SIDE OF A BARRICADE AND I WAS SAYING, 'WHAT DO YOU MEAN YOU'RE MANAGING THE NEWS? WE OUGHT TO BE ON THE OTHER SIDE. WE OUGHT TO BE TAKING A LOOK AT WHAT'S HAPPENING'. AND I RESENTED THE FACT THAT THEY KEPT US IN THE DARK."

Harvey responded: "I THINK ONE OF THE PROBLEMS THAT THE PHILADELPHIA POLICE OFFICERS HAD IS THAT THEY MAY NOT HAVE KNOWN IF MOVE HAD ACCESS TO TELEVISION, RADIO OR WHATEVER WE WERE SAYING OUT HERE, THAT WOULD GIVE THEM SOME IDEA WHAT THE POLICE STRATEGY WAS."

I watched in the van as Kasey began describing her morning experience with building enthusiasm.

"WE WERE WATCHING AS THINGS WERE UNFOLDING THIS MORNING AND WE SAW STRIKE FORCE AFTER STRIKE FORCE, VAN AFTER VAN COMING AND OFFICERS IN THE MOST MACABRE MAKEUP, WAR MAKEUP THAT ALMOST

LOOKED LIKE 'APOCALYPSE NOW', COMING IN WITH UH, UH, MACHINE GUNS AND UNBELIEVABLE WEAPONRY. WE SAW PLAINCLOTHESMEN. WE SAW TRAFFIC PATROLS. WE SAW AN ARRAY OF POLICE AND YET WE DIDN'T HAVE THE INFORMATION AS YOU SAID, AND WE WERE FORCED BACK FROM OUR ORIGINAL, BARRICADED POSITIONS ABOUT A BLOCK AND A HALF AWAY FROM MOVE HEADQUARTERS."

Harvey took it back from her and in the monitor, I saw the white helmet of our horse cop moving closer to Harvey's back.

"Oh, shit," I said aloud. I jumped out of the van and watched, sure we were about to catch hell again. The sergeant looked relaxed this time, almost enjoying his horsy ride. He and a uniformed officer gently asked the crowd surrounding Harvey to get on the other side of the barricade, which had now been extended up the sidewalks. This now put the crowd on one side of the barricades and Channel Ten reporters on the other side, inside the police perimeter, free of crowd harassment. This was good.

Harvey turned his head towards the mounted sergeant and gave him a wave and a "thank you". The horse cop waved back, smiled and trotted back towards our other van which he had ordered us to get the fuck out of just a couple of hours ago.

There were now several uniformed officers behind Harvey as though they were guarding him. This was the first break we had gotten all morning, other than not being shot, of course. We felt we wouldn't be moved again. I began to relax a little.

In the street, all sense of time was lost. I felt like I had worked long enough and was ready to go home. I looked at my watch. It was only 10:30. I climbed back into Mini 1, plopped down in one of the chairs and watched our air. Larry Kane had now taken over as primary anchor with Steve at his side. Steve had laid the groundwork the past four hours.

In the control room, Archer had many questions. What's the deal now? Is everyone dead? Did they surrender in secret? What the hell was all the shooting about if they didn't get them?

At the assignment desk, John Mussoni was reminded of

that awful day in 1977 when he was managing editor at WEEI radio in Boston. The station's traffic helicopter crashed into an apartment building in suburban Quincy, killing the pilot and a reporter. He couldn't help but think that today might be the day someone at Channel Ten might be killed in the line of duty.

In New York City, Steve Cohen sat in a courtroom, waiting his turn to testify, worrying about his employees getting hurt.

In Mini 1, I sat watching TV. I had been out here since about 3:30am. The morning shooting and the fear that accompanied it was now just a blurred memory. I closed my eyes for a moment. I sat perfectly still with my eyes closed, the sound of television just a drone. Then the cellular phone rang, jolting me back to reality.

"Mini 1," I answered.

"Tommy? It's Karen."

"Karen. How wonderful of you to call. How are you?"

"Fine. Are you alright?" she asked.

"Yeah," came the answer, "I just realized I've been here since three in the morning and have no idea when I'll ever see my wife again."

"The stuff's really been looking good," Karen said. "Jay even mentioned it at the morning meeting."

"Great. Chalk up another couple of share points. Listen, we have absolutely no information out here. We've got a couple of crazed MOVE supporters in this crowd talking about police brutality. But we have no idea what the hell's going on at the house. Do you know anything?"

"That's the reason I called," she said, finally getting a word in edgewise. "Inspector Kramer just told me the whole operation's at a standstill."

"What do you mean?"

"I mean they had this plan, see, a neat and tidy plan to arrest the MOVE people. Well, they've been at it since about 5:30 in the morning and they've gotten nowhere."

"You mean none of the MOVE people has surrendered?" I asked.

"That's right. In fact, Kramer overheard Brooks on the two-way radio and it sounds like the whole damn operation is going wrong." Leo Brooks, the city Managing Director, was the number two man directly under the Mayor. He was theoretically the police commissioner's boss.

"So, they haven't gained shit?"

"You got it," replied Karen. "Oh, I almost forgot. Did you hear about the photographers the police took into custody?"

"No. Not Pete, I hope."

"No, no. Apparently, a Channel Three cameraman and a USA Today photographer were hauled out of a house behind the barricades."

"Jesus Christ."

"And an Inquirer photographer was discovered in another house. I hear the cops really roughed him up, tore apart his camera and ripped out his film." This was the second Inquirer photographer to lose his spot on Osage Avenue. None of us knew about the first one until well after the fact. Bottom line, four other photographers from two newspapers and one TV station had been discovered. Ours was still safely hidden.

"Can I use all that?" I asked.

"Sure," Fox answered, "just attribute it to police sources."

"Oh, Kasey says two cops were slightly injured during the operation. Can you confirm that?" I asked.

"I haven't heard that, but I'll check it right away."

"You're terrific. Call if you hear anything more, OK?"

"You bet. See ya." She hung up in a hurry.

I was incredulous. Was it really possible that nothing was accomplished by all that shooting? What about that big explosion, what the hell was that all about? And the teargas that had just wafted through here. Had the whole god damn operation been a failure?

I relayed the information to Harvey who immediately reported it.

In the sky, I noticed a helicopter circling low. I looked at it closely and saw the ARCO logo, which meant Walt MacDonald was in the air.

Walt did traffic reports, sponsored by the Atlantic Richfield oil company. He did them for various radio stations during drive time, and for Channel Ten. His service was called the ARCO GO PATROL, and it had been part of the Philadelphia media scene for years. Walt's helicopter was equipped with a television camera and a small microwave transmitter. Walt was in the sky, accompanied by a police officer. They flew over the MOVE house to get an aerial view, which was beamed back live to Channel Ten.

I was watching Walt's live picture in the van. He was flying damn low, maybe a hundred feet or so. His live camera looked directly onto Osage Avenue from above, showing a picture no one else could see. He was struggling to keep it steady. At first, he locked onto the bunker. His live picture actually showed two structures on the roof--the large one that hung over the front of the house and a smaller one towards the rear. There was all manner of debris strewn across the roof including planks, canvas and random pieces of wood. Also present, though not readily visible until later examination of the videotape, was at least one gasoline container. The bunker was still being pummeled by water.

Walt described his live picture, then moved his camera a bit to show the street. There was a huge pile of debris in front of the house, as though it had been thrown out the front window. In fact, it had been blown out.

I peeked out of the van and Harvey was standing still, arms folded and watching TV on the monitor at his feet. Larry was doing some Q & A with Walt in the chopper. Harvey was learning with the rest of us the degree to which the MOVE house had been ravaged by the morning battle.

Behind our van on 61st Street was a small gathering of people who had been occasionally yelling at the police, calling them baby killers. From within that small group of men and women emerged Charles Thomas with Louise James Africa at his side. They walked towards our live location. I motioned to

Charles to come over to me. He did so, leaving Louise standing on the sidewalk, with a dazed look about her. I knew Charles wanted to interview her live. I was scared shitless about that idea.

"What's she gonna say?" I asked as he walked over to me.

"What do you mean what's she gonna say? She's pissed and she's upset. She's the owner of the house She has a side of the story we haven't told yet." Charles obviously felt strongly about this.

"What if she calls everyone mother fuckers on live TV?"

"She won't do that. She won't do that. I think she'll be alright." Charles sounded confident. I was shaking my head. "Look, fuck it. I'm gonna do it. This needs to be on."

I surrendered but thought I should call Mike to let him know what was coming. I forgot the control room number and dialed the newsroom instead.

Charles rejoined Louise on the sidewalk and began bringing her over to the camera position where Harvey was back on live. I sat with the phone to my ear. It rang and rang and rang and no one answered. Ten rings, 15 rings. There was no receptionist to answer phones; it was whoever in the newsroom felt like it at the moment. At this moment, no one felt like it.

Too late! As it rang for the 20th time, Harvey brought Charles into the live shot and the camera widened-out to show Charles standing next to Louise James. He was commencing the interview.

"LOUISE JAMES IS THE MOTHER OF FRANK AFRICA, WHO IS INSIDE THE MOVE HOUSE. SHE IS ALSO THE OWNER OF THE HOUSE AT 6221 OSAGE. MISS JAMES, HAVE YOU HAD ANY CONTACT AT ALL WITH THE POLICE ABOUT EITHER YOUR HOUSE, OR ABOUT FRANK?"

Charles pointed the microphone at her mouth. The camera zoomed in on her. The frame filled with her big afro and her small face, twisted in anguish and anger.

"THE ONLY CONTACT THAT I HAD WITH THE POLICE WAS A PHYSICAL CONTACT," she answered, spitting out the word "physical". Her lips twisted with emotion. "I RAN DOWN THE STREET. I WAS YELLING THAT MY S-SON WAS IN THAT H-HOUSE." Her lower lip quivered, her head looked to the ground and tears started to pour down her cheeks. She was momentarily unable to continue. The sound of her voice was replaced for several seconds by the sound of the helicopter. Into the frame a hand came to rest gently on her right shoulder. From my vantage point I saw Charles comforting Louise as she began to break down on live TV. "I WAS YELLING THAT MY SON WAS IN THAT HOUSE. MY BROTHER WAS IN THAT HOUSE. THE CHILDREN WERE IN THAT HOUSE." Her voice began rising in pitch and volume through the tears. "AND I WAS RUNNING TO THEM BECAUSE I HEARD THE SHOOTING." Her crying made her pause again.

Suddenly, her eyes became clear and anger erupted. "AND I TOLD YOU THOSE COPS WERE INSENSITIVE! THEY NEVER EVEN HEARD ME SAY THAT WAS MY SON IN THE HOUSE." Her voice was now a hysterical scream. "THE COPS SIMPLY GRABBED ME, DRAGGED ME DOWN THE STREET AND THREW ME BEHIND THE BARRICADES! I WANNA KNOW WHERE WILSON GOODE IS THAT HE CAN ALLOW SOMETHING LIKE THIS TO HAPPEN! WHERE IS THE MAYOR! I WANNA TALK TO HIM!"

Archer's sphincter clanged shut like a steel door at NORAD. He was helpless. It was up to Charles to control Louise. So far, the F word had not found its way to her lips.

Onlookers had now moved closer to the barricade as they watched the hysteria of a woman whose son and brother had been the subjects of 90 minutes of police gunfire and explosions. There were a few more minutes of Louise's fierce, verbal attack against the Mayor when Charles ended the interview. He led her off to rejoin her supporters. They began walking slowly away, Louise sobbing, her friends comforting her with arms around her shoulders and waist.

Harvey back on the air: "THE EMOTIONS OF EVERYBODY ARE TRYING TO RIDE HIGH NOW. WHAT WE HAVE NOT SEEN AND WHAT WE ARE STARTING TO HEAR FROM THOSE

AROUND US AT THIS POINT IS WHERE IS WILSON GOODE?.".

The Mayor had gone to City Hall. Reporter Suzanne Bates had ascertained that the Mayor was in his office but would not come out and would not answer questions.

Somewhere around 10:40am, the team of police led by Lt. Powell in 6223 Osage set of a final explosion, a heavy blast that was felt a block away. The blast blew out the entire front of both 6223 and 6221 Osage. Earlier explosions set off by the Powell and Connor teams had damaged the walls between the MOVE house and the houses on either side. The police could peer through holes made by their bombs and see what appeared to be yet another bunker inside the MOVE house. It was made of heavy wood, perhaps tree trunks or railroad ties and it had gun ports carved into the walls. Nothing in the intelligence gave a clue that this thing existed.

In the basement of the MOVE house, Birdie Africa and the other children had been herded into the garage. Railroad ties lined the garage walls. The one window at the front of the cellar was boarded up. Birdie was huddled under a wet blanket with his mother, Rhonda Africa, and one of his MOVE brothers, Phil. He was uncertain how much time had passed. He hadn't heard the rat-a-tat of guns for a long time but he had heard plenty of explosions. He had seen Frank James, Raymond Foster and Conrad Hampton Africa upstairs before. He hadn't seen John Africa, whom he knew as Ball, all morning.

At one point, the men came into the basement to check up on everyone. Conrad, who Birdie knew as Rad, came into the basement and said, "They got some mean bombs out there." He had tied a rag around his face to help him breathe through the teargas. The gas had hurt Birdie's eyes. He was told to keep his head under the wet blanket. Birdie felt water under him. It had been streaming into the basement through the front window as the squirt gun continued its assault on the bunker. Most of the water ran off through a drain in the floor. Looking around him, Birdie saw that all the kids were with him in the garage. His mother was under the blanket with him. Ramona and Theresa Africa were over there. All the men left again, to go upstairs.

A little bit after 11 o'clock, Archer's phone in the control room rang. It was Jay.

"Hello?" he answered.

"Looks pretty quiet out there, huh?" Jay observed. It had been quiet at 61st and Pine for several hours now. The big explosion that rocked the immediate vicinity of 62nd and Osage at 10:40 was neither heard nor felt by us. The information flow, as meager as it was, had now dried up completely.

"Yeah," said Mike, "and I'm running out of things to put on TV."

"OK. Let's leave it for now. In less than an hour, we're back on for the noon news anyway." Jay's decision made sense.

"Good," agreed Mike.

At about 11:10am, Channel Ten switched from the live drama in West Philadelphia to the network feed of The Price Is Right.

Mike ambled down the steps to the newsroom. Steve Levy left his anchor chair and headed directly for the bathroom. Both men had been strapped-in for the past five hours with no break.

Now that we were off the air, our van could finally feed Tom Watson's video back to the station. Raylena Fields watched as it was transmitted in from Mini 1. The first shots were of the police moving in under the early morning darkness, shots of the officers putting on their vests, blue and white cars with lights flashing and the shot of the dark van with stakeout officers inside wearing greasepaint and wielding Uzi's. The videotape turned to daylight and the sounds of gunfire were heard. Watson's camera bobbed up and down as he and Kasey ran for cover. There was Kasey, crouched behind a car. The sound of bullets ricocheting was incredible to Ray.

"We're at war," Raylena said to the microwave technician who monitored the tape as it came in. "Christ, we're really at war!" She madly took down time code notes of all the Watson tape. Finally, the tape feed was finished, and she was met by Mike Archer.

"I need you to put together a tape insert for Harvey, an open for the show and a tease. Make them look different," he told her. With only about 45 minutes to air, it was a tall order to fill, but not impossible.

Reporter John Blunt was assigned to take the air check tapes from Raylena and her notes and put together highlights of Harvey's live coverage when the shooting was the heaviest. Another producer was to grab the tape of the live interview with Louise James and cut a chunk of that for Charles to wrap. And yet another person was assigned to take in late tape from Kasey. She had gotten the only police interview of the morning, only after going to the command center and being a nuisance to the police brass who came and went there.

In the newsroom, typewriters were clattering like mad. The show producer was cranking out teases, lead-ins and miscellaneous copy stories for later in the show. Steve Levy was typing lead-ins to live shots. Karen Fox was typing her latest fact sheet for distribution to all the producers, Archer and Newman. Raylena and John Blunt were in editing booths with technicians, calling out time code numbers and watching the editors work their magic.

I had spent about 10 minutes on the cellular phone with Archer as he laid out how the noon show would look. Harvey would be on at the top, reporting the main story. Charles Thomas would wrap a piece of his interview with Louise James. Dennis would wrap a piece on reaction from the neighborhood, using the tape he and Artis shot earlier. By now, all tape had been shipped back to the station. Everyone had their instructions and it was time for all who had been standing to sit for a while. Tony Gore was rooting through the van for something.

"Looking for something?" I asked him.

"Yeah, more camera batteries," he replied, looking through some piles of gear. "Do you know that mast camera battery hasn't been changed since 5:30 this morning?"

"So?"

"So, those batteries rarely last for more than an hour with constant use. That thing's been in use since we went on the air at 6. Now it's 11! I can't believe it's lasted this long."

The mast camera picture never wavered, never dimmed and was always steady. It provided a non-stop source of live video through five hours of coverage even though it had been left on auto-pilot in Mini 2, which we were forced to evacuate.

"I've gotta change that battery," Tony said resolutely, stuffing a couple fresh ones into a satchel. "Wanna come?"

"Sure, they can survive here without me for a while," I said. "Let's go."

The idea that the police would simply part the Red Sea to allow us access to Mini 2 was absurd, but I figured we had to try. Knowing we wouldn't be able to walk up Pine Street to the van, we set off up Delancey Street, which was parallel to Pine, and hoped we would be able to bullshit our way into Mini 2.

THE STANDOFF

I n the news on May 13, 1985: Bruce Springsteen married model Julianne Phillips. General Electric pleaded guilty to defrauding the Defense Department out of $800 thousand dollars. The sexual assault trial of Dr. Samuel Lyness was going to the jury. Executives of the New Jersey amusement park Six Flags Great Adventure went on trial for neglect, one year after eight teenagers died in a fire in the park's haunted house. The Delaware River Basin Commission was meeting to decide whether to declare a drought emergency. Actress Selma Diamond died. And Channel Ten began a week-long campaign to educate people to the dangers of colorectal cancer. But there was no question what the lead story would be on the noon news.

There was the usual station identification, then the director called out "Roll Tape B" and Raylena's special open faded up from black. The sound of shooting began, then Larry Kane's voice:

"IN WEST PHILADELPHIA, GUNFIRE RINGS OUT AS POLICE MOVE IN ON MOVE. IT BEGAN AT 5:50 THIS MORNING, WHEN GUNFIRE ERUPTED FROM THE MOVE COMPOUND AT 62ND AND OSAGE."

The director called, "Take camera 2", and Larry and Steve appeared again on the screen.

Larry: "GOOD AFTERNOON EVERYONE. AFTER TWO WAVES OF THAT GUNFIRE, THE TENSE STANDOFF REMAINS BETWEEN MEMBERS OF THE BACK-TO-NATURE GROUP MOVE AND PHILADELPHIA POLICE. THERE IS NO EVIDENCE OF CASUALTIES INSIDE THE MOVE HOUSE, AND THERE IS ALSO NO INDICATION OF WHAT IS GOING ON INSIDE. WE DO KNOW THAT TWO PHILADELPHIA POLICE OFFICERS SUFFERED MINOR INJURIES. AND AT NOON, SIX HOURS LATER, THE

149

STANDOFF CONTINUES."

The noon producer sat in the control room, watching the story come together on the air. Archer was there with her. Harvey was back on live, relating the story of the morning shootout and talking over the tape Raylena had cut for him. In the newsroom, all work had ceased and all eyes were on the monitors. Harvey wrapped his report and Larry took over again.

"THE CITY'S FIRST, OFFICIAL REACTION TO THIS MORNING'S CONFRONTATION WITH MOVE CAME ABOUT 10:30 THIS MORNING WHEN LIEUTENANT AL LEWIS OF THE PHILADELPHIA POLICE DEPARTMENT MADE THIS OFFICIAL STATEMENT."

The director yelled "Roll tape B," and video of a thin, black man with a moustache and thick glasses rolled. "Take it!"

Lt. Lewis of Police Public Affairs read the statement: "THE INVITATION FOR THE MOVE MEMBERS TO EVACUATE AND SURRENDER WITHOUT HARM WAS ISSUED AT 05:35 HOURS BY COMMISSIONER SAMBOR. AT 05:58 HOURS THE FIRST SALVO WAS FIRED FROM THE MOVE RESIDENCE AT POLICE AND POLICE RESPONDED WITH CONTROLLED FIRE, ONLY IN A REACTIVE POSTURE. AND THERE HAS BEEN NO FIRE FROM THE MOVE HOUSE SINCE 07:30."

It took 26 seconds for Lewis to read the few lines. It was the only official acknowledgement that anything had occurred in West Philadelphia that morning.

Larry: "SUZANNE BATES HAS BEEN AT CITY HALL ALL MORNING, COVERING THE REACTION OF OFFICIALS. SHE'S LIVE RIGHT NOW INSIDE CITY HALL WITH THE VERY LATEST. SUZANNE?"

Suzanne: "WELL LARRY, THE MAYOR IS STILL HOLED-UP IN HIS OFFICE RIGHT NOW. HE'S BEEN HERE SINCE BEFORE EIGHT THIS MORNING. OF COURSE, HE HAS BEEN IN CONTACT WITH THE COMMAND POST ALL THROUGH THE NIGHT AND AT 4:30 THIS MORNING HE BEGAN MEETING WITH MEMBERS OF THE CITY COUNCIL. HE ARRIVED AT CITY HALL SHORTLY AFTER THAT AND HAS NOT COME OUT OF HIS OFFICE SINCE

150

AND HAS DECLINED TO TALK TO REPORTERS UNTIL THE SITUATION IS RESOLVED."

Suzanne looked like she was in a hallway. Her voice resonated in the empty space. Instead of speaking to Suzanne or any reporter, the Mayor sent his press secretary to do the talking. Karen Warrington told Suzanne the Mayor had known of the potential for violence and that he was "pensive" this morning but was continuing to monitor the situation from his office.

The broadcast continued through Dennis' report on the neighbors' reactions, Charles' reprise of the Louise James interview and John Blunt's wrap of Harvey's performance during the morning. MOVE had comprised the entire top of the noon news, about 12 minutes worth. After a two-minute commercial break, other stories were reported including the colorectal series and the weather forecast.

It had turned into a gorgeous day in Philadelphia. The clouds had melted away and the sun was shining brightly. It felt unseasonably warm, too.

Tony and I had made our way to the corner of 62nd and Delancey, a block from Mini 2. The corner was mobbed with people pushing against the police barricades. Channel Three's van was here. I looked way down 62nd Street, past Osage to about Larchwood, and saw a Channel Six van. There were many police officers on guard at the barricades. Tony and I approached one of them.

"Excuse me," said Tony. "I'm from Channel Ten. I wonder if I can get to my van over there to change a battery."

"What the hell for?" spat the cop.

"Hey man, some of that equipment needs constant power or it'll get hurt, you know? I just need to run in and change a battery."

"Wait right here," said the officer, as he turned and walked towards one of the plainclothes men wearing a POLICE armband.

To me, Tony said, "I just need ten minutes to lower the mast, put in the new battery, then raise it again. I'll be in and out before they have a chance to figure out what I'm doing."

The officer returned.

"The boss says OK, but just one of you."

I stayed put and watched Tony walked through the barricade to Mini 2, unlock the sliding door and let himself in. About a minute later, I watched the mast slowly come down, section by section, until it was fully collapsed and the camera was within reach. Tony climbed onto the roof and began doing what he had to do.

Around me were people with many questions: Was it over yet? When could they go home? Did they kill MOVE? What about the children?

Before I knew it, Tony was squeezing back through the barricade and making his way through the crowd towards me.

"You should see those cops pushed up against the window of our van," he said. "They figured out they can see the bunker on the monitor inside."

"You didn't leave the door unlocked, did you?" I asked cautiously.

"Are you crazy? When I changed the battery on the toy camera, I did manage to zoom the lens in a little more, so the picture is tighter on the bunker now."

"Roncaglione would love you for that," I said.

We walked back down Delancey Street towards Mini 1. It was getting to be around one o'clock now, and Tony and I were hungry.

"What do you think, Karen," Jay was asking. "Don't you think we should bring Pete Kane back so we can get his tape on the five o'clock news?"

Karen had gone around on this one several times with Jay.

"No way, Jay. Once he's out, he'll never get back in. Besides, we don't know that this is over yet." Mussoni had just gotten off the phone with Suzanne at City Hall. Jay was pressuring her to get Mayor Goode to talk. John asked her what the prospects were for Goode to emerge. Not good, she answered. For the first time all day, John began to feel a little bored. It was clear the police had failed and it looked like the Mayor was hiding. The only city officials who had done any talking were members of city council. Among them was Lucien Blackwell, who had spent the early morning with the Mayor in his kitchen. There had been nothing further from the police since the 26-second statement from Lt. Lewis at 10:30 in the morning.

Jay Newman was also pensive at this hour. He had decided to keep the regular, daytime programming on the air until something happened to warrant cutting in again. He thought it was important now to look back and assess what had happened. He felt good about his decisions so far. His phone rang.

"Hello, Jay Newman."

"Hi Jay, it's Steve." It was the lunch break in the trial and Steve Cohen dashed over to the phone booth to check in. "What's happening?"

Jay related everything that had happened since his last call. He told him he was planning a one -hour noon show instead of the usual 30 minutes and that there was no further reason to break into programming any more until something happened.

"Everyone all right out there?" asked Steve.

"Everyone is fine, a little tired maybe," answered Jay.

"Pete Kane OK?"

"He's fine. We made him a reporter this morning."

"Great. Any union problems with that?"

"Shit, I don't know."

"I gotta go back into court," said Steve. "Keep up the good work."

"Thanks."

Inside his secret perch on 62nd Street, Pete Kane and his companion were starting to sweat their asses off. Since there was no power, the air conditioner was useless. They had both stripped down to their T-shirts and were drinking warm sodas from the dead refrigerator. Pete had stopped smoking four months ago. He started again yesterday and was now on his second or third pack of Newports.

"Man, it is hot in here," he complained.

"Wish we could open up a window," Gary responded.

"Wait, I have an idea," said Pete. He walked back up to the bathroom and opened the skylight. It offered a tiny breeze. He peeked into the toilet, scrunched up his nose and closed the lid again.

He joined Gary downstairs and soon his thoughts turned to lunch. There were those pork chops. Hell, they'd spoil anyway unless someone ate them. With all the windows closed and no fan for ventilation, Pete cooked pork chops in the Parkers' kitchen.

As for those of us at Mini 1, it was now time to think seriously about food. There is an unwritten rule that field producers get lunch. After making a list of what everyone wanted, I decided I would just buy the first food I could find at the closest place.

"Just don't get me any meat," said Dave Harrington. "Chicken, turkey, filet of fish is OK, just no beef."

I collected some money from each person, stuffed it in my pocket and set off. I felt a little uneasy leaving my post but I was starving. I walked east on Pine Street towards 60th. The farther away from our van I walked, the more relaxed I became. I could feel MOVE and the tension drifting away the further east I walked. I was leaving the war zone and walking back into a normal neighborhood. Many of Philadelphia's old neighborhoods are studies in contrasts between the old and the older. This part of West Philadelphia was old. Most of it was in decent shape but some of the row homes were falling apart and neglected. I reached 60th Street and turned right, or south. This was once a vibrant business district with stores of every kind lined up for blocks. There was a kosher meat market within shouting distance of a storefront church and a hoagie shop. As I walked along the strip, I noticed a number of the shops had been closed for a long time. Some had fallen into ruin and were boarded up. Many still remained, although they had metal fencing on their windows. As the only white face on the street, I stood out. There was a business-as-usual feeling on the street. Deliveries were being made, people were double parking to run into stores, a 46 bus made its usual stops and the traffic lights signaled green, yellow and red. This was Philadelphia as I knew it, not that insanity I had just walked away from.

I saw a sign at a corner store that said SANDWICHES. I went in and found a neat little neighborhood store that indeed sold pre-made sandwiches, sodas, chips, combs, cough drops and cigarettes. I got a couple hoagies, a couple ham-and-cheese and a chicken sandwich for Harrington. I took a six-pack of cold sodas out of the refrigerator. I glanced at the cigarettes behind the counter and asked myself if this should be the day I start again. After more than seven months without, I decided to hold out a bit longer. The bill came to about $15. I got a receipt and headed back to my assigned place on a street corner where time had stood still.

Tony Gore, meanwhile, figured it was time to change the battery in the mast camera again. He made his way back up Delancey Street to the same barricade and talked to the same cop who again asked his superior. Tony was allowed in again to attend to Mini 2. As he approached the van, he again saw a number of cops crowded around the sliding door window, peering at the image on the monitor inside. They were fascinated by that bunker shot.

"Excuse me, can I get in here please," said Tony, extending a key towards the sliding door to unlock it. The officers made a path for him and one of them spoke up.

"That sure is a good view of that rooftop, buddy," said one of the officers. "Do you mind if one of us monitors that shot from inside your van?"

"Well, I don't know," responded Tony. He was playing it coy. "I guess so, but I'll have to stay with the van."

"Let me check that with my superior," said the officer. "I'll be right back."

He walked away and Tony proceeded to lower the mast again. He changed the camera battery and wiped off the lens, then slowly raised it 50 feet back in the air. He panned it back and forth, checking the picture. The shot looked good.

The officer returned.

"My boss says, OK, you can stay."

Tony nodded and showed the officer where to sit in the van for the best view of the monitor. The officer gazed at the shot with a portable radio in hand, ready to report any movement. Tony stepped away from the van and walked into Dee's to grab a soda. He was finally back where he wanted to be, close to the action and with the approval of the police.

As the afternoon progressed and the quiet at MOVE continued, the police officers at Mini 2 loosened up a bit and chatted easily with Tony. They told him MOVE had some heavy fire power in that compound but that they had some heavy stuff, too.

"This isn't general knowledge," confided one of the officers, "but they're trying to bring a crane down here to knock that bunker off."

Tony made a mental note of that and later called the station to get our helicopter up to shoot aerials of the crane being moved. But by that time, the crane idea had been abandoned. Tony was also told that all news helicopters were banned in the immediate Osage Avenue area. At one point Tony complained to the officers about how the teargas had made its way all the way up to 61st Street in the morning.

"Here's a trick for you," said one of the officers, "in case you ever get caught in teargas again." The officer went over to a privet hedge behind Dee's and ripped off a handful of the small leaves. "Grab a handful of leaves like this and breathe through them." He put the handful up to his face and showed Tony. "The chlorophyll helps neutralize the teargas. The leaves also release oxygen to help you breathe."

Tony was hoping he wouldn't have to test it.

Suzanne Bates had called the newsroom from City Hall to report the Mayor had scheduled a news conference for 3:00pm. We would carry it live.

Karen was keeping track of something she had heard from Inspector Kramer during one of their telephone conversations. He mentioned there was talk of bringing in a crane to try to knock the bunker off the MOVE roof. The idea took her back to her conversation four days ago with former Police Commissioner O'Neill who had thought of using a weight suspended from a helicopter to knock the bunker off. Now, on the police scanner, she heard bits and pieces of messages that indicated preparations for traffic detours to make way for a crane, even a police escort. Later, it was revealed the crane idea was abandoned for several reasons. It was feared the crane would not have room to maneuver properly in the narrow streets; the crane's reach was not long enough to actually reach the bunker over other rooftops; it was feared the crane operator might get shot.

So, once again, the bunker taunted the police. It remained standing despite a five-hour barrage by 700,000 gallons of water under high pressure and a 90-minute torrent of machine gun and rifle fire. The bunker survived. How could it be eliminated? How could the police win with that thing glaring at them?

At City Hall, Mayor Wilson Goode was preparing to go before reporters. The news conference would be held in room 202, the Mayor's Reception Room, where all his formal news conferences were held. It was this room Suzanne had staked-out since the morning. Usually, the Mayor's news conferences had a standard cast of characters. The City Hall reporters had their office right down the hall and were always the first ones in their seats. Many times, our camera would be the last to show up due to a general climate of apathy towards City Hall events shown by our news operation. Today however, we were the first ones there. We had been waiting since 9:30 in the morning.

The Mayor entered the room. The TV lights went on and Channel Ten interrupted its regular programming. After a brief intro by Larry Kane, the director switched to the City Hall live shot where W. Wilson Goode stood at a podium.

"We have a standoff," he began. "The members of the organization are barricaded inside. Uh, we are assessing the situation at this time and, uh, are trying to determine what step to take next. There are, in fact, some negotiations going on now and we are hopeful to be able to resolve it and talk them out," the Mayor continued. "However, we are determined that they should not remain in the house."

I had been back at the van and only noticed by accident that the Mayor was on. I glanced at the monitor as I finished the dregs of my hoagie and saw him on our air with the words Live/City Hall superimposed over the bottom of the screen.

"Hey, Harvey," I called over to him. "The mayor's on."

Harvey jumped in front of his little monitor and put his earpiece on so he could hear. My imprudent shout also attracted some spectators to the van. A few people stuck their heads in to watch the mayor. I figured what the hell, it's everyone's story now and I turned up the volume so they could all hear.

"Do you have any plans to go to the scene, to go to Osage Avenue?" Suzanne asked the Mayor. His response came without hesitation.

"Uh, no I think it's inappropriate for an executive to be there. I have two, uh, three very capable people there, Leo Brooks the Managing Director, Greg Sambor the Police Commissioner and Bill Richmond the Fire Commissioner. I don't I think I'm needed at the scene."

"Oh, man," came the response from one of the spectators

watching on my monitor.

The Mayor was asked questions about all phases of the operation, especially the shooting barrage. He said it was a police operation and that it was in the hands of the police commissioner. He said there was no word from inside the MOVE house. He made it clear he would not telegraph any police plans for fear MOVE had a television and might be watching.

And what about the children who were believed to be inside the compound-- wasn't there a safer way to solve the MOVE problem?

"I don't think there was any other way, other than this way," the Mayor responded. "And I don't take it as any kind of easy decision to take into my hands a decision regarding children. And therefore, I hope, and I pray with all of the might I have to God that those children will not be injured, will not be hurt. Uh, we'll do everything we can to prevent that. But the kind of violent confrontation that these people are involved in can lead to no positive conclusion, in my view."

The crowd around Mini 1 was now growing as word spread that the mayor was on.

"Mr. Mayor," asked a reporter. "Should the negotiations with the community leaders fail, what's the next step?"

"Uh, we intend to evict from the house. We intend to evacuate from the house. We intend to seize control of the house."

"How are you going to do that?"

"Uh, we will do it by any means necessary."

Christ, I thought, you've already tried water, teargas, smoke, machine guns and explosives. What's left?

The Mayor had agreed to one last attempt at negotiating with MOVE. The negotiators were a hastily formed coalition of neighborhood leaders and the mother of MOVE member Theresa

Brooks Africa. The police escorted them close to 6221 Osage where they shouted through a bullhorn.

"We tried to negotiate with the MOVE members inside," recalled Stanley Vaughn, "but there was no response. We told them that they couldn't win and we pleaded with them that they had children and that they could send the children out. That would help ease the situation." The bullhorn plea was not acknowledged, and after a half hour, the negotiators left.

At about 4 in the afternoon, the cellular phone in Mini 1 rang.

"Hello," I answered.

"Hi, it's Karen."

"Hi."

"Did you see Goode?"

"Most of it, yeah. What do you think's on his mind?"

"I don't know," she said, "but I do know they want this to end before dark. They're real worried that they blew it, but they don't want the thing dragging into tomorrow."

She paused, rooting through some notes. "They're gonna try something before sunset."

"When's sunset these days?" I asked, glancing at my watch.

"I guess 7:30 or so."

"Jeez, I can't wait," I said, sighing with exhaustion. I had recently passed the 12-hour mark on this story.

"Talk to you later, Tommy."

"Bye." I slowly hung the phone back on its cradle and rested my hand on it for a few moments. Then, I picked it back up and dialed my house.

"Hello?"

"Hi, it's me."

"How are you?" asked Marianne, sounding concerned but not as worried as I thought she might be.

"I'm beat to shit. They have no idea when this is gonna end. Have you been watching?"

"I haven't turned the set off since I got up. That Harvey is great! Walt Hunter was good, too. Channel Six hasn't done shit."

"I have no idea when I'll be home. Christ, that shooting was something."

"You were real close to it, huh?"

"Yeah. Then there was the teargas later. That was some nasty shit. Look, I think I better go. I'll call you later."

"Alright, sweetie. I love you."

"I love you, too."

Outside the van, the crowd had grown considerably in size since the mayor went on TV a little more than an hour ago. About a hundred people were now gathered around the truck. Behind me, where Louise James and her supporters had been lingering in the morning, she had collapsed in the arms of her companions and was carried away, crying hysterically. That incident, along with the mayor's news conference and the 85-degree temperature all contributed to a growing undercurrent of anxiety at 61st and Pine.

One block west at 62nd and Pine, Jim Barger had now joined Tony in Mini 2. Once Tony re-established our beachhead there, we figured it would be smart to have a two-person crew with Mini 2 again since anything could happen down there. Also, fresh technicians had arrived to take Mini 1 into the night, if necessary.

Jim arrived at Mini 2 to see a policeman sitting in the van. The cop had three stripes on his sleeve.

"Hi," said Barger, introducing himself. The sergeant gave him a quick handshake before returning his gaze to the monitor.

It was Jim's impression that the police had taken over the van, although there was never any overt power play along those lines. The important thing in Jim's mind was to maintain Mini 2's position here. If the trade-off was allowing the police to look at the monitor in the van, so be it. The sergeant and the other officers here were friendly enough.

Jim reached into the van, grabbed its camera and recorder and began shooting video. He shot the police around the van, the police up and down 62nd Street and a helicopter that had made occasional passes overhead. Its markings were of the

Pennsylvania State Police.

One of my hardest jobs thus far was now upon me--to get Harvey Clark and Dennis Woltering to sit down somewhere quiet and write their pieces for the early news. Harvey and Dennis, like me, were now into their 13th hour on this story. From my own experience, the hardest thing to do sometimes is to step back to get a broad view of a story you've been close to for so long. They were trying to do that now, sitting in separate station cars with the doors closed, writing their pieces.

"This is microwave control to Mini 1," crackled the two-way radio in the van. I picked up the microphone.

"Mini 1 here," I responded.

"Ah, roger Mini 1, when might we expect track from Harvey and Dennis?"

Track is another word for recorded narration. Harvey and Dennis were writing those tracks now.

"Give us another couple of minutes," I said into the mike.

"That's a roger, Mini 1. Call us when you're ready to feed."

I put down the mike and Harvey appeared at the van door with his script in hand. I switched places with him, letting him climb into the vacant seat inside so he could close the door and record his track without outside noise. Dave Harrington was with him, throwing the right switches to make the transmission happen.

Meanwhile, we had been joined by fresh technicians. Don Overton, Suzy Goldstrohm and Frances Harty arrived together, driven down by a station courier. Don was hired by the station in 1981 when management was in the market for so-called super techs who could both shoot and edit video, plus work a live van. All during the 1960's and 70's, the technicians at Channel Ten for the most part were either sound technicians or shooters or editors, but usually not a combination. After 1980, when film was being phased out, the station sought to bring in people who could do all those duties without new training. Don was one of the first, newly hired people during this period. He was a skinny guy with a receding hairline who had sinus problems that sometimes prevented him from going up in the helicopter.

Suzy was to be married in a month. After working as a technician for five years, she had decided to marry and move to Michigan. At age 29, she was looking forward to a new life out of the business as a wife and mom. She saw this as perhaps the last, big story she might ever work on. Suzy was thin, attractive and had beautiful, straight, long, brown hair.

In the nine years since she left Temple University, Fran Harty had been a model and a clothing buyer. She joined the station in 1975, finished school and the following year had a camera on her shoulder. Fran's aesthetic sensibilities were later reflected in her marvelous editing talent. Fran was a tall woman who also had beautiful long, sandy hair.

A collective decision was made to relieve Tony in Mini 2 and let him go home, since he'd been on the scene longer than any of the other techs. He would be replaced by Fran. I called down to Mini 2 to ask Barger to inform the police of the intended switch. An officer escorted Tony up to 61st Street and escorted Fran back down to Mini 2 to join Jim Barger. At Mini 1, Don and Suzy took over van operations leaving Dave as a roving camera. Harvey, Dennis, Kasey and Charles were all with me at Mini 1, while Suzanne was still at City Hall.

Police intelligence over the preceding months indicated that MOVE may have dug tunnels from under its compound to other locations in the Cobbs Creek area. MOVE had indeed bragged over the bullhorn that they would blow up the whole neighborhood if their imprisoned members were not released. And there were the sightings of gasoline being hoisted onto the roof. Those threats increased police fears of an underground network of tunnels originating at 6221 Osage and possibly leading to other homes on the block or even to Cobbs Creek Park.

The possibility of MOVE members escaping, I surmised, was probably the main motivation for the police commissioner and the managing director to cling to the goal of getting MOVE out of its compound before dark. There were also complaints from some of the neighbors who were itchy to go back to their homes.

These factors, along with an unspoken mandate to finish the job, led to the continuation of the eviction operation. There was agreement among the police commissioner, the managing director and the mayor that the operation should continue, rather than be halted and resumed tomorrow.

At the command post at the geriatric center, police commissioner Sambor, fire commissioner William Richmond and managing director Leo Brooks gathered at about 4:30pm. Sambor had invited the Bomb Squad chief, Lieutenant Powell, and Bomb Squad officer William Klein to the meeting. Powell and Klein had spent a harrowing morning together in 6223 Osage, being shot at while trying unsuccessfully to smoke MOVE out of its house.

In later recollections, Brooks said he heard Sambor approve the construction of an explosive device designed to destroy MOVE's rooftop bunker and blow a hole in the roof so that teargas could be pumped into the house. The explosive would be delivered by helicopter. Commissioner Richmond was assured that the explosive would not cause a fire. At the time, Richmond was unaware that at least one can of gasoline was present on the roof.

Managing director Brooks got on the phone to inform the Mayor of the plan.

◆ ◆ ◆

5:00pm, Channel 10 News, Live At Five, Larry Kane, anchor: "GOOD EVENING EVERYONE. IT IS NOW BECOMING A MARATHON STANDOFF. ELEVEN HOURS OF TENSION, AS THE STREETS OF PHILADELPHIA BECOME A BATTLEGROUND IN FIRST, A WAR OF BULLETS, AND NOW, A WAR OF NERVES."

It was a war of nerves, a war we were fighting at 61st and Pine with a crowd of people that had grown steadily in size all afternoon. By five o'clock, many people were home from work and walked over to have a look. Many others had watched all day on television and came from other neighborhoods to see for themselves. The crowd was restless. Among them were several self-proclaimed MOVE supporters. They shouted out challenges to the police officers guarding the barricades.

"Don't kill MOVE babies!" one would shout.

"Stop the brutality!" shouted another.

I noticed one of them was just a few feet from the barricade that kept the crowd separated from Harvey and Dennis. He was a slim man with a beard, short hair, khaki shorts and a buttoned shirt. He stood defiantly, peering through sunglasses with his arms folded and shouting epithets at no one in particular.

Several times during the day, a car with a bullhorn attached to its roof cruised slowly by with demonstrators shouting over a microphone.

"We want Mayor Goode! We want Mayor Goode here!"

Someone on the crowd shouted, "Put a stop to this mass murder! That's what it is--MASS MURDER!"

This generated a smattering of applause from the spectators, but the reaction from the majority of the crowd was one of wariness. There was no sense that the crowd was moving to support the dissidents, although a few people silently nodded their heads.

The five o'clock news was well along, reporting virtually nothing new except that a neighborhood coalition had been formed to try to negotiate with MOVE. Harvey and Dennis live-wrapped the reports they had tracked an hour ago. Occasionally, Harvey and Larry referred back to the mast camera shot of the MOVE bunker. Because Tony had adjusted the lens when he changed the battery, the bunker appeared much closer. In fact, it filled the screen, revealing details of its construction.

At Mini 2, Jim and Fran marveled at the bunker shot as the police sergeant stared at it hard. Jim had been shooting video infrequently. The scene around the van hadn't changed since he arrived. However, he did notice, as did we at Mini 1, that the State Police helicopter had made a number of low passes over the neighborhood. I found the noise made by the chopper distracting to our live shots. It appeared to be concentrating its passes in the area of the MOVE house, probably surveillance to supplement the view the cops were getting from our mast camera.

"Live at Five" was covering the MOVE story from top to bottom, with a total of four reporters at the scene, one at City Hall, a photographer in a secret location behind police lines and several other reporters back at the station doing sidebars. All the best of Tom Watson's tape of the gunfire made air as did highlights of Harvey's play-by-play of the morning shooting. Dennis Woltering's interviews with neighbors reflected two basic opinions-- either a flat rejection or guarded support. The closer the people lived to the MOVE house, the more they seemed to subscribe to the latter. But a chilling reality emerged in Dennis' report. He had had trouble getting many people to talk about the morning gun battle because they feared MOVE might get revenge sometime later.

"After this is over," remarked resident Dierdre Thurmond, "will we still be safe? I mean, will there be some conflict? Can we walk up and down our neighborhood without being fearful that something could break out?"

Kasey and Charles recapped their morning experiences. Suzanne reported on the mayor's news conference and did another live interview with Councilman Lucien Blackwell. Blackwell had been the only other city government representative to talk all day, although he knew little more than we had been able to find out on our own.

Steve Levy presented a report on the actual warrants that were the basis of the whole operation. Karen had obtained a copy of the warrants charging Frank, Conrad, Ramona and Theresa Africa with a half dozen crimes that included making terroristic threats, possession of explosives and rioting. Roseanne Cerra reported on the raid on the MOVE house in Chester, where police found five children eating dog food and a woman named Mary Robbins, wife of MOVE member Alphonso Robbins Africa. Philadelphia police had feared that MOVE members might try to flee the Osage Avenue compound and hide in the Chester house. The raid was designed to coincide with the Philadelphia operation.

I watched from my perch inside Mini 1 and learned about all these things along with every other viewer. Harvey remained on standby at the live camera. The fact that there was live TV going on energized the crowd around us even more. Individuals became more vocal about their particular views on the police, on MOVE, on the children, on the social structure of America, on the presence of television.

Up the street inside Mini 2, there was a brief flurry of excitement as the sergeant and Fran Harty thought they saw someone on the MOVE roof. They wound the tape back and studied what appeared to be a person moving. They wound it back again and again. The sergeant reported this over his radio. Whoever it was, he didn't appear in the picture for long. Then, he was gone.[24]

Back at the station, Archer had come back down to the newsroom after spending only the first ten minutes of the show in the control room. Gary Herman, the regular show producer, was now in the control room. Without an ongoing, breaking-news situation at the scene, Archer felt he didn't need to baby sit.

John Mussoni had been relieved at the assignment desk by the night editor. John was on the phone, trying to line up interviews with city council members and community leaders while his replacement was getting a final briefing from Karen.

Out on the street, I was annoyed that our helicopter, along with everyone else's, had been banned from the air space, especially now that this State Police chopper was making low passes over the MOVE compound. It would have made for great aerial pictures.

At Mini 2, Barger had the camera out again and was shooting a few random pictures. Just eleven years ago he was moving a toilet from one room to another on his first day on the job at Channel Ten. How he ended up moving a toilet when he was hired as an electrician, he still couldn't figure out. He'd gotten a degree in electronic engineering from Philadelphia Wireless and became a broadcast technician. He had come a long way since hauling the toilet.

The police sergeant had his portable radio to his ear when he stuck his head out of the van.

"Hey Jim, come here a minute," he said.

"What's up," Jim responded.

In a hushed voice that only Jim could hear, the sergeant said only, "Keep your eye on that helicopter." He immediately returned his gaze to the monitor.

The State Police helicopter wasn't visible at the moment but the sound of its rotor cutting through the air could be heard somewhere in the distance.

Jim took the sergeant's advice. He mounted the camera on his shoulder and got into position to focus on the chopper as soon as it returned.

The first 15 minutes of "Live at Five" was solid MOVE coverage. After a two minute commercial break, co-anchor Alan Frio read some of the other news of the day and introduced Terry Ruggles' report on the drought situation.

At Mini 1, we had a temporary break from live TV. Harvey and Dennis had put their microphones down. Don took his eye off the viewfinder and Suzy relaxed for a few minutes in the van. I glanced at the air monitor and saw that the show was in a commercial break. I looked at my watch: 5:26.

A block away, Barger heard the helicopter noise getting louder and he began to roll his camera, glancing down quickly at his recorder to make sure tape was rolling. The helicopter came into view from behind a row of houses a block or two away. He followed it closely, zooming in to fill the frame. As it got closer, he could see a side door open and a man's leg hanging out. In fact, he saw all of the man through the open helicopter door, sort of leaning out. The man was wearing sunglasses and a white vest.

Jim stopped down for a brief moment to re-aim his shot over the MOVE house, suspecting something was about to happen. Of course, from the ground at 62nd and Pine, he couldn't see

168

the bunker. So, he aimed the camera at the point where the helicopter would have to hover, kept the shot a bit wide and held his breath.

The helicopter came into the frame and Jim immediately zoomed into the open, side door. It slowly approached, steadily descended, then hovered directly over the unseen MOVE roof. The chopper was almost totally silhouetted by the sun. From the open door, an arm emerged and tossed something out. The object fell out of the frame and the chopper immediately climbed out of the picture.

Jim's heart was pounding. He knew he had to hold the shot over the MOVE roof, where something had just been dropped. He zoomed out a little bit, then stood as still as he could with the camera rolling. It took 45 seconds for something to happen.

THE BOMBING

I t sounded like one of the ending booms of a good fireworks display, the kind that really rocks the neighborhood. It jolted me from my late afternoon malaise and set the crowd around us buzzing.

Harvey was barking into his microphone.

"Get me on! Get me on! There's been an explosion!"

I picked up the two-way microphone and called microwave control, telling them to get us on. We were still in the commercial break.

At the station, Mike Archer walked past the news director's office when Jay shouted at him.

"Mike! I think you'd better get back up there. It looks like there's been an explosion at MOVE."

Mike hustled back upstairs, saw Harvey ready to go and gave the OK in Larry's ear to go to him. A commercial for Francesco Rinaldi spaghetti sauce was wrapping up. The break ended, and Larry was cued.

"WE'VE JUST BEEN ADVISED THERE'S BEEN SOME SORT OF EXPLOSION AT THE MOVE BUILDING AT 62ND AND OSAGE. WE'LL GO DIRECTLY LIVE TO HARVEY CLARK RIGHT NOW AT THE SCENE. HARVEY, WHAT'S GOING ON?"

Harvey had settled into the rhythm of the afternoon, his face appearing tired during the last few hours. But now, his brow was tied up in that terrible knot again.

"LARRY, ABOUT TWO SECONDS AGO, THE STATE POLICE HELICOPTER PASSED OVERHEAD. CHARLES THOMAS TOLD ME THAT IT MADE A LOW PASS OVER THE MOVE HEADQUARTERS AND SOMETHING WAS DROPPED ON TOP OF THE COMPOUND."

Inside the house on 62nd Street, Pete Kane was on his belly.

He had been raiding the refrigerator when the explosion hit. To him, it sounded right overhead or next door. He hit the floor, crawled out of the kitchen, crawled up the stairs into the bedroom and over to his tripod. Whatever blew up shook the whole house. He climbed up to his camera and cautiously peeked out the window. No one seemed to be running or panicking. He began rolling.

In the garage of 6221 Osage, Birdie and the Africa family felt the whole house shake. Seconds before the explosion, the MOVE men had rejoined the women and children in the fortified garage. The dogs were there, too. Birdie and the other children were crying, frightened by the loud blast.

Fifty feet above Mini 2, the mast camera saw the explosion. It was recorded on tape and burned into the minds of Frances Harty and the sergeant who were looking at the monitor. The blast had thrown debris into the air and caused a momentary flash of flame near the bunker. But the bunker still stood. The device had essentially missed its mark.

Outside the van, Jim's camera had also rolled through the whole thing. When it blew, he saw only a spray of debris and a puff of smoke rise from the unseen roof.

It was 5:27pm, almost 12 hours since the police began their mission to arrest four MOVE members. Karen Fox heard someone in the newsroom say, "They dropped a bomb!" She quickly turned up her monitor and saw Harvey describing to Larry the sound he had heard.

"Jesus Christ," she said. She picked up her phone and tried to confirm what had happened out there.

Pete Kane was reporting live by phone to Larry on the set.

"LARRY, WE HEARD A LOUD EXPLOSION AND A LOT OF DEBRIS CAME FROM THE FRONT OF THE MOVE HOUSE. THERE'S WHITE SMOKE COMING FROM THE HOUSE AND THE STAKEOUT SQUADS ARE SLOWLY MOVING INTO THE SCENE, HIDING BEHIND THE BUILDINGS AND CARS RIGHT NOW."

Larry: "HOW LOUD WAS THAT EXPLOSION?"

Pete: "IT WAS VERY LOUD. IT SHOOK THE BUILDING WE

ARE IN AND YOU COULD HEAR GLASS BREAK AROUND US."

Photographer Frank Goldstein was at the station now and watched on a monitor. He'd returned yesterday from covering a Sixers game in Boston and had gone to Chester with Roseanne earlier in the day. He heard what was happening now.

"Let me go down there and help," he told Mussoni. John said OK and Frank took off for 61st and Pine.

Archer was back in the control room and watched the monitors. The mast camera shot was not being transmitted when the explosion hit. Now he went back to it but it didn't show much except for a small trail of white smoke emanating from the roof.

He stayed with the formatted show for now, which meant going next to John Blunt's feature on a local author who had studied MOVE and was writing a book on the group. Medical reporter Cherie Bank presented her special report on colorectal cancer, part of a station project to educate and offer free screenings.

In Mini 1, Jim and Fran were jumping out of their skin to get someone back at the station to take in their tape. Even though the mast camera was not transmitting live when the explosion happened, Fran was rolling tape in the van, thank god. Thus, they had two different angles of the explosion, pictures no one else in Philadelphia--not even most of the police--had yet seen. Jim loaded his tape into a machine and cued it up to the moment the helicopter entered the frame before the device was dropped. Only one tape could be fed at a time and Frances had the close-up of the device actually exploding next to the bunker. I never figured out why they didn't feed the mast camera shot first.

Jim finally got someone in the microwave control room to give them a window to feed tape. He transmitted his tape back. After that, the police sergeant wanted to keep tape rolling on the close-up of the bunker in case anyone came out. This left no way to send back tape to the station because it tied up the one and only tape machine. Frances grabbed the mast camera tape of the blast and dashed out of the truck and up the street towards the other van.

Up the street, I was standing close to Harvey, keeping an eye on the dissident in the khaki shorts who was shouting rather close to our camera position. I suddenly saw a figure running up 61st Street towards us. It was Frances. I ran over to the opposite sidewalk to meet her and she shoved a tape into my hand.

"This," she huffed and puffed, "is the explosion." She was trying to catch her breath to tell me. "This is the thing exploding", she said breathlessly, "from the mast camera."

I grabbed it and she turned and jogged back down 61st Street towards Mini 2. I walked over to our van and handed the tape to Suzy.

"Feed this back when you can," I said. She nodded, took the tape from me and put it aside because Harvey was about to go live again.

Jim's ground-level tape of the rooftop explosion was turned around at the station and made the air about 15 minutes after the event actually happened.

Larry Kane: "AS HARVEY CLARK REPORTED JUST MOMENTS AGO, APPARENTLY THE LAST-MINUTE NEGOTIATIONS FAILED AND SOMETHING HAPPENED ABOUT 10 MINUTES AGO WHEN A STATE POLICE HELICOPTER DROPPED SOMETHING." He described Jim's tape as it played on the air. "AND THERE YOU SEE THE EXPLOSION AFTER THE STATE POLICE HELICOPTER DROPPED WHAT LOOKED LIKE A BOMB RIGHT IN THE MIDDLE OF THE MOVE COMPOUND. YOU SEE THE EXPLOSION RIGHT THERE. HARVEY SAID IT HAPPENED 30 SECONDS AFTER THE DEVICE WAS DROPPED, APPARENTLY SOME SORT OF TIMED EXPLOSIVE."

Jay's eyes were riveted to the three TV sets in his office tuned to channels three, six and ten. He saw nothing on the first two like what he was seeing on his station. No one else had shown video of the device exploding. His people were the first to get it on.

It was 5:40 and at the assignment desk, Karen Fox madly made phone calls to anyone who might have known what was dropped on the MOVE house. Kramer had left for the day after helping Fox as best he could through the morning and afternoon hours. Her source of inside information had dried up. It was as though she was starting from scratch on a brand new story, digging for that primary source who was as close as possible to the epicenter.

At 61st and Pine, the unrest among the spectators was becoming unsettling. The dropping of the device and the explosion convinced the dissidents that the police were simply trying to wipe out whoever was in the MOVE house, including the children. It also won-over a number of other spectators who, until now, had tried to remain open minded about the situation. The dissident in the khaki shorts, who had been shouting epithets much of the afternoon, was now more agitated than ever and began directing his tirades at me as I walked by him to go from Harvey's camera position to the van. He would look me right in the eye and follow my eyes with his while shouting, "Y'all are murderers! Y'all helping them kill!" The first few times, I walked by without acknowledging him. I made it to the other side of the barricade, where I approached a uniformed policeman who was standing guard. The khaki man's attention had been distracted for a moment.

"Officer", I said, "there's a guy standing over there with sunglasses and khaki shorts who's got one hell of a big mouth." I stood aside to let the officer's gaze find him.

"The guy mouthing off right now?" he asked.

"That's him. I think he might be trouble."

"Appreciate you pointing him out. I'll keep an eye on him," promised the officer.

"Thanks."

I climbed back under the barricade, away from our camera and back towards the van. As I walked by my friend, he pushed my shoulder and said, "Mother fucking killers!" I wheeled around and swung my arm up to knock his hand off me.

"What's your fucking problem," I yelled at him. "We're not killing anyone!" I grabbed his wrist and threw it aside.

"Don't you touch me, mother fucker!" he snarled. "Don't you EVER touch me, motherfucker! I'll bring you more trouble than you got now, boy!"

He took a step towards me and I took a step back. His glare could melt a rock and I was now convinced he was an unstable individual. I backed off as the people immediately surrounding watched us, waiting for something ugly to happen. It didn't.

The police officer I had spoken to had his back turned the entire time, gazing at something on the horizon. I looked to see what was so damn interesting that he couldn't come to my rescue. A plume of smoke was rising from Osage Avenue.

"I'm going on," said Harvey to me. "That place is starting to burn."

Harvey stood poised, ready and waiting for the director's cue in his ear. I looked at the air monitor in the van, and Larry was on the air.

"THERE IS A NEW DEVELOPMENT AT MOVE HEADQUARTERS AT 62ND AND OSAGE. WE'LL GO LIVE RIGHT AWAY TO HARVEY CLARK AT THE SCENE. WHAT'S GOING ON, HARVEY?"

The director called for the switch to Harvey's live camera. Harvey heard "go" in his ear.

"LARRY, BEHIND ME YOU CAN PROBABLY SEE--WE'LL TRY TO PUSH IN TO GET A LITTLE TIGHTER SHOT OF IT---THAT SATCHEL CHARGE OR WHATEVER THE EXPLOSIVE OR BOMB THAT WAS DROPPED ON THE MOVE COMPOUND JUST A FEW MINUTES AGO, HAS APPARENTLY STARTED A SERIOUS FIRE. IT IS NOTHING BUT BLACK SMOKE. UH, THERE WERE A FEW SIRENS THAT MAY HAVE EITHER BEEN FIRE ENGINES OR AMBULANCES, DON'T HAVE ANY IDEA WHICH. BUT THERE IS APPARENTLY A--NOT APPARENTLY, THERE IS--A SERIOUS FIRE. YOU CAN SMELL THE SMOKE FROM HERE."

As Harvey spoke with the black smoke rising behind him, more voices in the crowd began making themselves heard.

"I told you they just out to kill 'em!" shouted a woman.

"They tryin' to burn 'em out now!" came another voice.

"Get the children out!" came another.

The air was thick with tension and the smell of smoke.

I turned my attention back to the TV. Larry was talking over the live picture of the smoke plume being provided by Harvey's camera.

"RIGHT NOW PETE KANE IS A LITTLE CLOSER THAN HARVEY ON OSAGE AVENUE, ABOUT A HALF BLOCK AWAY FROM THE HOUSE. WHAT DO YOU SEE FROM YOUR DIRECTION, PETE?"

Pete talked on the telephone.

"LARRY, WHAT I SEE IS A LOT OF BLACK SMOKE. IT'S VERY THICK. THERE ARE FLAMES SHOOTING FROM THE ROOF AREA OF THE, UH, EITHER THE NEIGHBORS' HOUSE OR THE MOVE HOUSE." Pete's voice was describing the live picture coming from Mini 1's camera. On the screen the words "Speaking: Pete Kane, Cameraman" were superimposed.

Pete: "SEVERAL OF THE HOUSES ARE ON FIRE NOW."

Larry: "SEVERAL OF THE HOUSES? NOT JUST THE MOVE HOUSE?"

Pete: "NOT JUST THE MOVE HOUSE, NO, LARRY. THERE ARE SEVERAL HOUSES ON FIRE. RIGHT NOW THERE ARE STAKEOUT GUYS MOVING DOWN THE STREET, GETTING CLOSER TO THE MOVE HOUSE."

Larry: "OK. PETE KANE WE'LL STAND BY WITH YOU AND WITH HARVEY CLARK AND WE'LL GET BACK TO YOU IF THERE ARE FURTHER DEVELOPMENTS. THICK BLACK SMOKE IS POURING FROM THE ROOF OF THE MOVE HEADQUARTERS AND APPARENTLY SEVERAL HOMES NEARBY ARE ON FIRE."

With that, Larry stopped talking and looked over to Alan, giving an unexpected, nonverbal cue. Alan and sportscaster Meltzer were caught staring at their desk monitors. Alan lifted his eyes abruptly and spoke to the camera.

"WELL, LET'S TURN OUR ATTENTION NOW TO AL MELTZER. A LOT OF SPORTS NEWS GOING ON, PARTICULARLY WITH THE FLYERS UNDER A LOT OF PRESSURE TO WIN TONIGHT."

It was an absurd segue, to be sure. Meltzer was a trooper, reading from the teleprompter about the Flyers' must-win situation in tonight's playoff game with Quebec. He had only been on about a minute when he got a message in his ear to wrap.

Al: "AND WE HAVE A BREAKING STORY HERE AND YOU HAVE IT, RIGHT LARRY?"

Larry: "WE HAVE A PICTURE OF WHAT'S GOING ON IN WEST PHILADELPHIA RIGHT NOW. LET'S TAKE A LOOK AT IT, A LIVE PICTURE OF THE HOUSE IN WEST PHILADELPHIA. THERE YOU SEE THE ROOF OF THE HOUSE. WE'VE BEEN WATCHING THAT SCENE ALL DAY. EARLIER WE SAW THE WATER BEING POURED ON IT BY THE SNORKEL GUNS. NOW WE SEE A RAGING INFERNO ON THE ROOF OF THAT HOUSE!"

The mast camera showed a carpet of flame on the roof to the left of the bunker, sending billows of smoke into the air. There was no water being put on it by the squirt gun. There were no sounds of sirens.

Karen watched as Larry described the picture. She kept one ear on the fire scanner. No fire equipment was being dispatched to Osage Avenue. How could that be, she thought. The fire commissioner himself was there. Couldn't he see the smoke and flames?

Archer watched from the control room as the flames licked the MOVE roof. It was exactly 12 hours ago he was in this same room, watching Harvey and Charles dodge bullets and watching the fire department squirt guns pound the bunker with water. He now saw that same rooftop on fire and no water anywhere.

Larry: "LET'S TAKE ANOTHER LOOK RIGHT NOW AT THE BREAKING SITUATION AT 62ND AND OSAGE, NOW IN ITS 13TH HOUR, AND THIS FIRE ON TOP OF THE MOVE BUILDING SEEMS TO HAVE GOTTEN COMPLETELY OUT OF CONTROL."

The fire had reached the bunker and had engulfed it.

Larry: "IRONIC THAT THEY TRIED WATER TO DESTROY IT AND NOW FIRE DESTROYS IT. HARVEY CLARK IS STANDING BY LIVE. WHAT DO YOU SEE FROM YOUR VANTAGE POINT?"

Harvey: "LARRY, IT'S NOT WHAT I SEE; IT'S WHAT I DON'T HEAR. THERE'S BEEN NO SOUND OUT OF THE MOVE HEADQUARTERS SINCE 7:20 THIS MORNING. THERE'S NO IDEA WHERE THOSE PEOPLE ARE, HOW MANY PEOPLE ARE STILL IN THE HOUSE, HOW MANY MAY BE CHILDREN."

Larry: "ARE THERE PHILADELPHIA FIRE DEPARTMENT UNITS ON THE WAY TO TRY TO STOP IT FROM SPREADING TO THE OTHER BUILDINGS?"

Harvey: "LARRY, UH, YOU KNOW, I'VE SEEN VERY FEW FIRE ENGINES AROUND. NO SIRENS, NO INDICATION THAT THERE'S ANY BIG OR FAST ATTEMPT TO COME IN AND, UH, UH, PUT THE FIRE OUT."

With those words, the flames atop MOVE headquarters suddenly grew, as though fed by a newfound source of fuel. The flames on the roof jumped ten feet or more into the air.

From his vantage point on the ground, Pete Kane saw the entire top half of the house become engulfed in flames and part of the roof collapsed into the second floor. Flames also licked out of the houses on either side of 6221 Osage. Right in front of his perch, Pete saw firemen standing with police officers, watching. Not a drop of water had been put on the fire since the explosion sparked it almost an hour ago.

From Mini 1, it appeared the smoke was becoming thicker and blacker and it filled the sky. It must have been visible for miles. The smoke and flames being shown on live TV begged an answer to a disturbing question: WHY DON'T THEY PUT THE FIRE OUT?

FIRE AND CALM

"It's the worst day of my life," said Earl Watkins, who once lived across the street from MOVE. "I feel so sorry for all of them, MOVE, the police and all. I wish there had been another way, you know? I really wish there had been another way."

Earl and his wife Pearl had left their home the day before, hopeful that the MOVE problem would be solved once and for all. They had prayed for MOVE, the police and all their friends as the evacuation began Sunday morning. Now, Earl stood at a police barricade telling Dennis Woltering his feelings as a plume of black smoke billowed from the little street he had called home.

"Something had to be done but I still think they could've handled it a little better. I really think so."

"You think negotiations early on perhaps," began Dennis.

"You can't negotiate with MOVE. They know everything!"

Steve Cohen rode a quiet elevator 24 floors up the building known as Black Rock, CBS corporate headquarters on west 52nd Street in Manhattan. After a day of grueling testimony in a six-year old libel case, he now faced what would surely be some of the toughest news decisions of his career, and he had to make them by long distance.

He walked through a quiet hallway to the office of Neil Derrough, president of CBS Television Stations, his boss. He walked past the reception area and into a conference room. Derrough was there, watching a television getting a live feed of WCAU.

There were perfunctory greetings and a handshake. Then, Cohen picked up a phone and dialed Jay Newman in Philadelphia. As he waited for Jay to answer, he watched the TV and saw for the first time what his people were doing. He saw the live picture of the fire, flames on the rooftop. He heard Harvey and Pete describing the slow but steady spread of the fire. He was able to glean that it had been almost an hour since the bomb explosion that apparently sparked the fire.

"Hello, Jay Newman," came the voice on the other end of the phone.

"Hi, it's Steve. I'm in Neil's office at Black Rock. We're watching your air. Why aren't they putting that fire out?"

"That's the question we're all asking," said Jay. "But here's a more pressing question for us right now: should we pre-empt Rather, and stay with this?"

No one could remember the last time the CBS Evening News was pre-empted in favor of local programming. It's something that wasn't done lightly, especially by an owned station. "That's not a call we want to make lightly," Steve reminded Jay. Jay knew this, of course, and didn't make the suggestion lightly.

"Look," Jay said. "They're not putting the god damn fire out. It's been spreading since it started. We're talking about a threat to public safety at this point."

Jay had made a dozen calls to Archer in the control room during the past 40 minutes, trying to assess how serious the fire threat was. He had made a call to the assignment desk and found out that Karen hadn't heard one fire engine dispatched to fight the fire since it started. As the hour approached 6:30pm, the decision on the Evening News had to be made.

Cohen talked with Derrough. Both consulted with Van Gordon Sauter, president of CBS News. Cohen made the final call.

"OK, Jay," he said over the phone, "we'll blow out all regular programming as long as you think we need to stay with this."

"Fine, I'll be in touch." Jay hung up. Steve hung up. Both returned their eyes to their monitors.

◆ ◆ ◆

6:30PM. Instead of Dan Rather and the CBS Evening News, Philadelphia viewers who were tuned to Channel 10 saw anchorman Larry Kane.

"WE HEAR SOME NOISE IN THE BACKGROUND, OF PEOPLE YELLING. ARE THOSE JUST THE PEOPLE WHO ARE WITH YOU HARVEY?"

There was no announcement that the Evening News wouldn't be on. Larry simply continued the live description of what was going on at MOVE.

Harvey: "LARRY, WHAT WE'VE GOT HERE IS A GROUP OF PEOPLE WHO ARE VERY SYMPATHETIC WITH MOVE. THEY FEEL THAT THERE WAS AN OVERREACTION HERE AND MAYBE IT DOES NOT HAVE TO GO THIS FAR. UH, THERE'VE BEEN SOME VERY, VERY ANGRY INDIVIDUALS HERE."

No shit, Harvey, I thought, still remembering the near-fight I got into with my man in the khaki shorts. My role as field producer had become more of a security officer, keeping people away from the equipment, away from the van's open door and away from Don Overton who was operating the live camera on Harvey. Each time I asked people to give us some breathing room they became more irritable, even offended. Yet, without us there for them to get information, they'd have no reason to even be there.

We were soon blessed by the arrival of a real security guard. Pete Wiggins was a senior man at WCAU's security firm, Wells Fargo. Pete was of medium height, stocky build and had a friendly demeanor. He wore no uniform. He fit right into the sea of black faces around us at 61st and Pine.

He had been watching on television and saw the angry crowd at our live location. He later said, "Those boys needed me," referring to Harvey and the rest of us, "so I went there on my own."

I had seen him at the station before, so I recognized him.

He introduced himself to me just as Pete, and perched himself at the open side door of our van. He had a way of immediately sizing someone up. He seemed to have no trouble keeping the folks away from the open van door. His eyes scanned the crowd, looking for trouble.

My eyes were scanning, too. They found Frank Goldstein arriving in his marked station car and trying to park across 61st Street from us. He was able to squeeze his car into a corner spot.

On the roof of our van, Dave Harrington had set up his camera on a tripod and was shooting video of the fire cooking in the distance. He also took several shots of the crowd around us as Harvey stood on the other side of the barricade, microphone in hand, talking live on TV. Frank started unloading his camera gear.

Charles and Kasey had finally left. Night reporter Kris Long had been driven to the scene and had lost himself in the neighborhood to talk to people about the catastrophe unfolding around them.

At 6:32pm, one hour and five minutes after the fire began, the Philadelphia Fire Department squirt gun that had sat idle all afternoon was turned on, along with a second squirt gun that had been set up next to it. Co-anchor Alan Frio was the first to notice it.

"APPARENTLY, THEY'RE MAKING A MOVE TO CONTROL THAT FIRE NOW," said Alan, interrupting Larry who was on the air. "WE CAN SEE THERE IS WATER BEING POURED ON IT."

Larry paused as they watched the squirts turn on and streams of water enter the mast camera shot of the burning bunker.

"WATER IS BEING POURED ON FROM THE RIGHT HAND PORTION OF YOUR SCREEN THERE," said Larry, describing the live picture. The squirts appeared to be pouring water on the fire. And for the first time I noticed that the bunker was gone. The symbol of MOVE's defiance had finally been erased. But the cost of its destruction was starting to escalate.

"THE NIGHTMARE OF THIS MORNING HAS SPREAD

THROUGH THE EVENING," reported Larry, "AND THIS IS CERTAINLY A MACABRE AND NIGHTMARISH DAY WHERE A GAME BEING PLAYED OUT HAS TURNED INTO A VERY DEADLY GAME IN WEST PHILADELPHIA."

As the squirt guns were turned onto the MOVE roof, fire fighters turned on a ground hose right in front of Pete's house on 62nd Street, aiming the water at the burning MOVE house.

"THIS IS SOMETHING THAT COULD HAVE A PERMANENT IMPACT ON THE YOUNG PEOPLE IN THAT AREA," Larry offered. "I KNOW FROM THE TENOR OF YOUR VOICE, HARVEY, THAT THIS HAS AFFECTED YOU. UH, IT'S CERTAINLY AN UGLY ENDING, ISN'T IT?"

Over the voices of Larry and Harvey, the mast camera shot of the roaring fire burned itself onto the television screen.

Harvey: "LARRY, A VERY UGLY ENDING. ABOUT HALF THE PEOPLE OUT HERE WITNESSING THIS ARE CHILDREN. MOST OF THEM ARE JUST BIG-EYED, TRYING TO FIGURE OUT WHAT THIS IS ALL ABOUT. THEY'RE CONCERN OF COURSE AS CHILDREN, IS THAT CHILDREN JUST LIKE THEMSELVES, ARE OR MAY HAVE BEEN KILLED IN THIS VIOLENT END TO THE MOVE CONFRONTATION."

In the crowd, a man yelled loudly as Harvey tried to do his report.

"How many mother fucking kids have you killed?" came his angry cry. He cursed and screamed, at no one in particular.

Dennis Woltering interviewed another MOVE neighbor, Harry Waters.

"This is a travesty. This is not what we expected when we elected Wilson Goode mayor. You know, bombs, houses burning, this is no good."

On the 24th floor of Black Rock, Steve Cohen and Nell Derrough were now joined by CBS News president Van Gordon Sauter, all three with experience at local stations during the turbulent 60's and early 70's, all with experience covering demonstrations and riots. They now watched a failed police action against a group of radicals generating strong emotions in an unwieldy crowd.

Steve remembered watching Detroit explode in 1974 when he was executive producer at WXYZ-TV. A white policeman had shot a black youngster, sparking riots in the Livernois section. It was a dangerous time in a city known as the murder capital of America. Detroit epitomized everything that was wrong with urban America. The Philadelphia of 1985 could hardly be compared with the Detroit of 1974, but the potential for a riot was definitely there and it troubled Cohen and the others who watched Channel Ten with him now. Ratings were not on Cohen's mind. There would be plenty of time later to fight the ratings war. He had not even seen what Channels Three and Six were doing. Competition was not important to Cohen right now. Presenting accurate reporting in a calm manner was. So far, he had seen nothing that indicated otherwise on his station.

Eventually, the pizza came and the three CBS executives sat nineteen floors above New York City, watching a neighborhood in West Philadelphia go up in flames.

Rob Feldman was eating pizza in the Channel Ten control room along with the entire technical crew. He had been at the station for over 13 hours, first monitoring the live shots, then producing the 6 o'clock broadcast. Now, his show had run overtime, pre-empting the CBS Evening News. In between brief communications in Larry's ear, he chomped on pizza. The direct line from the news director's office rang for the millionth time. Rob snatched the phone.

"Yeah," he said.

"Just stay on that roof shot," said Jay on the other end. "I can't get enough of that roof shot."

Apparently, someone at City Hall was also entranced by that

roof shot. Karen Fox took a phone call.

"Hello, this is Karen Fox."

"Yes, this Is Karen Warrington." Mayor Goode's press secretary.

"Yes, Karen?" inquired Fox.

"Where's your truck?" Warrington asked.

"I beg your pardon?"

"Where's your truck?"

"You mean our live van?"

"Yes." Warrington sounded demanding in her tone, and Fox didn't like it.

"It's out there with all the other live vans," Karen answered tersely. "I don't know exactly where it is."

Warrington made no other demands, nor did she offer any explanation of why she wanted to know where the van was. The conversation ended and Fox went directly to Jay.

"Karen Warrington just called," she relayed to Jay in his office, "wanting to know where our microwave van is. I think Goode is thinking about commandeering it."

Jay immediately called Mini 2 and got Jim Barger on the cellular phone.

"Is everything OK there?" asked Jay.

"Yeah, the cops here are all very nice," said Jim. "They're just watching our roof shot very closely. The fire commissioner's even been here."

"I want to put you on the air, Jim," said Jay quickly. "Just call on the live line and we'll have you do a quick phone report on what the police are doing at the van. OK?"

Jim paused for a moment. "Uh, sure."

Jay played it smart. He would put Barger on live television to reveal to the world that the police were using the mast cam for surveillance. Then, Goode would have to leave it alone.

At about 7 o'clock, Larry Kane introduced Jim Barger to the viewers.

"RIGHT NOW, WE UNDERSTAND THAT PHILADELPHIA POLICE ARE USING OUR CAMERA. AND CHANNEL 10

CAMERAMAN JIM BARGER IS ON THE PHONE. WHAT'S GOING ON THERE, WHAT ARE THEY DOING, JIM?"

Jim's voice was heard over a telephone, as the screen showed what was left of the MOVE roof burning.

"WELL LARRY, THEY'VE TAKEN OVER OUR TRUCK SOMEWHAT AND THEY'RE USING OUR PAN UNIT FOR OUR MICROWAVE TO PAN BACK AND FORTH ON THE ROOFTOPS. WE HAVE A CAMERA MOUNTED ON TOP OF THE MICROWAVE ANTENNA AND THEY ARE PANNING THAT BACK AND FORTH TO KEEP AN EYE ON THE ROOFTOPS TO MAKE SURE THERE'S NO MOVEMENT UP THERE. THEY ALSO USED IT BEFORE THEY DROPPED THIS LARGE, EXPLOSIVE DEVICE TO MAKE SURE THERE WERE NO PERSONS UP THERE."

Larry: "SO THEY'RE USING OUR CAMERA AND OUR MICROWAVE TRUCK AS A SURVEILLANCE UNIT, IS THAT CORRECT?"

Jim: "THAT IS EXACTLY WHAT THEY ARE DOING."

Only two people on earth knew why no one was putting out the fire and Mayor Goode was not one of them. After the fire started, it obviously had destructive potential. This was a fact not lost on the police commissioner who had been stymied at every turn by the existence of that bunker. Here was an opportunity to get rid of it once and for all. Somewhere around 6:10, Commissioner Sambor approached Fire Commissioner William Richmond on the street. He had an idea to let the fire destroy the bunker before it was extinguished. He asked Richmond if he thought the fire could be controlled after the bunker was destroyed. Richmond thought it could. Sambor and Richmond decided letting the fire burn would destroy the bunker, and eliminate MOVE's high ground advantage over the police. Neither Richmond nor Sambor had any idea what the status of the people in the house was. No one had seen them. Apparently, no one had escaped. And no one had seen any of the children.

Mayor Goode had been watching the fire spread on Channel Ten in his office. After a time, he became puzzled over the fact that the fire was not being put out. He heard Pete Kane's report about the flames spreading to other homes. He finally became alarmed enough to call Managing Director Leo Brooks and order him to put out the fire. Brooks had already given the order to the police commissioner. The police commissioner later claimed he relayed the order to the fire commissioner. The fire commissioner denied ever receiving the order.[25] So the fire burned as firefighters looked on, as the fire commissioner looked on. It wasn't until the bunker was destroyed, and the MOVE house and those on either side were burning brightly, that the fire commissioner gave the order to strike out the first alarm. The squirts directing water onto the MOVE roof were doing no good, because any fire fighter knows you have to attack a fire from inside, from its source.

The one hose that had been set-up in front of Pete Kane's perch on 62nd street was also too little, too late. It wasn't until the first fire alarm was struck that the Philadelphia Fire Department was ordered to fight the fire in the traditional way. That didn't happen until almost 7 o'clock, about an hour and a half after the bomb triggered it.

Janice Walker's house was two doors away from MOVE. A pair of large eyeglasses rested on her broad face, and sweat was beaded on her brow. She was crying as Dennis Woltering interviewed her.

"I'm sure it's just destroyed and it's just not fair," she declared through teary eyes. "We've been there over 20 years and we didn't have to go through this. It's just not necessary." Her voice broke and tears flowed down her face. "It's just not necessary."

"The city said it tried to negotiate," Dennis offered her. "It said there was no other way."

"I can understand that. I want to know who's gonna pay for it now. That house is paid for. We don't owe nobody for it. I want to know who's going to replace it now. My family had all of their dreams, all of their aspirations tied up in that house."

"You blame the MOVE group for this?" asked Dennis.

"I blame everybody. I'm not gonna give it all to them because

I grew up with Louise James."

"Tell me why you blame everybody," said Dennis.

"Because, it's just not necessary. They knew they had a no-win situation. You knew they had a no-win situation. It just seems to me there should have been some other way to work this out. The fire was not necessary!"

With each interview, with each plea for sanity, with each cry for justice, the crowd became charged with more negative energy. People like Janice Walker and Earl Watkins were not radicals. They were row-home dwellers like thousands of other people in Philadelphia. Their homes meant as much to them as a million-dollar mansion to a family on the Main Line.

Don Overton was born in a row house, too, in Clifton Heights, just outside the city. He watched Janice Walker crying through his viewfinder. The sun was going down and it was making Don's job a little easier. All afternoon, he had been shooting due west, into the sun. It created a terrible backlight problem because it meant Harvey was almost a silhouette in front of a bright background. To compensate, Don had set up two, 1,000 watt stand lights, one shining on each side of Harvey's face. It helped light him more but it made Harvey even hotter under the 85-degree sun.

Don was beginning to feel hotter, too, not because of the lights or the weather but because the voices coming from behind him were getting more hostile by the minute. With his eye glued to the viewfinder, he couldn't see what was happening behind him.

I stood near the door of the van, listening to Harvey on the monitor with Pete Wiggins the security man. Harvey was on autopilot. It seemed as though he knew what to say without thinking about it. His narrative came naturally again, unfettered by fatigue. The fire had now become the second part of the story, the second half of the 1985 MOVE saga.

Tom Watson heard the bomb explosion as he sat with his brother, drinking scotch and water at the Turtle Crossing bar in Upper Darby, just a few blocks on the other side of the county line from Cobbs Creek. The bartender switched the TV to Channel Ten in Tom's honor and they watched Harvey and the fire for a while. At around seven, Watson went home exhausted and went right to bed.

A few miles further into Delaware County, Bob Roncaglione stood next to a pitching machine on his son's little league field. He was manning the machine as young boys batted the balls into the outfield and other boys chased the balls and tried to throw the runners out. Behind Bob, as baseballs were projected towards home plate from the machine, black smoke rose from West Philadelphia. When he saw it, he thought about where he was. On a balmy, spring night, he was here on a ball field, enjoying a normal relationship with his son. The boys ran around the field, tagging bases, catching fly balls and yelling at each other. Their parents urged them on, yelling their names and slapping their backs when they did well. Back where the smoke was coming from, boys and girls the same age might be dying. The children of 6221 Osage didn't play little league baseball with their parents. They played John Africa's game of politics by rules they probably didn't understand. And now, thought Bob, their world was coming to an end.

Tony Gore watched on a TV set at the station. This has got to be the end of Mayor Goode, he thought. John Mussoni had long since been relieved at the desk. Yet, he couldn't leave. He wandered into Jay's office and sat down on one of several chairs facing the three TV sets. Gordon Hughes, the station's program manager, was there waiting for Jay to get off the phone. Finally, Jay hung up.

"Steve agrees," he said to Gordon. "As long as the fire burns out of control, we stay with it. No breaks, no commercials."

He finally noticed John's presence in the room, and was annoyed.

"If you're not doing something for this broadcast," he said sternly to John, "I don't want you here." John was both hurt and impressed by Jay's desire to stay focused.

Steve Cohen reported to the others in the New York

conference room.

"The fire is burning out of control. We're going to stay with it for the duration. No commercials, no breaks. Jay feels Larry can handle it on the air and he has the support in the field to sustain it." It was a report Steve was proud to give his superiors, although the destruction of a neighborhood in his home town was hardly the scenario he would have chosen for the occasion.

By 7:30, fire hoses crisscrossed the area around the MOVE house, although there was apprehension among the firefighters. None wanted to get too close since MOVE members were still assumed to be in their house, or perhaps somewhere in the neighborhood, with guns. Firefighters took positions in homes across the street and across the alley from MOVE.

Pete Kane saw a sudden flurry of odd activity. Directly across 62nd Street, a firefighter began hacking away at the front door of a home with his ax as several police officers with rifles drawn stood prone behind him, waiting to get inside.

Jim Barger and Frances Harty saw a number of police officers begin running down Pine Street into the small walkway that connected Pine with MOVE's back alley. Another firefighter began hacking at a door on Pine Street with a half dozen stakeout officers behind, waiting to get in.

Harvey Clark abruptly interrupted Larry's narrative.

"LARRY, LET ME BREAK IN JUST FOR A SECOND. APPARENTLY THERE'S SOME SHOOTING BREAKING OUT HERE BEHIND ME IN THE 6100 BLOCK, IF WE CAN GET A PICTURE HERE, UH, LARRY--"

A plainclothes police officer was briskly walking right towards us on Pine Street, waving his hand and trying to tell us something.

Harvey: "WHAT YOU SEE RIGHT NOW IS A POLICE OFFICER, RIGHT IN FRONT OF OUR CAMERA, WHO IS CLEARING THE 6100 BLOCK OF PINE STREET."

The officer, with his POLICE armband visible, came right up behind Harvey and waved him aside.

"Move away, they're shooting!" he said. He motioned for us to move out of the street and onto the sidewalk, a distance of only a few feet. A second plainclothes officer jogged in behind him to help.

"HARVEY, WHY DON'T YOU GET UNDER COVER THERE," responded Larry. "YOU CAN STILL TALK TO US. I'D RATHER YOU WERE PROTECTED--THERE'S A MAN RUNNING WITH HIS CHILD THERE--AND I THINK IT'S BETTER FOR YOU TO STAY BACK."

I didn't know what that cop was talking about. We heard no gunfire, saw nothing threatening at 61st and Pine.

Birdie Africa definitely heard the shooting. After spending what seemed like hours in the garage of his house, smoke began invading their sanctuary. Conrad Africa grabbed little Tomaso, opened the garage door and tried to take him out. Birdie remembered hearing gunfire. He remembered it sounding like do-do-do-do-do-do, like shots fired one right after another. Conrad came back into the garage with Tomaso clinging to his stomach. By now all the adults were in the basement and garage and Birdie remembered them yelling out the front, basement window and out the garage door, "The kids are coming out."

The children were crying. The basement and garage were filling up with smoke. Everyone was out from under the wet blankets that had helped protect them from the tear gas.

"The kids are coming out," Birdie recalled someone yelling. It became harder to breathe. It got hotter and the smoke became thicker and all the children were crying.

"The kids are coming out!" is all that Birdie could remember someone saying, as Ramona Africa opened the garage door again and stuck her head out.

Tomaso was now face down in Rhonda's lap and she was slapping his back. Tomaso had stopped crying. He had stopped moving.

It was time for Birdie to move. He bolted for the open

garage door and saw Ramona already outside in the small yard. Tree went out next, followed by Phil. Birdie remembered Ramona helping Tree and Phil climb up the retaining wall to the walkway in the alley. Then she helped Birdie climb up, too. He remembered watching Tree and Phil run down the alley towards Cobbs Creek Parkway. He did the same, as behind him he saw his house on fire. The other adults were still inside, as were the two other girls. He remembered only himself, Ramona, Tree and Phil escaping. Then, he fainted.

The next thing he knew, he was being fished out of a puddle of water by a policeman who led him to Cobbs Creek Parkway. He saw Ramona there, but not Tree and Phil.[26]

"I think the danger of anyone being alive in the MOVE house is probably slim," said Milt Williams, an Osage Avenue neighbor who came to the barricade at 61st and Pine to talk live with Harvey Clark. "I think the firemen should concentrate on the lower end of the block to help save our properties."

"What do you stand to lose there?" asked Harvey.

"Well, everything we own."

At this point, no one knew the reason for the new delay in fighting the fire. The police later reported gunfire coming from the rear of the MOVE house. Thus, firefighters were ordered to retreat. On several occasions, firefighters moved in and retreated again, claiming they heard gunshots, or maybe something that sounded like gunshots.[27]

The fire continued to cook. Commissioner Richmond had decided that the loss of property was acceptable, if it meant avoiding a loss of firefighters' lives.

By 8 o'clock, the sun had set. Twilight cast blue light over the bizarre and awful scene. The black smoke was no longer just a plume, but a wall rising behind the 6100 block of Pine Street. The story had achieved a life of its own. It transcended any petty news judgments made by news directors, general managers or field producers.

I was now dead tired, yet wired. After watching the interviews with Earl Watkins and Milt Williams, I was

convinced I was witnessing an utter disaster. These people were watching
their homes go up in flames and nothing was being done about it.

A few blocks south of us, Dennis Woltering and Frank Goldstein had been looking for a spot to get some high shots of the fire. Around 62nd and Larchwood, they found some people on the roof of a row house, watching.

"Excuse me," shouted Frank. "Can we come up to take some pictures?"

"Sure you can," came the response, "but you gotta pay."

"OK," said Frank. As he did so, a reporter from Channel Three overheard and got in on the action. Frank, Dennis and Channel Three's reporter and crew went into the house and up the stairs to a second floor porch. From there, they all climbed a ladder to the roof and forked over ten dollars per station to stand there and take pictures.

And what pictures they were. From this vantage point, Frank saw stakeout officers with rifles drawn on rooftops in the foreground as towering flames leapt up behind them from Osage Avenue. A wall of fire filled Frank's viewfinder and smoke bellowed into the air. One policeman with a blue helmet was perched behind a chimney, as though waiting for something to happen down below. The fire churned away with no end in sight.

At one point during Harvey's non-stop narrative, Don Overton zoomed the camera past Harvey down Pine Street. There stood Jim Barger, hunched over his tripod-mounted camera, as he shot the black smoke rising up from the point where, two and a half hours ago, he had shot a helicopter bombing MOVE headquarters. Jim's pictures were also being shown live, from the closest vantage point any camera had to the fire.

The star of the day had been retired for the night. The mast camera had sat taped atop Mini 2's antenna mast, quietly recording everything that happened on the MOVE roof from 6am until the fire destroyed the bunker about 12 hours later.

Because Chuck Satiritz thought of it, promoted it, and coddled it, and because Bob Roncaglione and Tony Gore maintained it and protected it, Philadelphia was given its only view of the fire from its inception to its out-of-control fury.

At 8:16pm, the mast camera's shot of the bomb blowing up on the MOVE roof finally made the air for the first time since Frances dashed it up to me at 5:40. Because Harvey had been on live non-stop, there was no window to send the tape back to the station. Suzy had held onto it until Harvey was given a break around 8 o'clock when Archer re-ran Kasey's piece on the morning shootout, then went to Larry for another recap. It was a brief rest for Harvey, but long enough for Suzy to transmit the tape back to the station where it finally made air. I watched it on the monitor in Mini 1 as Larry ad-libbed a description. It was a movie explosion. It didn't look real. It looked almost choreographed.

Pete Wiggins had been doing a good job of keeping the pain-in-the-ass spectators away from our van. But someone nearby must have had a television set tuned to us because just two minutes after we replayed the bomb explosion, someone began chanting, "Murder! Murder!" A number of people in the crowd joined in. Larry picked it up as background noise, and immediately went to Harvey for an explanation. Harvey was trying extra hard to keep calm.

"LARRY, AT THIS POINT PEOPLE ARE STARTING TO BUILD UP IN THE AREA. UH, YOU KNOW, I'M NOT GONNA SAY THAT THESE FOLKS ARE EVEN NECESSARILY MEMBERS OF THIS COMMUNITY. WHAT WE'RE GETTING HERE, UH, APPARENTLY WITH THE TELEVISION COVERAGE, THERE'S A LOT OF PEOPLE COMING FROM AROUND PHILADELPHIA, EXPRESSING WHATEVER THEIR BELIEFS ARE ABOUT WHAT HAS HAPPENED HERE. BUT NOW OF COURSE WITH THE LIGHTS--UH, I THINK WE HAVE TO KEEP IN MIND THAT THERE ARE A LOT OF YOUNG PEOPLE, I THINK, REACTING QUITE A BIT OUT OF SHOCK."

Steve Cohen snapped the phone off the receiver and quickly

dialed Jay.

"Hello, Jay Newman," answered Jay.

"It's Steve. Keep off that 'murder, murder' stuff. It's inflammatory. I don't want to make things any worse out there."

"OK, bye," snapped Jay. This was not a situation he had much control over.

In the newsroom, Karen Fox had watched Channel Three report that Ramona Africa and a child had been rescued from the burning house. She had been working desperately to confirm that and had finally done so. She typed out the information and gave it to reporter Bill Baldini, who had been planted at a live camera in the newsroom. His function was to give updates on any information Fox could develop by phone, independent of Harvey's reports. Baldini reported that Ramona Africa had been taken to Miseracordia Hospital for treatment of burns. He also reported that one child was in the hospital for treatment of second degree burns. And, the fire was now at four alarms. Bill did his report and tossed it back to Larry.

Larry now referenced the monitor over his shoulder. It was Overton's shot down Pine Street past Harvey, and it showed flames for the first time.

"HARVEY, WHAT'S IT LOOK LIKE NOW FROM YOUR VANTAGE POINT?"

As Larry asked the question, Overton's picture filled the screen. Flames began jumping out of the front door of a house on Pine Street.

"LARRY, I THINK THAT'S--THAT IS, UH, ABOUT HALFWAY UP THE BLOCK FROM 62ND AND PINE. THEY'RE GETTING READY TO LOSE THIS SIDE OF PINE STREET, LARRY."

As the crowd became aware that Harvey was live again, they began shouting "Murder! Murder! Murder!" again. One of them reached over and toppled one of Overton's 1000-watt lights. Don stepped away from the camera to pick it up off the ground. As he did so, someone tipped over the other light. As it hit the ground, the light bulb shattered. Don had no idea when the station was coming back to him live so he scrambled back behind his camera and framed Harvey in the shot. Larry tossed it back to Harvey again, without warning.

"WHAT'S THE FIRE LOOK LIKE FROM YOUR STANDPOINT NOW, HARVEY?"

"IT'S BEGINNING TO SPREAD INTO PINE STREET. YOU CAN LOOK BEHIND US NOW AND YOU CAN SEE MANY, MANY OF THE HOUSES OVER THERE ARE NOW BEING ENGULFED IN FLAMES."

The crowd now shouted "Murder!" with no organized chant at all. It was a free-for-all. People shouted "Murder!" because other people around them shouted it. When Harvey began talking, that was their signal to begin yelling.

"PEOPLE SHOUTING MURDER, MURDER, MURDER IS WHAT'S GOING ON HERE. I WANT TO REITERATE AND SAY THAT IT IS MY BELIEF THAT MOST OF THESE PEOPLE ARE NOT FROM THIS WEST PHILADELPHIA COMMUNITY AND AT THIS TIME ARE HERE FOR ATTENTION MORE THAN ANYTHING ELSE."

I watched as angry people pressed in on Overton's back as he tried to shoot. Harvey was cleared from his live shot again.

"We've lost audio, shouted Suzy from the van. I quickly waded into the crowd that had smothered us, looking for the audio cable and found that it had been disconnected. Overton had stepped away for a moment to help me search for the problem. As he looked back up he saw the camera start to tip and fall to the ground. He was close enough to be able to scramble towards it and partially break its fall.

Harvey's eyes now searched the crowd around us and they didn't like what they saw. Don was picking up his camera. Suzy was reconnecting an audio cable that someone had pulled out. Pete Wiggins' hands were doing overtime, holding people back from the van.

"Murder! Murder! Murder!" continued the chant from people with fire in their eyes. Pure emotion had taken over. Some of the young men had gathered at the van and were mustering a force to begin rocking it.

"Let's get the fuck out of here," I shouted to Pete.

"Right! Let's go now!" He helped Suzy, Don and I throw our gear into the van. No cables were neatly coiled, nothing was placed in its assigned spot. Everything was just tossed in. I was more scared than when the shooting broke out early in the morning. This was bullshit. I snatched the radio mic off its clip.

"This is Mini 1 to microwave control, do you copy?"

"Roger, Mini 1", came the voice back at the station.

"We are shutting down this live shot. People here are destroying our equipment. We are evacuating our position. Tell them not to come back to us."

Suzy jumped into the driver's seat. Don sat next to her. I sat in the seat behind them. Harvey flagged down Frank who had finished shooting with Dennis. The three of them escaped in Frank's car. Pete Wiggins stood in front of Min 1 and physically shoved people out of its way. Suzy started it up, put it in gear and slowly inched forward. Wiggins walked ahead, parting the crowd to make room for the van. He waved her forward, thrusting his body into the sea of agitated people. She followed him slowly. He walked backwards through the mob, looking behind him to check his path, constantly signaling for Suzy to keep on moving. Around him, people shouted and cursed. He guided the van through the mob like a tugboat pulling a freighter. After about a half block, the crowd suddenly thinned out. Pete jumped in the side door and Suzy sped off with Frank ahead of us in his car.

I was huddled in my seat, my eye on Suzy's foot as it pressed on the gas pedal. I had to go to the bathroom real bad again.

❖ ❖ ❖

"Four members of the MOVE organization did come out of the rear of their home," Mayor Wilson Goode told a news conference at 8:43pm, "and started firing at officers between Pine and Osage Avenue." It was his opening statement, delivered as the fire was going strong.

"The difficulty for the fire department in fighting the fire is that we know there are MOVE members in the alleyway back there, uh, with guns, and we are concerned about the protection of the firefighters. So, if there is concern about why the firefighters are not in the alley fighting the fire, it is because we did, in fact, see four members come out. They did, in fact, engage police in gunshots and that was the last that we saw of them."

The Mayor again faced reporters with apparent confidence in his information.

Suzanne Bates' question: "Mayor, we've heard chanting out there by the neighbors. There are reports there's a mini kind of riot situation underway. What's being done to take care of that?"

His answer came without hesitation.

"I'm aware of the fact that there's a lot of frustration out there and a lot of concern. We do have our people in the area. And I want to just speak directly to the people of this city. And that is, this is a very difficult problem. We are doing the very best job that we, in fact, can do under very difficult circumstances. There is no perfect way to bring this to a conclusion. We'll do our very best from this point on to preserve lives and protect property. It is very difficult because at this time we are aware that there are people in that area who, in fact, have weapons and who, in fact, have engaged in gunfire at this point."

"Mr. Mayor," came a question from another reporter. "If you could turn the clock back 24 hours, is there anything that you would've done differently that would've yielded a different result?"

Again, his answer came quickly and confidently.

"Oh, I don't think so. I think that you will find tomorrow morning a lot of people who want to play Monday morning quarterback, uh, Tuesday morning quarterback. I stand fully accountable for the actions that took place tonight. I will not try to place blame on any one of my subordinates. I was aware of what was going on and therefore I support them in terms of their decisions. And therefore, the people of this city will have to judge the Mayor, in fact, for what happened."

I didn't hear the Mayor's news conference. Neither did Harvey, Dennis or any of the technicians with us. We were circling the area in two vehicles, looking for a safe place from which to go live again. Frank had turned onto busy Walnut Street which ran parallel to Osage and about six blocks north.

"Follow me," he said over the radio. "I think I know where we can go."

I felt safe for the first time in hours. My heartbeat began slowing down a bit and I started breathing normally again. We were locked in our nice, safe van with no more screaming, chanting people around us. Pete Wiggins had gotten us away safely. Now, Suzy drove Mini 1 slowly behind Frank as he led us to the west side of the MOVE operation.

I noticed we had circled the geriatric center and were heading back onto Cobbs Creek Parkway, right back to Osage Avenue, but on the side I hadn't seen all day.

"There's a police roadblock there," I said into the radio.

"Don't worry about it," was Frank's response. "I think we'll be alright."

Frank drove down Cobbs Creek Parkway to Locust Street and turned on his left turn signal. He slowly drove his LTD around a police barricade and drove through to Locust Street, unchallenged.

"Just follow me," he said over the radio.

It worked. We drove through as though we belonged there and no one even gave us a second look.

Back at City Hall, Mayor Goode continued with his report.

"What we have out there is war," he said resolutely. "And I knew from the very beginning that once we made that decision, to go in there, it would, in fact, be war, because they intended to have a violent confrontation."

"Mr. Mayor," came the final question, "for the last few years, Philadelphia has tried to live down a fairly rotten reputation. What do you think this is going to say about Philadelphia?"

"I think that it says that we have a difficult problem and that we dealt with that problem and that we'll go on and build our city. I don't think that any city in America is free from problems. I think the issue here is whether or not we are willing to stand up and deal with those problems. What I hope it will say is that we had a problem, we dealt with it. It did not turn out in the best possible manner but we dealt with it and that the Mayor of the city is a stand-up guy who takes responsibility for what he does."

Frank led us onto Locust Street which ran parallel to Osage about three blocks north. Suzy guided Mini 1 along the very quiet block, unchallenged and virtually unnoticed by any police. Our two vehicles slowed down as we searched for a place to park. There was plenty of space on Locust, at its intersection with tiny Hirst Street, to park Frank's car and our van. We climbed out of our vehicles. We were suddenly somewhere else, a quiet place with no crowds, no police and no other press. I checked the street signs at the corner, to make sure we hadn't gone too far away. The signs said Locust Street and Hirst Street. We were three blocks away from 62nd and Osage. Then, I looked south on tiny Hirst Street and could see the orange glow seeping over the roofline at the end of the block.

"Let's get set up. Let's get on again," commanded Harvey. But it wouldn't happen with the snap of a finger. A new microwave signal had to be established. The tripod, camera and portable lights had to be fished out of the mess in Mini 1. Suzy, Don and Frank scrambled to get the equipment hauled out of the van where it was hastily dumped during our frantic evacuation.

Several blocks from our position, a tired but wired Pete Kane and his companion made their move to leave their secret location inside the Parkers' house. The fire had gotten too close for comfort. The whole neighborhood was burning down, including houses just a hundred feet away. It was getting hotter and hotter and who knew how much longer before they would put the fire out.

Pete gathered his camera, tripod and accessory bag. Gary

shared the load. They weighed their options and figured the back door would be their safest exit. They cautiously cracked the door open and peeked out into ithe alley. There were fire fighters and police officers scurrying around. Radios chattered, men mumbled and an occasional, distant siren was heard. There was only one way to handle their sudden presence among the police and firefighters, act like they belonged there. They boldly opened the Parkers' back door and walked out, taking time to pull the door shut and lock it behind them. Without hesitation, they walked right out into the alley and into the chaos. They were roundly ignored. At the point where the alley emptied onto Pine Street, Pete and Gary parted with a handshake, ending a relationship that lasted 26 hours.

Pete looked around him as he walked a short distance and took a deep breath of fresh air. It wasn't that fresh actually, tainted by the raspy smell of smoke. The first sight to greet his eyes was the bright orange paint job that said "10 NEWS" on the side of Mini 2. It was there, just where he had left it the night before.

"Hey, Pete! You OK? How you doing," shouted Frances from inside the van.

"A little tired," he shouted back with a big grin. He walked over to the van and peeked at the monitor. He saw a picture coming from a camera very close to the inferno. It must have been Mini 2's camera.

"Where's your camera?" he asked Fran.

"Jim Barger's on it. He's right over there in the middle of the street."

Pete peeked around the van towards Pine Street and there was Jim, hunched over a camera in the middle of the street.

"Mini 2 to microwave," said Frances into her radio.

"Go ahead."

"Pete Kane is out. He's with us here."

"Is he OK?" asked the voice.

"Fine," answered Fran.

Pete stood by Jim as he aimed his camera at the inferno

on Pine Street. Jim's camera was now the primary live camera, recording incredible scenes of destruction. Flames were shooting through the Pine Street homes, destroying them one by one in giant gusts. Swirls of gray smoke mixed with the bright, orange flames to create a terrible picture. Stakeout officers with their rifles hoisted in the air were silhouetted by the orange brightness behind them.

Jim's face went blank for a moment as he strained to listen to an instruction being given over his headset from the control room. Mike Archer was telling him to put Pete Kane in front of the camera.

"They want you on, Pete," Jim said. "You up for it?"

"Yeah, OK," Pete responded, still dazed by what was going on around him.

Jim pivoted his camera slightly to line Pete up in the frame.

"Take a step or two back," he said. Pete complied. Jim gave him his two-way radio so he could hear Larry's questions. "Get ready, coming to us." It was 9:17PM.

Larry Kane: "WE ARE TOLD RIGHT NOW THAT PETE KANE, THE CHANNEL TEN CAMERAMAN, IS STANDING BY LIVE. HE IS NOW OUT OF THE AREA HE WAS IN." Larry got the cue from the control room at the last moment, and there was some confusion over whether Pete was ready yet.

"PETE ARE YOU--HE WILL BE THERE--WE'LL BE ABLE TO TALK TO HIM ABOUT WHAT HE SAW ON--"

"LARRY?" Pete was heard asking on live TV.

"OK, WE CAN HEAR YOU. DO WE HAVE A PICTURE OF HIM?"

The picture appeared on the screen, a dark image of a man wearing a CBS Sports cap, holding a microphone in one hand and a portable radio in the other.

Larry: "PETE CAN YOU HEAR ME NOW?"

Pete: "YES I CAN, LARRY."

Larry: "HOW FAR AWAY WERE YOU ACTUALLY FROM THE SCENE OF MOVE HEADQUARTERS?"

Pete: "I WAS A HALF A BLOCK AWAY ON 62ND STREET AND WE HAD A CLEAR VIEW OF OSAGE DURING THE WHOLE

EVENT DOWN HERE, FROM BEGINNING TO THE END, WHEN WE CHOSE TO, YOU KNOW, GET OUT WHILE WE COULD."

Larry asked questions and Pete answered, but he looked out of it. He was tired and overwhelmed.

Fire Commissioner Richmond had ordered six alarms be struck, an order that summoned firefighters and equipment from across West Philadelphia, Southwest Philadelphia and downtown. For the past two hours though, he hesitated to send the men in to fight the flames close up because of the consistent police reports of gunfire in the alley, and then the supposed escape of MOVE members from the house. By 9:30PM, however, it became clear that any threat from that alley or the homes adjacent to MOVE was nonexistent because the alley and homes were obliterated. So, at 9:30PM, four hours after the bomb sparked the fire on the MOVE roof, the Philadelphia Fire Department finally began to throw everything it had against the raging fire. The department, with a national reputation for excellence, could finally do what it did best, after sitting by helplessly until it was too late. Men in helmets and protective coats ran hose lines through the streets. Some set up deluge guns--large hoses anchored to the ground with strong tripod-like devices. Others lashed hoses to hydrants, tightening them quickly and then filling the hoses with water pumped directly from the Schuylkill River. Water streams were directed where they should have been from the beginning--at the base of the flames and at adjacent buildings exposed to the heat. The fire emergency band was alive with dispatchers barking orders, battalion chiefs calling in for their assignments and fire marshals checking in.

Jim Barger's camera on Pine Street caught a shot of flames and sparks shooting through yet another Pine Street house as a policeman walked into the frame holding his rifle erect in his right hand, silhouetted by the bright orange background.

The flicker of the flames lit up the monitors in the Channel Ten control room where Rob Feldman had retreated into a corner to simply watch. The color reflected on the white pizza boxes and aluminum soda cans that littered the control room.

Harvey was back on, live from Locust and Hirst Streets. Rob couldn't exactly place where that was in relation to the fire. The orange glow Harvey pointed to over his shoulder looked very distant. Some kids behind him were waving to the camera.

The director punched back to Barger's camera where it was clear that firefighters were finally on the case. Harvey was running out of things to say. Larry's concentration was beginning to ebb. The fire would now run its course. Rob walked over to Mike Archer, who was at the producer's console.

"I think we ought to wrap this soon, don't you?" he asked Mike.

There was no answer right away. Mike picked up the direct line to the newsroom to get one more update on the progress of the fire. Thirty-six homes were involved, he was told. He hung up the phone in disbelief. Thirty-six homes. Mike didn't know the number was more like 50, and more were yet to fall.

I was on the cellular phone in Mini 1 with someone back in the newsroom, getting the 11 o'clock marching orders for Harvey, Dennis and Kris Long who was to join us. Each would do a tracked report for the top of the show and then remain available to go live through the broadcast. Tonight, it would be expanded beyond its usual 30 minutes. I hung up the phone and turned the van's monitor on to air and saw Larry. My watch said 9:48.

"SO THE HEADLINES IN THE CITY OF PHILADELPHIA, PENNSYLVANIA, TONIGHT--PHILADELPHIA FIREFIGHTERS ARE BATTLING A SIX ALARM FIRE THAT HAS ENCOMPASSED ONE WHOLE CITY BLOCK, MAYBE AS MANY AS 36 HOMES. THE MOVE HEADQUARTERS HAS BEEN DESTROYED WITH THE HELP OF A STATE POLICE HELICOPTER AND A FIRE THAT SPREAD OVER A BLOCK AND A HALF. THE SEARCH CONTINUES, ACCORDING TO MAYOR GOODE, FOR AT LEAST

THREE MOVE MEMBERS WHO ARE ARMED AND DANGEROUS. ONE WOMAN IS IN CUSTODY, AN APPARENT MOVE MEMBER, RAMONA AFRICA. AN UNIDENTIFIED CHILD IS UNDER TREATMENT AT CHILDRENS' HOSPITAL."

Larry's gaze at the viewers never wavered as he recapped what had happened over the past four hours.

"MAYOR GOODE HAS SAID HE STANDS BY HIS POSITION AND WILL STAND BY THE DECISIONS OF HIS COMMISSIONERS IN THIS SITUATION AND HOPES TO HAVE MORE INFORMATION TONIGHT. WE'LL BE JOINING YOU AT 11 O'CLOCK TONIGHT FOR AN EXPANDED EDITION OF THE CHANNEL TEN NEWS UPDATE, AND WE'LL UPDATE YOU FROM EVERY IMPORTANT LOCATION IN THIS CONTINUING AND BREAKING STORY."

Finally, Larry ended his marathon, three-and-a-half-hour anchor stint.

"I'M LARRY KANE FOR CHANNEL TEN NEWS, AND AFTER A COMMERCIAL BREAK, WE'LL BE JOINING THE MISS USA PAGEANT IN PROGRESS."

I felt uneasy about being on this quiet street. It was too much of a contrast to go from a hotbed of dissent and despair to a totally quiet setting. I thought we were missing something. I looked around. Across the street from our van was a large field enclosed by a fence. About 100 yards across the field was a big building that looked like apartments. We were behind the geriatric center and about a two block walk from its front door. One of us had to go there so see what we could find out.

"Harvey," I called over to him. He approached, interrupting his conversation with Charles Thomas who had mysteriously appeared again. "I'm gonna take a walk over to the geriatric center. Maybe someone there is talking."

Harvey shook his head. "Those mother fuckers aren't gonna say shit to you or anyone else tonight. But go ahead; I guess it couldn't hurt."

He went over to rejoin Charles and I began walking back the way we came on Locust Street. I hadn't walked since lunch and it felt good to move around. I also craved being alone for a little while.

Locust Street was deadly quiet. Except for the smoke smell in the air, it felt like just another night in West Philadelphia. Locust emptied out onto Cobbs Creek Parkway and I turned right. Here it was brighter and noisier. Police cars and fire engines cruised by but they were not in a hurry. The pace was slow, the mood relaxed. This was not the war zone Tom Watson and Kasey Kaufman experienced 18 hours ago. A couple police officers glanced over at me as I walked by, then went back to their conversation.

Aside from a couple of unmarked police cars and several blue-and-whites parked at the curb, there was very little activity at the geriatric center. I came upon a white door that led into the side of the building. Occasionally, a uniformed officer would walk in or out, or a man in a suit would walk in or out. This door obviously led to the command center. I stood on the sidewalk, watching the comings and goings. After just a couple of minutes, a radio reporter I had known for years noticed me standing there and came over.

"Hey, Kranz, nice to see you working for a living," he said.

"At least I know work when I see it," I shot back with a smile on my face. This guy was not a threat, but now that he saw me hanging out at the doorway, he decided he would do the same.

"Who's in there?" he asked.

"Everybody, from what I understand."

Suddenly, I recognized the man coming out of the door. It was Captain Dooley of homicide. I had talked with him many times over the phone on various jobs and seen him on TV, but never met him.

"Captain," I said as he approached. "Tom Kranz," I said as I extended my hand.

"Tom Kranz! How the hell are you? I'm Gene Dooley and

I don't know anything." He seemed relaxed, almost playful. I figured if he came out of the geriatric center, he must have known something.

"What's going on in there," I asked. "Is this thing over finally?"

"Honest to god, Tom, I don't know anything. My role here is a very limited one."

"Who's in there who could help us out, you know, give us a quick interview on the status?"

"Jeez. Uh, the deputy commissioner is supposed to be on his way, I know that."

"OK, I'll look for him. Nice to meet you finally, Captain."

"Same here, Tom. See ya," and he waved and walked away.

A couple minutes later, deputy police commissioner Robert Armstrong appeared, walking towards the side door. I approached.

"Hi, Commissioner, my name is Tom Kranz from Channel Ten," I offered, extending my hand again.

"Hi, Tom, Bob Armstrong. What can I do for you?"

"Can you give us an update on what's going on out there tonight?" I asked.

"No, I really can't, I'm just getting here."

"Would you mind seeing if anyone inside could come out and give us just a few minutes?"

"I'll see what I can do," he answered with sincerity, and he smiled as he walked into the geriatric center.

By now, my radio buddy was looking impressed that I knew who these two guys were. He and I chatted for a few minutes when deputy commissioner Armstrong came back out.

"The police commissioner will be coming out at 11 for a news conference. He'll answer all your questions then. OK?"

"Great. 11 o'clock?"

"Yes, that's right."

"Thanks for checking, Commissioner. Nice to meet you," I said, shaking his hand one last time.

"Nice meeting you, too, Tom. Good night." He disappeared

back inside.

Bob Armstrong was named a deputy police commissioner after spending his life with the Philadelphia Police Department. He was a soft-spoken, deeply religious man. The Inquirer once reported that he was referred to within the department as "Father Bob". It happened that his son Tom was a production assistant at Channel Ten. Even with that connection, it seemed people went out of their way (certainly I did) to not take advantage of Tom's relationship with the number two man in the police department.

I looked at my watch. 10:15pm.

"I gotta go," I said to my buddy. "See you at the news conference?"

"Absolutely," he said.

I began walking back towards Mini 1. I had to get a reporter and a camera to the news conference. I started to feel recharged, with another assignment to tackle. The pace of my walk picked up. I almost started jogging but caught myself for fear of drawing attention. It never occurred to me that this would be just the neighborhood where those three, missing MOVE members might be hiding.

When I arrived back at Mini 1, a small crowd of neighborhood kids had gathered and people on Hirst Street began peeking out their doors to see what was going on. It turned out that Charles didn't go home after all, but spent the night roaming the neighborhood. He returned to offer his presence on the air and it was accepted. Kris Long had arrived and would report on the residents' reaction to the fire. Dennis would retell the story of the residents' reaction to the gunfire earlier in the day. And Harvey would he the field-anchor. The cellular phone rang.

"Hello, Mini 1."

"Hi, Tommy, it's Fox."

"You still there, too?" I asked.

"You bet. This is a whole, new story now. Let me give you the latest facts as we have them, OK?"

"Go ahead."

She rustled some papers and mumbled, then began.

"The fire's at six alarms, still not under control. You know about that other fire in southwest Philly? That one's a four-alarmer and they're afraid it's causing a water pressure problem at the hydrants. The official line is that at least three MOVE members are believed loose in the neighborhood somewhere. Two others are in custody. There was some confusion about that earlier, but it is only two, Ramona Africa and a male child. Ramona refused treatment at Miseracordia Hospital and the boy is at Children's." She paused to leaf through more notes. "The latest we have on the number of homes burning is 36 but that's expected to increase. No one knows if anyone is left in the MOVE house, dead or what. That whole neighborhood is being treated like a crime scene. Cops have sealed it off and are securing it for the investigation. I think that's it."

"Have you heard something about an 11 o'clock news conference by Sambor?" I asked.

"No. Is there one?"

"Yeah, at our location. We'll cover it."

"Are you safe where you are now? I saw that *murder, murder* shit before."

"It's quiet here, yeah," I said, as a few more people from Hirst Street gathered to see what was going on here.

"OK, Tommy. Listen," she said with a pause. "Good job out there. Excellent job. You guys were really something."

"Thanks, Karen. You weren't too bad yourself."

"I've known you longer than anyone at this station," she said smiling. "I'm never surprised that we work well together."

"Take care, Karen."

"Bye."

It was 10:30. All four of the reporters at Mini 1 had slots in the 11 o'clock news, so there was no one left to cover the Sambor news conference. We were also out of live vans, so we would have to cover it on tape only. The responsibility fell upon me, with Frank as my photographer.

"Should we take a tripod?" Frank asked.

"Nah, we better stay loose in case we have to move," I answered. Frank put a new tape in his recorder and gave me a bag containing batteries. We set off towards Cobbs Creek Parkway and that side door to the geriatric center.

What a horror for Philadelphia, thought Steve Cohen, as he pushed away an empty pizza box from the table in the conference room at Black Rock. He remembered how the eyes of the world turned to Chicago in 1968 during the Democratic Convention when the police lost control of themselves. It was an image that still haunted that city. Would the events of this night, broadcast live on his television station, haunt Philadelphia for years to come? His people had performed a mind-boggling feat, to stay on live with very few glitches for hours at a time. He was proud of how the coverage came together on the air, yet saddened that it chronicled such an utter disaster.

His newsroom in Philadelphia was rumbling with one, final burst of energy. Writers banged their typewriters. Buttons clicked and tape cassettes whirred in the editing booths as the recorded pictures of the disaster were reproduced on tiny screens. The 11 o'clock producer, had his right ear to a phone with Newman, his left ear to a phone with reporter Lorrie Yapczenski. She was called in on her day off to cover Ramona Africa's arraignment at police headquarters and she was checking in to see when she might get on. The Miss USA Pageant would soon wrap-up and our viewers would shortly be thrust back into the drama in West Philadelphia.

Frank and I stood outside the entrance to the geriatric center, watching for some sign that a news conference was about to begin. Other reporters had gathered, too, but none that I recognized. This was definitely the "B" team covering this event. Everyone's primary reporters were either about to go on live television or were back at their newspapers writing for tomorrow's morning editions.

Just a few minutes before eleven, two uniformed police officers emerged from the door and looked warily at the assembled press corps.

"The Commissioners and the Managing Director will be out in a minute," said one of them, and turned around to go back inside.

"Where will they have it?" someone asked.

"Across the street at the rec center," said the officer over his shoulder as he walked inside.

After another minute or so, they emerged, Commissioners Sambor and Richmond, and Managing Director Brooks. Sambor wore a dark jumpsuit and navy blue, baseball cap. Richmond wore a plaid, flannel shirt and jeans with a baseball cap. Brooks wore a suit and tie, and was sweating. They walked through the reporters as Brooks gestured over towards the building at the recreation center across Cobbs Creek Parkway. The two police officers followed them, and we trailed along. The photographers already began jockeying for position, trying to anticipate where the Big Three would stand. I followed Frank, whose short legs moved quickly to keep up with everybody else. Brooks more or less led the procession to a concrete area in front of the rec center's activity building where he turned around to face the reporters. Sambor and Richmond followed in turn.

"Are we all ready?" Brooks asked.

"Hold on a minute," came a desperate cry from a photographer whose camera was being momentarily stubborn. He jiggled his recorder, messed with his zoom and smacked the camera with a fist. That did it.

"OK, sorry."

Managing Director Brooks began with his version of the latest on the search for the three escaped MOVE members. His rambling monologue also detailed how the neighborhood was being sealed off, how the burned out homes would be secured so their owners could inspect them in the morning and how the thrust of the operation against MOVE had turned towards neutralizing the bunker.

It sounded familiar. There was no news here. Commissioner Sambor then spoke.

"At no time," said Sambor in his terrible, whining monotone, "did any police position fire in an offensive posture. It was purely in a defensive posture. That was during the entire day. As a result of being unable, in any other manner, by crane--we were looking at every possible means of securing the roof, and eliminating the advantage MOVE had with that bunker--and one thing the Managing Director left out is they had steel plate around that bunker--we developed an explosive entry charge that was dropped on the building and succeeded in eliminating the threat from the roof."

Absent were the biting questions that would have peppered Sambor's answer if the "A" team of reporters had been present including Harvey, Tia O'Brien from Channel Three, Vernon Odom from Channel Six and Jan Gorham from WIP Radio. Instead, the questions were lame and uninformed. This group of reporters was waiting to be lectured, not hungry for the story of the century. Admittedly, even I didn't have the presence of mind to ask the questions that needed to be asked. At that point in the day, I was just happy to point a microphone and make sure Frank's recorder was picking it all up.

Frank was having trouble maintaining his position.

"Shove the mike closer to them," he said to me as he tried to shove his camera lens between two people standing in front of us. The Big 3 were simply standing in the open air, with no amplification at all. Their police guards made us maintain a healthy distance, so there was a fear our audio would not be strong. After Frank and I had shifted, we settled-in on a response by Fire Commissioner Richmond.

"When the charge was dropped, a subsequent incipient fire started up on the roof. The thought was that it would catch the bunker and it would drop into the second floor, which it subsequently did. When the fire started to move, there were shots fired. Firefighters backed down to defensive positions.

Consequently, the backing down allowed the fire to move. It's a dense, residential area. It's got back alleys. It was a hot fire and we had the winds. And consequently, we have about 50, 60 houses involved since that time."

I felt a tapping on my shoulder. I turned around and there was Charles. Man, he really got around.

"Great, you're here." I handed him the microphone and talked into Frank's ear. "Pop that tape so I can run it back to the truck and cover the rest of it with Charles."

Frank stopped shooting, leaned over and popped the tape out of the recorder. I practically ripped it out of the chamber, pushed my way through the other reporters behind me and dashed away towards Mini 1. I hadn't run at full speed since that time in Boston when I and three friends ran down Boylston Street to make a late show at the Jazz Workshop. That was 13 years ago.

I was huffing and puffing after what seemed like a mile but was really just about 2 blocks. I was now turning the corner onto Locust Street and had Mini 1 in sight. My pathetic body was crying out for me to stop and I did seconds later at the side door of the van. I shoved the tape at Suzy, totally winded.

"Radio", I managed to spit out. "Hand me the radio mike, please." Suzy rewound the tape and prepared to ship the tape back to the station. I glanced at the air monitor and turned up the volume. It was around 11:15.

Suzanne Bates was still at City Hall and was once again interviewing Councilman Lucien Blackwell. Larry jumped in at the end of Blackwell's first answer.

"COUNCILMAN BLACKWELL, LARRY HERE. FIRST OF ALL, I WANT TO THANK YOU VERY MUCH FOR JOINING US LIVE THIS MORNING ON SEVERAL OCCASIONS AND HELPING DISSEMINATE INFORMATION THAT WAS IMPORTANT FOR PEOPLE OF THE AREA. THAT WAS A REAL PUBLIC SERVICE, AND THANK YOU. QUESTION TONIGHT: AH, THE MAYOR IS OBVIOUSLY STRAINED UNDER THE CIRCUMSTANCES. WHAT HAPPENED IN WEST PHILADELPHIA TONIGHT WITH THE MOVEMENT OF THE FIREFIGHTERS, THE LACK OF MOVEMENT

IN THE EARLY HOURS? WAS IT JUST THE DANGER OF THE MOVE GUNMEN, OR WAS THERE SOMETHING ELSE BEHIND THE SCENES?"

"LARRY, I THINK WE HAD TO BE VERY CAUTIOUS TODAY. WE HAD SOME GUNFIRE THIS MORNING. IN THE LAST CONFRONTATION WITH MOVE MEMBERS WE HAD AN OFFICER KILLED. CERTAINLY, WE DON'T KNOW WHAT HAPPENED IN TERMS OF THE FIRE. I'M SURE THE MAYOR WILL CONDUCT A FULL INVESTIGATION, AND AFTER THE FACTS ARE KNOWN HE WILL REPORT THEM TO THE GENERAL PUBLIC. NO ONE EXPECTED THIS TO HAPPEN TODAY."

Suzanne: "CAN YOU TELL US WHAT WILL BE DONE FOR YOUR CONSTITUENTS WHO LOST THEIR PROPERTY IN THIS TREMENDOUS FIRE?"

Councilman Blackwell: "WELL FIRST I'M SURE THAT THIS CITY HAS AN OBLIGATION TO MAKE SURE THAT ANY PROPERTY LOST WILL BE REIMBURSED."

"Microwave, this is Mini 1," I barked into the radio.

"Go ahead, MINI 1."

"I've got some tape to feed you. Is there a writer back there to watch it?"

"Not right now."

"Well, I'll feed it anyway. It's Sambor and Richmond at a news conference that's still going on. I think they'll want to get it on right away."

"Roger, MINI 1. Let me put a tape in my machine to record it. Stand by."

Suzy had the tape cued up and ready. Sambor's face flickered, as the tape waited to be let loose.

"OK, Mini 1, let 'er rip."

Suzy hit the "PLAY" button and the Sambor tape was pumped back to the station.

"That's all you should need for now," I said into the mike.

"Standby. Checking tape."

Another silence over the radio.

"Did Charles find you OK?" asked Suzy.

214

"Yeah, he showed up. That guy always shows up."

"Mini 1, your tape is good. Any more to feed?"

"That should do it for tonight. Thanks!"

"Roger that."

The fire on Osage Avenue and Pine Street was just about out now. Barger's live picture showed a pathetic flicker of flame hiding behind a darkened hulk that was once a city block. He had to zoom in tightly to get a shot of that flame. When he shot wide, the picture showed smoke rising from the block but an unclear view of the devastation that lay behind the row of relatively untouched homes on the west side of 62nd Street. Flood lights cast a blue glow over the neighborhood and painted sharp shadows of firemen and police officers as they patrolled.

The fire was virtually out. The hysteria had also burned itself out. A cooler breeze funneled through the streets. West Philadelphia now had a scar on its face, but for the next few hours, it would still be shielded by the darkness.

My eyes were hurting and I wanted to go home. I twisted my wrist to see my watch. 11:48. I sat back inside Mini 1 and turned my attention to the TV.

"AND RIGHT NOW," Larry went on, "WE UNDERSTAND THAT LORRIE YAPCZENSKI IS LIVE AT THE ROUNDHOUSE, THE POLICE ADMINISTRATION BUILDING AT 8TH AND RACE, WITH SOME LATE INFORMATION. LORRIE, WHAT DO YOU HAVE?"

Lorrie, Karen and I all worked together at WCAU radio in the 70's. Lorrie was an excellent writer with good police contacts. She had worked as a print journalist, writing for Associated Press and Ebony Magazine before hitting the airwaves. Lorrie was supposed to be off today, but was called in because there was no one left to cover Ramona's arraignment at the Roundhouse. And she was not unwilling. Ironically, she was the freshest reporter on staff despite her starting time of about 10pm. The director switched to her live, outside the Roundhouse.

"LARRY, RAMONA AFRICA IS BEING QUESTIONED BY HOMICIDE DETECTIVES HERE AT THE ROUNDHOUSE. SHE WAS BROUGHT HERE ABOUT 9 O'CLOCK AFTER SHE WAS ARRESTED, AND IT IS EXPECTED SHE WILL BE ARRAIGNED WITHIN THE NEXT HOUR OR SO. THAT WOULD BE ABOUT SIX HOURS AFTER HER ARREST. SHE WAS ARRESTED ABOUT 7 O'CLOCK, AND THAT WAS COMING OUT OF THE MOVE COMPOUND WITH A CHILD. POLICE ARRESTED HER THERE AND TOOK HER TO MISERACORDIA HOSPITAL WHERE SHE REFUSED TREATMENT, THEN BROUGHT HER HERE TO THE ROUNDHOUSE. SHE WAS ARRESTED AT 7 O'CLOCK. THAT WAS APROXIMATELY AN HOUR AND A HALF AFTER THAT BOMB DROPPED, SO SHE STAYED IN THE HOUSE FOR SOME TIME ACCORDING TO MY SOURCES."

Lorrie was eager to spill all the information she had gathered, after waiting forever outside the Roundhouse.

"MY SOURCES ALSO TELL ME THAT THE BOMB--THEY DESCRIBE IT TO ME AS A C-4 PLASTIC EXPLOSIVE, WHICH IS SUPPOSED TO BE ONE OF THE SAFEST, AND ONE OF THE MOST MODERN DEVICES OF THAT KIND. RIGHT HERE AT THE ROUNDHOUSE, ASIDE FROM RAMONA AFRICA'S PRESENCE, IT'S VERY QUIET. POLICE OFFICERS ARE COMING AND GOING, SHAKING THEIR HEADS IN DISBELIEF."

By the time Lorrie had gotten off the air, the fire in the Cobbs Creek neighborhood had finally been declared under control by Commissioner Richmond. It took just seven hours to burn down what dozens of families had built-up over a lifetime.

12:08AM. Larry Kane: "LET'S LOOK AT THE LIVE PICTURE OF THE SCENE IN WEST PHILADELPHIA. IT IS ALMOST SERENE AND QUIET RIGHT NOW. PHILADELPHIA POLICE AND FIREFIGHTERS STILL ON THE SCENE CLEANING UP AFTER AN ENORMOUS, SIX-ALARM FIRE THAT BEGAN IN THE MOVE HOUSE, AND FULLY INVOLVED 50, 60 HOMES. WE DO KNOW FROM BILL BALDINI, WHO'S BEEN IN CONTACT WITH THE FIRE DEPARTMENT, IS THAT TWO FULL CITY BLOCKS HAVE APPARENTLY BEEN WIPED OUT BECAUSE OF THAT FIRE

TONIGHT. THE MOVE CONFRONTATION IS OVER, BUT STILL SOME UNANSWERED QUESTIONS."

There was no more tape to cut. No more scripts to write. All the "best" video and sound were shown on TV. Jay Newman allowed the 11 o'clock news to extend beyond midnight with the hope of getting the mayor for a live interview.

Out of nowhere, a man who introduced himself to me as a CBS field producer for Nightwatch appeared at the van's door. He babbled something about using our cellular phone for air-cue for an interview with Managing Director Brooks.

"Hang on just a minute," I said to him. "Let me find out what the deal is with our crew." I hadn't been informed yet but Don and Suzy had been assigned to remain on the scene overnight, with Lorrie as their reporter. They would stay hot in case anything happened and Lorrie would report for the early morning cut-ins. And, they would do this guy's live shot for the network. I called the station, and found someone who knew about this CBS guy. Our technicians were rigging up some system to pipe CBS air sound through our cellular phone.

This field producer, meanwhile, was crazed. He didn't seem to know where he was, what he was covering or why. He only knew he had an interview lined up with Leo Brooks, and nothing was more important. Little did I know that CBS was doing something right also. Producer Jude Dratt, after going to school all day with Karen Fox, had spent the past hours on the telephone lining up interviews with Philadelphia officials, clergy and community leaders for the Morning News, a program that would be devoted almost exclusively to the Philadelphia Story of 1985.

But I couldn't have cared less what CBS did. Nothing anyone else did on MOVE could possibly have equaled what I had experienced. No TV coverage, even our own, could relate the things I saw with my own eyes and felt in my heart during the last 21 hours.

Harvey, Dennis and Kris appeared together for one, last live shot at 12:18AM, to try to sum up what they had experienced on sensory and emotional levels.

Kris: "I WAS JUST UP ALONG PINE STREET AND OSAGE AVENUE. AND WE'VE ALL SEEN THE PICTURES OF BERLIN IN 1945, AND QUITE HONESTLY IT LOOKS LIKE THAT. MOST OF THE HOMES ARE JUST SHELLS. THEY HAVE BEEN TOTALLY GUTTED BY THE HEAT AND SMOKE AND WATER."

Dennis: "THIS HAS BEEN AN INCREDIBLE ORDEAL. FROM THE VERY BEGINNING THIS MORNING AT 5 O'CLOCK AS WE WERE WATCHING THE SWAT TEAM GATHER, THE UTILITY LINES BEING CUT, THE GAS LINES BEING PURGED, IT SEEMED ALMOST LIKE A DREAM. YOU COULDN'T REALLY BELIEVE THIS WAS HAPPENING. AND THEN THE GUNSHOTS RANG OUT ABOUT 6AM. AND THEN THE TEARGAS WAFTING OVER TO THE AREA WHERE WE WERE. FINALLY, THIS AFTERNOON WHEN THE BOMB WAS DROPPED, THE BIGGEST EXPLOSION ALL DAY, AND THEN THE FIRE-- IT JUST WAS AN UNBELIEVABLE ORDEAL, I MEAN STEP AFTER STEP AFTER STEP WAS HARD TO BELIEVE IT WAS HAPPENING AS IT WAS HAPPENING."

Harvey: "I THINK WHAT WE HAVE TO KEEP AN EYE ON IS THE FACT THAT THERE ARE AT LEAST, WHAT WE'RE BEING TOLD NOW, UP TO 60 HOMES THAT MAY HAVE BEEN DESTROYED, AND PEOPLE OUT OF THEIR HOMES. THERE'S A LOCAL CATHOLIC CHURCH THAT'S PUTTING THOSE PEOPLE UP, AT LEAST SOME OF THEM. OTHERS ARE STAYING WITH RELATIVES. A LOT OF THOSE PEOPLE LEFT LAST NIGHT WITH THE UNDERSTANDING THAT THEY WERE GOING TO BE OUT OF THEIR HOMES FOR 24 HOURS. THEY LEFT EVERYTHING BEHIND."

Finally, the Mayor showed up at our live camera at City Hall. Larry went to him. Goode looked tired and drained. His eyes looked puffy. He stood before the same podium at which he had held his two news conferences earlier, except now he spoke only to our camera and Larry Kane.

Larry: "MAYOR THIS HAS TO BE ONE OF THE MOST DIFFICULT DAYS OF YOUR 18-MONTH ADMINISTRATION IF

NOT THE MOST DIFFICULT. WE SAW YOU AT THE AFTERNOON NEWS CONFERENCE AND I WAS WATCHING YOUR FACE VERY CLOSELY. I'VE COVERED YOU FOR A LONG TIME. YOU LOOKED VERY MUCH IN CONTROL, BUT EXTREMELY SAD."

Mayor: "UH LARRY, I THINK THAT SAD IS A GOOD WORD. I THINK THAT ANY TIME THERE'S A POSSIBILITY THAT LIFE IS LOST ONE HAS TO BE SAD. AND IN FACT IF THE LIFE THAT IS LOST IS THAT OF A CHILD, YOU HAVE TO BE DOUBLY SAD. AND THEREFORE I DON'T FEEL ANYTHING BUT SADNESS DEEP DOWN INSIDE OF ME. THERE MAY HAVE BEEN SOME YOUNG PEOPLE WHO LOST THEIR LIVES."

Larry: "MAYOR, ONE FINAL QUESTION. WE MENTIONED EARLIER TONIGHT THE FACT THAT THE IMAGERY PRESENTED TO THE NATION OF THIS EPISODE IS KIND OF HARD TO COUNTER. PEOPLE WILL SAY IT'S ANOTHER URBAN CONFRONTATION IN PHILADELPHIA. HOW ARE YOU GOING TO DEAL WITH THAT?"

Mayor: "WELL, I THINK THAT BASED UPON THE INTERVIEWS THAT I'VE HAD, I THINK YOU COUNTER IT BY SAYING THAT WE HAVE THIS REVOLUTIONARY GROUP IN THE CITY, AND THE CITY DEALT WITH IT IN A VERY STRONG AND FIRM MANNER AND THAT WE SHOULD, IN FACT, DO SO IN THE FUTURE WHEN WE HAVE GROUPS LIKE THAT."

Larry: "MAYOR, THANK YOU FOR JOINING US."

It was now almost 12:30am. In the final news decision of the day, the producer told Larry in his ear to wrap it up.

"RIGHT NOW FOR ALAN FRIO AND EVERYONE AT CHANNEL TEN NEWS WHO'S PARTICIPATED IN OUR NON-STOP COVERAGE THE LAST SEVERAL HOURS, I'M LARRY KANE. GOOD NIGHT, AND THANKS FOR BEING WITH US."

The director dissolved to a wide shot of Larry and Alan on the set. "Channel 10 News" was superimposed under them momentarily. At 12:26AM, the Channel 10 News faded to black.

"I'm gonna get some sleep, then be back in the morning," said Harvey Clark, his last words to me before he trudged off to find his Corvette.

Kris went off to shoot some more pictures for his overnight report on the fire aftermath.

Charles had finally disappeared for the night.

Dennis was standing in front of the camera, his arms dangling at his sides, waiting for a barely audible cue from CBS to do his Q and A on Nightwatch. Twelve years ago, as a writer for Voice of America in Washington, he had written about the fall of Saigon. Tonight, he would report on the fall of Osage Avenue.

Pete Kane had left a while ago, without fanfare.

I said some quick goodbyes to Don and Suzy, who had survived some of the worst harassment of their careers, and began my search for the station car Tony Gore and I had driven here some 21 hours ago.

Frances Harty had gotten a new partner to take her into the night after Jim Barger was relieved. He had spent most of the past five hours hunched over a camera trained at the MOVE fire.

By 1:00 AM, the Red Cross had begun serving coffee and donuts to the firefighters, police officers and reporters at the geriatric center.

Frank Goldstein drove his station car through the streets of West Philadelphia and center city, turning onto northbound I-95 to head home to Bensalem Township. He found himself on Street Road around 1:30 AM when he saw the flashing red lights of a police car in his rear-view mirror. He checked his speed, then looked back in the mirror. He'd never been stopped before on this road. Many of the police officers here knew him.

He slowed down and pulled to the shoulder. He watched in his side view mirror as the officer climbed out of his cruiser and walked slowly toward Frank's marked, Channel 10 car. Frank began reaching for his license and registration.

"How you doing tonight?" the officer said with a pleasant smile.

"Fine, officer."

"You work for Channel Ten, huh?"

The answer was obvious, since Frank's car had "10 NEWS" plastered all over it. "Sure do," Frank answered.

"Were you at MOVE?" asked the officer.

"Yeah, as a matter of fact I was."

The officer stood at Frank's door in the night breeze. He looked down at the ground, a little embarrassed, then back at Frank. "Could you tell me about it?"

"Sure," said Frank with relief. He climbed out of his car, sat on the hood and for the next 30 minutes told the Bensalem policeman what happened in West Philadelphia.

TOM KRANZ

PART 3

TOM KRANZ

EPILOGUE

On Tuesday, May 14, 1985, the Medical Examiner's van would arrive, confirming what we all knew, that people were dead in there. After another couple days of digging, remains of eleven people were hauled out in orange zipper bags, carted away on gurneys and sealed-up at the ME's office. Under the same rubble, police found the remains of two .38 caliber revolvers, two shotguns and a .22 caliber rifle, but no automatic weapons. MOVE had bragged of much bigger weaponry, but no evidence of it was found. There was also no evidence of the underground tunnels police believed might have existed.

The 61 homes that were destroyed by the fire included those of Earl and Pearl Watkins, Milt Williams and many of the other people familiar to television viewers. Mayor Goode went to the shelter at St. Carthage's Church and promised to rebuild everyone's home. At a news conference that same week, he promised to do so by Christmas. It seemed like an awesome task to rebuild an entire neighborhood in just seven months.

The Parkers' home was not destroyed, though it sustained some water damage from the firefighting effort.

The Philadelphia Police Department's homicide squad, led by Captain Gene Dooley, began its investigation into what happened May 13, 1985. The results of that investigation were never formally announced because they were to be forwarded to a special commission appointed by the Mayor to learn the facts behind the disaster. Critics said the information should have been immediately forwarded to a county grand jury, which would then have the power to recommend criminal charges. The Mayor's special commission had subpoena power, but could not indict. It was merely a fact-finding body.

In the days immediately after the disaster, the news media were especially concerned about learning the nature of the explosive used in the bomb dropped from the helicopter. Lorrie Yapczenski had reported the night of the fire that the device was made of C-4. It was just a mention, almost a throwaway. At the time, we weren't concerned about what the bomb was made of, as much as we were concerned about what damage the bomb had inflicted. Later that week, police Commissioner Sambor categorically denied that the bomb was made of C-4, a powerful military explosive. He said it was made of DuPont Tovex, a less powerful commercial explosive used in mining and demolition. Subsequent follow-ups by the newspapers and our station eventually led Sambor to admit that he did not know, at the time, what explosive was used.

It was revealed three years later that the policemen who were in the two teams in the houses on either side of MOVE headquarters had also used C-4 in trying to blow holes in the walls. Their efforts destroyed the entire front of the MOVE house. Explosives experts testified that C-4 generates heat when it explodes, unlike Tovex. It also renders a more forceful explosion than Tovex. They also testified that the Bomb Squad officers who handled the stuff and constructed the bomb dropped on the MOVE house really didn't know the differences.

Because of fear, peer pressure and the general media hysteria concerning the makeup of the bomb during the months after the MOVE incident, several police officers lied to investigators about the use of C-4. Again, the truth didn't come out until May 1988. The thrust of the media coverage of the C-4 cover-up danced around the theory that the policemen involved were trying to kill MOVE, or at least do more damage than they were actually authorized to. The central question was, were these police officers renegades, out to get even with a group that killed one of their own in 1978? The debate over this question continued for some time to follow.

The 250 people who once lived in the neighborhood were

moved to an apartment complex in southwest Philadelphia. Most had lost everything. Their children received counseling. The adults became pawns in complex and tiresome legal battles over which they had little control. One of them reached a breaking point some months later and shot his lawyer, almost killing him.

The new homes were not ready by Christmas. The developer in charge of the rebuilding project, Ernest Edwards, was fired by the city because of cost overruns and other irregularities. A new developer had to pick up the pieces. Edwards was subsequently convicted of defrauding the city by stealing money earmarked for the rebuilding project.

The families finally began moving in over a year after the homes were destroyed. Many of the roofs of the new homes leaked badly and had to be repaired, a final turn of the screw for those embattled people.

A nationwide outpouring of giving helped the people of Osage Avenue and Pine Street put their lives back together. There were donations of clothing, toys and money. Earl Watkins, who lost jazz albums he had collected over a lifetime, got a start on a new collection from people who donated their treasured LP's to him. There was a concert to benefit the families who lost their homes.

Ultimately, Philadelphia taxpayers paid an almost $30 million for the MOVE disaster, including the total cost of rebuilding the neighborhood and legal fees for lawyers to represent the Mayor, the police and fire commissioners and the managing director.[28]

But perhaps the biggest hurdle yet to be faced by the city would be the civil suits filed by those who lost property or loved ones in the disaster. Included were suits by 69 residents, Michael Ward, known formerly as Birdie Africa, Ramona Africa, and families of the deceased MOVE members. The city continued to face the prospect of paying millions of dollars in damages.

The Mayor's special commission, which became known as the MOVE Commission, spent the entire month of October,

1985, hearing testimony. The hearings were televised live on WHYY, the public television station. Testimony was heard from everyone involved except for a handful of police officers, members of the Bomb Squad and the morning insertion teams, who invoked their Fifth Amendment right against self-incrimination. They later testified before the city grand jury.

Four police officers won disability pensions for psychological stress they continued to experience more than two years after the incident. Among those was Officer James Berghaier, who pulled Birdie Africa out of the water he fell into face down upon his escape. Berghaier told Harvey at a chance meeting many months later that he had been targeted for harassment by fellow officers, evidently for breaking ranks and saving Birdie Africa.

Louise James and her sister, Laverne Sims, did the Phil Donahue Show and the college lecture circuit. Louise filed suit against the city to regain ownership of the house at 6221 Osage Avenue. Mayor Goode said she would never regain ownership.

Following the MOVE Commission's extensive effort to discover all the facts surrounding the disaster, two grand juries were convened to seek possible criminal charges. A Philadelphia County grand jury, empaneled at the request of Philadelphia District Attorney Ron Castille over a year after everything happened, took almost two years to complete its investigation. It had the power to recommend criminal charges. The grand jury was empaneled on May 15, 1986. Its findings were announced on May 3, 1988 by District Attorney Castille. The grand jury's conclusion speaks of "this City's greatest tragedy" as an "epic of government incompetence." It details an operation marked by "political cowardice in its inception, inexperience in its planning and ineptitude in its execution. Even the ensuing investigations were marred by deception.

"While the conduct of City officials in handling MOVE is entirely unacceptable, it is not the proper subject of criminal prosecutions. Applying the law to the facts as we found them, no charges are warranted. Yet we do not exonerate the men responsible for this disaster. Rather than a vindication of those officials, this report should stand as a permanent record of their morally reprehensible behavior. This City, its leaders and citizens must never forget the terrible cost of their misjudgments."

No one had been charged with any crime. Moreover, it was made public six months after W. Wilson Goode was re-elected to a second, four-year term as mayor of Philadelphia.

Several months later, on September 20, 1988, a federal grand jury completed its investigation into possible civil rights violations. A news release from the office of Assistant Attorney General William Bradford Reynolds, head of the Justice Department's Civil Rights Division, noted that the grand jury considered statements from over 250 witnesses in the course of its 16 month investigation.

Quoting Reynolds news release: "The probes yielded no indictments."

WCAU-TV enjoyed a couple of days of critical acclaim immediately following the disaster.

"Coverage by WCAU-TV (Channel 10) was the most aggressive and pervasive," wrote David Bianculli in the May 14th, 1985, Philadelphia Inquirer. "Channel 10 often was the only local station televising news coverage."

The next day Bianculli wrote: "The coverage by Philadelphia's local TV stations was responsible and informative and the station deserving of the most praise, clearly, is WCAU-TV, which devoted hours more air time to the story than its competitors."

David Friedman of the Daily News chose to dwell on the fact that the city's number one rated television news organization, WPVI-TV, did the least coverage of all.

"If being Number Two means trying harder, then being Number One means not trying hard at all," he wrote on May 14, 1985. "How else can one explain the shockingly inadequate coverage presented by Channel 6's vaunted Action News' team?"

His critique continued: "Channel 6...had virtually no live presence to speak of at all at Osage Avenue, especially during yesterday's crucial early-morning hours, other than brief cut-ins...at 6:15am, 6:45, 7:25 and 8:25."

In the same article Alan Nesbitt, news director at WPVI, responded to the criticism: "We reported the story. We gave all the information we were able to get and then we got off. What would be the point of staying on indefinitely? You can't see too much. You're at least a block away from the action. You're relying on information that's tough to confirm, if it can be confirmed at all. And what you usually end up with is lots of air time devoted to reporters interviewing other reporters."

Since WCAU carried more MOVE coverage than the other station that day, more people watched it than the other stations that day. Therefore, in addition to providing a bona fide public service, WCAU scored its first ratings victory in years over WPVI. Nielsen ratings quoted in the May 15, 1985, Inquirer showed Channel Ten as the undisputed ratings winner after 5:30PM. Peak viewing came during the half hour beginning at 9:30pm when the station had a whopping 40% share of the television viewing audience, a share rarely seen on any television station, especially Channel Ten, except perhaps for an Eagles football game.

But the ratings euphoria at the station was short lived. Within two days, viewership returned to more modest levels despite an aggressive promotional campaign touting Channel Ten's wall-to-wall coverage of the MOVE disaster.

Perhaps the more lasting effects were felt by Harvey Clark and Pete Kane. In addition to becoming instant media darlings, both men enjoyed new respect in the community and among their peers for years to come. "STEADY IN THE FACE OF DANGER," read the headline over a feature article about Harvey in the May 15, 1985, Philadelphia Inquirer. There, next to a photograph of Harvey standing outside the van with a phone to his ear and an intense look on his face, were these

words written by Gerald B. Jordan: "The quickly spreading
fire forced him to move several times, and bullets pierced the
air during sporadic shootouts between police and members of
MOVE. But Channel 10 reporter Harvey Clark continued to talk
coolly to Philadelphia-area television viewers who sat stunned,
horrified, awaiting some bit of news, some assurance that the
conflagration they saw in West Philadelphia would soon end."

Pete Kane took his newfound fame to schools where he
did career day talks. He became a genuine source of pride for
everyone in the newsroom. It was so invigorating to see a good
guy do well. But there was also a dark side to his new fame.
He was being regularly harassed by Philadelphia police officers
who pulled him over for no apparent reason while driving his
Channel Ten car. It was apparent payback for being a secret
witness to the destruction of the MOVE house during an
operation that many still believe was aimed at killing all those
inside.

It was Pete and Harvey who went to New York a year
later to accept one of broadcast journalism's highest awards,
the Alfred I. duPont-Columbia University Award. The next day
WCAU general manager Steve Cohen brought the award, a silver
plated baton, into the newsroom. He invited the entire staff of
the television station into the newsroom for a little ceremony.

"Last night, we were proud to receive the highest award
a television station can get for journalistic excellence," he
announced, holding the silver baton high for all to see. "And I
want you all to share this award. The people watching our air on
May 13 of last year saw only the handful of people on the air who
got the credit for our coverage of the MOVE disaster. But this
award acknowledges the total effort it took to keep us on the air
that day, from the non-stop work of the sales department to the
patience of the traffic department to the newsroom production
assistants who got pizza and sodas and answered the phones."

He paused and looked across the silenced newsroom.

"This is YOUR award."

The room broke into applause. Then, Cohen began shouting

something about everyone forming a long line through the newsroom.

"I want to pass this baton down the line, so that everyone may touch it, read the inscription and share this moment."

For Harvey Clark, the MOVE incident was a career turning point. He got his own weekly public affairs program called "Channel 10: The People", complete with production staff and a raise. Harvey had climbed his way out of a bombed-out apartment in all-white Cicero, Illinois, in 1951, to become a celebrated reporter in Philadelphia.

By 2016, most of us had been long gone from Channel Ten. Careers took different turns, the TV news business changed and management turned over several times at WCAU. The station changed ownership and rode a ratings roller coaster.

Harvey Clark left the TV news business, as did I. Pete Kane retired in 2020. Karen Fox retired after many more years in the newsroom, as did Mike Archer. Larry Kane continued to work in television and radio well into 2016. Jay Newman went on to run a television station in Baltimore.

Michael Ward, the former Birdie Africa, returned to the home of his biological father later in 1985 and settled into what would be a more normal life for a teenager. In one of the cruelest ironies of all, the boy who was fished out of a puddle behind his burning house on Osage Avenue in 1985 died in 2013 at the age of 41, drowning in a hot tub during a Caribbean cruise.

Though John Africa died in the conflagration on Osage Avenue, MOVE remained active with a website and new outrage aimed at the 2008 Guinness Book of World Records which listed the incident in West Philadelphia as a "mass suicide."

For the residents of Osage Avenue, life would never be the same. Many of the rebuilt homes fell into disrepair and the block remains a silent monument to a catastrophe.

2020 turned out to be an eventful year as the city of

Philadelphia tried to close the book on MOVE. Philadelphia City Council issued a formal apology for the 1985 operation, coming on the heels of a police killing of a black man in the same neighborhood. W. Wilson Goode wrote an op-ed in The Guardian in which he said, "The event will remain on my conscience for the rest of my life."

The last of the so-called "MOVE 9" were released from prison. One, Delbert Orr Africa, who had been savagely beaten and kicked by police after the 1978 incident, died of cancer. Ramona Africa, who served seven years in jail on charges of inciting a riot, did an interview for the Vice News program *I Was There* in which she showed the burn scars which are still evident on her arm. "You can die any day of the week in this country being killed by police," she said. "People ought to take the lesson from me and stand up for what is right. As long as we can fight, we're going to fight."

To my great sadness, my friend and colleague Harvey Clark died in 2021 of liver cancer at age 76. After leaving WCAU in the early 1990s, he had an active and colorful life that included an unsuccessful run for Congress, a stint as Philadelphia City Representative under Mayor Ed Rendell and vice president of communications for the Philadelphia Gas Works. Harvey won two Emmys for his WCAU public affairs program *Channel 10: The People*.

The children of MOVE who died will always be remembered as the innocents of the debacle. For them, I have a private moment of silence every May 13.

WCAU-TV received the Alfred I. duPont-Columbia University Award for Journalism on February 6, 1986, in New York City. Accepting the award, from left to right, were Gordon Hughes, Station Manager; Jay Newman, News Director; Steve Cohen, General Manager; Harvey Clark, Reporter; Larry Kane, Anchor; Mike Archer, Executive Producer; Mike Beardsley, Assistant News Director; Pete Kane, Photographer.

Photojournalist Pete Kane, circa 1985

Iconic still frame taken from Jim Barger's video of Lt. Frank Powell dropping the satchel containing explosives onto the MOVE roof. Most of the key video of WCAU's coverage was handed over to the MOVE Commission for its investigation. News Director Jay Newman felt the footage belonged in the public domain.

Reporters Dennis Woltering and Harvey Clark

Charles Thomas reporting live

SOURCES AND CITATIONS

In addition to my own recollections and interviews, there are a number of other sources as marked by the footnotes throughout the book. Those citations are listed below.

---

[1] "Street Names of Philadelphia", by Robert Alotta, Temple University Press.

[2] Quotes from Smalls and Swans from the television program "The Burning of Osage", first aired on WHYY-TV. The name of the program was changed for syndication to "The Bombing of West Philly".

[3] Transcript of MOVE Commission hearings, October 9, 1985.

[4] Hardy Williams and David Richardson represented West Philadelphia in the state legislature. Cecil Moore was a city councilman and civil rights leader.

[5] Testimony before the MOVE Commission, October 10, 1985.

[6] Testimony before the MOVE Commission, October 9, 1985.

[7] Testimony before the MOVE Commission, October 9, 1985.

[8] Testimony before the MOVE Commission, October 8, 1985.

[9] Probable cause affidavit filed in Philadelphia Common Pleas Court.

[10] Recollections of Michael Ward from his interview by MOVE Commission chairman William Brown.

[11] Testimony before the MOVE Commission, October 11, 1985.

[12] As related by Earl Watkins and Margaret Lane on the program "The Burning of Osage," previously cited.

[13] It was August 8, 1984. Police had information that MOVE planned to observe the 6th anniversary of the big shootout in Powelton Village with some kind of violent display. Dozens of police were dispatched to Osage Avenue in anticipation of no-one-knew-what. After a daylong presence, they left after nothing happened. It was later revealed that an elaborate plan existed to arrest MOVE members in the house if violence did break out.

[14] Sony model BVP 100, bought by station a couple years earlier as an experiment because of its light weight, cost about $5,000. Standard issue street camera was Sony model BVP 300, costing upwards of $35,000 each. Both items are

obsolete now and small video cameras costing less than $5,000 are common place.

[15] Names are changed to protect privacy.

[16] Testimony before the MOVE Commission October 9, 1985.

[17] Interview with Charles Thomas aired on Channel 10 News, Sunday, May 12, 1985.

[18] Interview with Kasey Kaufman, Channel 10 News, Sunday, May 12, 1985.

[19] Testimony before the MOVE Commission, October 22, 1985.

[20] From "The Burning of Osage", WHYY-TV, cited earlier.

[21] At the time there were no early morning newscasts done by local stations in Philadelphia or most other major markets, only the five-minute updates, typically at :25 and :55 past each hour.

[22] Name changed.

[23] The interviewee, Irving Machlader, was awarded $1.25 million by the jury which found that although the story WCBS broadcast was factual, the station invaded his privacy by portraying him in a "false light". The jury verdict was overturned on appeal, a ruling which was allowed to stand by the U.S. Supreme Court.

[24] 1 later looked at the tape myself and there was indeed movement. However, it was so fleeting, it was impossible to make out who it was. Plus, the mast camera was zoomed in tightly to a scene that was really several hundred feet away, thus distorting the depth of field. My own conclusion after the fact was that the figure was a policeman on an adjacent roof who had merely shifted his position.

[25] There is considerable disagreement over when the Mayor actually gave the order to put out the fire. He has testified he did so around 6PM, about 20 minutes after the fire became evident. A report by a member of the MOVE Commission staff concludes the order actually came closer to 6:25, about 45 minutes after the fire was detected by our TV camera looking right at the roof.

[26] Recollections of Birdie Africa as told to MOVE Commission chairman William Brown.

[27] Police assigned to the MOVE alley testified that a male MOVE member, presumably Conrad Africa, emerged from the garage waving a rifle and began shooting. The police say they never returned fire. This account differs dramatically from Birdie's, which claims police fired unprovoked as Conrad tried to leave the garage with Tomaso. The differences in the two accounts have never been adequately reconciled.

[28] $29,916,801 paid out through the City Controller's office as of December 31, 1989. Figures supplied by Jonathan Saidel, City Controller.

ABOUT THE AUTHOR

Tom Kranz

Tom is an independent author and lifelong journalist, currently residing in New Jersey. The 1985 MOVE story was the most consequential of his career in local news, eclipsed later by the 9-11 attacks in 2001, coverage of which he helped manage for CBS affiliates. Today he writes novels and does freelance communications work.

BOOKS BY THIS AUTHOR

Liveshot: Journalistic Heroism In Philadelphia

Bullets flying. Choking teargas. Angry crowds chanting for justice. Eleven dead people, five of them children. This is the epic true story of the intrepid journalists of a Philadelphia television news department whose creativity and dedication brought the 1985 MOVE disaster to a live television audience.

Budland

Jail didn't sound so bad to Bud Remmick, who sacrificed his successful television news career, a small price to pay for erasing an abusive, blackmailing sociopath from the face of the earth. But the plan to ride out a lenient sentence starts to fall apart when prison life turns on him. Then his lawyer turns on him. Then, his wife. With nothing left but his own anger, Bud Remmick faces a reckoning with a lifelong dysfunction that plays out behind bars with a couple of unlikely co-dependents.

Killer Competition

Two years out of prison and trying to reinvent himself, Bud Remmick just wants to be a solid citizen. He volunteers as an EMT then gets a job in his old career, TV news. But after only a week, he discovers bad things swirling around him including a psychotic photographer who has been creating news stories and selling them to Bud's station for years. Bud is suddenly knee-deep in scandal and a murder investigation.

Time Travel Rescue: Escape From The 21St Century

Living in a wasteland that is beyond repair becomes too much for Rick who, like most of those left on the planet in 2212, works for the Big Five mega corporation. A chance, online meeting with a young hacker named Chen leads to a perilous journey through a wormhole back to the 21st century where he and Chen hope to set things right before they go terribly wrong. Unbeknown to Rick is Chen's propensity for violence and her murderous exploits complicate an otherwise altruistic mission.

Moon Rescue: Escape From The Dome

Moon Rescue: Escape from the Dome, speculates about a future Moon habitat designed as a final refuge for those escaping the slow destruction of the Earth due to unchecked climate change. Plans to make Moon habitation a stepping stone to a Mars mission–as speculated by NASA's Artemis program–are scuttled in the face of catastrophic fires, land erosion and rising temperatures on Earth. In the year 2067, the average temperature has risen three degrees. New York's Battery Park is under water. The beaches of the Jersey Shore are reduced to thin strips of sand. Huge portions of California have been reduced to burned hellscapes due to relentless fires and mudslides. Refugee camps dot the former state as survivors struggle to figure out what to do now that their homes, cars, all their worldly possessions have been lost. Storm shelters are mandated in major population areas to protect citizens from tornadoes, hurricanes and other severe weather caused by global warming.

Unknown to their lunar neighbors, Dome residents Sam and Leah Ragland are fugitives from the insurrection of 2055 during which Sam, then known as Enrico Janice Walton Stein, Rick for short, aided and abetted an armed invasion of the Planetary Commission's headquarters in Old Philadelphia that ended in bloodshed. Rick is a native of 23rd century Earth, a devastated environment of toxic bogs, dark rain and little direct sunlight, who traveled through a wormhole in an effort to halt the climate apathy of the 21st century.

Made in United States
North Haven, CT
04 October 2024

58302426R00150